D1350085

A0363

Africa World Press, Inc.

P.O. Box 1892
Trenton, NJ 08607

P.O. Box 48
Asmara, ERITREA

Book & Cover Design: Roger Dormann
Cover Photo: With the kind permission of *The Daily Dispatch*,
East London, South Africa

Library of Congress Cataloging-in-Publication Data

MacLean, Barbara Hutmacher, 1926-
  Strike a woman, strike a rock : fighting for freedom in South Africa /
Barbara Hutmacher MacLean.
    p. cm.
  ISBN 1-59221-075-9 (cloth) -- ISBN 1-59221-076-7 (pbk.)
  1. Anti-apartheid movements--South Africa--Biography. 2. Women civil
rights workers--South Africa--Biography. 3. Women political
activists--South Africa--Biography. I. Title.

DT1948.M33 2003
323.168'092'2—dc22

2003022917

About the Title

In 1956, thousands of women appeared at the seat of the South African government to protest extension of the infamous pass laws to cover women. "You strike a woman, you strike a rock," was an expression popular in that march, in a song and lettered on placards carried in the march.

Contents

Acknowledgements

This project began because Cecily van Gend, a long-time-ago neighbor from East London, South Africa, happened to be in London in 1996, at the same time as my husband, Fraser, and I. She was visiting a friend who had fled South Africa in the turbulent 1970s. So were we. All of us met over a dinner table—such a familiar gathering place in our shared pasts, so conducive to good conversation. We talked of the good old bad days and caught up with the latest news and gossip from the beautiful, drama-filled country that still possessed each one of us. Cecily, then on the first leg of a round-the-world journey, promised to come stay with us when she reached the U.S.

This book owes a great deal to Cecily. She arrived at our house with news of mutual friends and acquaintances and information on others who had and were influencing the exciting developments that had transformed South Africa. So many of the activists were women. We talked for hours and the idea of this book evolved.

When Cecily returned home, she forwarded contact information on women she knew and others she had learned about. My thanks to Cecily as well for her hospitality and the gift of space in her charming home during my weeks in South Africa.

Special thanks go to the women who trusted me with their stories. None of them probably have any idea of the weight of the responsibility I felt toward them. Other sincere thank yous to my friend and guardian angel Aldino Muller; to Sylvia Hagerty for her hospitality and help; to GlynWilliams, a fine editor, witty writer, and all around good guy.

Without that month-long residency at Hedgebrook, a retreat for women writers on Whidbey Island, maybe I would not be composing this acknowledgement. For the tranquility, time, and solitude to concentrate only on writing, my everlasting gratitude.

Thanks to P. Anna Johnson, a fellow writer and former publisher. She pointed this project in the direction of Africa World Press and her much respected friend at its helm, Kassahun Checole, publisher.

Charles Cantalupo edited the manuscript. I appreciated his professional skills as well as his care. I have had many pleasant and helpful fax and phone conversations with Angela Ajayi, Africa World Press Staff Editor. Thank you for your guidance, Angela.

Many thanks to my writers group here in Port Townsend whose members generously gave critiques, suggestions and most helpful of all, encouragement.

Jim Hladecek, computer guru and good neighbor, saved the day several times. Thanks so much Jim.

And finally, thanks for your patience, Fraser. I suspect it is not much fun being married to a writer.

Barbara Hutmacher MacLean
Port Townsend, Washington
December 2002

Introduction

Barbara Hutmacher was on the staff of the East London *Daily Dispatch* during some of the most turbulent years in the history of the newspaper, and of South Africa itself. She was features editor of a morning newspaper that was to become world famous because of the anti-apartheid crusading of its editor, the late Donald Woods.

As a person who showed courage in her personal life—there are not many women who have decided to develop their careers by traveling to a strange continent on a freighter from New York to Cape Town—she became intrigued by members of her own sex who had their own particular brand of bravery.

She had a three-month contract with the *Daily Dispatch* and then returned to her newspaper in California. During that relatively short period, the executives of the East London newspaper were as impressed with the demeanor and ability of Barbara Hutmacher as she herself became intrigued with South Africa and its people.

When she was offered the post of features editor at the *Dispatch* the following year, she immediately resigned from her paper in Ventura, California. In the next two years she developed significantly as a formidable writer and interviewer, the theme invariably being justice and those who sought to achieve it, despite obstacles in the form of state-legislated apartheid, or race separation.

The seeds of this book were sown at this time, and in the other periods that Barbara Hutmacher worked on the *Daily Dispatch*. She wanted to stay, and end her working days on the newspaper, but her intentions were disturbed by the tumultuous events in South Africa that adversely affected so many lives and institutions.

Donald Woods was banned for five years in 1977 by the apartheid government of the National Party, which effectively stopped him working as a journalist, and communicating with people—virtually house arrest. His banning came shortly after the death in detention of Woods' friend, political activist Steve Biko.

In the worldwide condemnation that followed, the government became increasingly nervous, and Barbara's companion, Fraser MacLean, chief photographer of the *Daily Dispatch*, had his temporary residence revoked. They had to return, reluctantly, to the United States, but in 1998, after a new democratic government had been elected, Barbara Hutmacher returned to South Africa to continue the work started in the 1970s.

This book is the result. In it she tells of some of the brave women who were unrelenting in their search for justice in the days of apartheid, despite tremendous pressures that included torture and family deaths, and their roles in the new South Africa. It is a significant addition not only to the literature of the anti-apartheid struggle, from a new aspect, but topically emphasizes that the struggle for equality and justice is never-ending.

Glyn Williams *
East London, South Africa

---

*Glyn Williams was with the *Daily Dispatch* for 27 years. He was editor from 1987 to 1983. Prior to that, he was the leader (editorial) page editor.

I
卌 *Arrival*

Pretoria's traffic-choked center looked like Any City U.S.A.

"Y ou must not, *must not*, leave the hotel day or night," Ella announced to the bus filled with Americans on a South African tour. We were, at that moment, coming into the suburbs of Pretoria, our stop that night. Pretty, perky, professional guide Ella Bauer, third-generation South African, had preceded that brief, unconditional announcement with a prosaic listing of the evening's schedule—a lecture on the Anglo-Boer Wars, a late dinner in our hotel.

I had never been in Pretoria, but knew a little about it. I had lived and worked in South Africa in the early and mid-1970s. Danger lurking on the streets of Pretoria in 1998 came as a surprise. In the bad old days of apartheid, Pretoria had often been referred to as the heart of white Afrikanerdom. In Cape Town, which we had just left, those of us on this Elderhostel tour had been free to come and go as we wished. The only restriction had been the center of Cape Town at night. That had seemed appropriate to just about any big city anywhere in the world, particularly to visitors in an unfamiliar country. And even that had not been absolute. One night Ella arranged taxis for those wanting to see a Zulu musical in a downtown theater. I had read about Johannesburg's high crime rate in U.S. newspapers, but never a mention of Pretoria in that context.

I recalled that twenty minutes or a half hour before Ella's announcement, I had looked out the bus windows and thought *this*

1

could be Seattle. Or Chicago. We had flown into Johannesburg from Cape Town, boarded a modern bus at the airport and sped along a first world highway with the first world skyscrapers of Johannesburg in the distance. People around me spoke American. I had thought then that perhaps in Pretoria, I would get a sense of the new South Africa. In and around Cape Town, where the tour had started a week earlier, not much looked different than it had twenty-plus years earlier. Whites still drove BMWs and Mercedes and lived in what appeared to be all-white neighborhoods behind walls in big houses with bars on the windows. Blacks still lived in sprawling townships with the look and smell of poverty.

The advisory over, Ella returned to tour guide: that brick tower on the hilltop, the Dutch-descended Afrikans people's monument to their pioneer past; those old-fashioned, adobe-colored buildings, pillared and imposing, wide steps leading to stern entrances, were government offices. Pretoria is and was South Africa's executive capital; the judicial center remained in Bloemfontein; Cape Town was the legislative capital of government. In the center of Pretoria, Ella pointed out city government buildings, a civic theater. Those tall trees lining the downtown streets? Jacaranda. A couple of months before—this was early January—the pale purple blooms would have been spectacular. At lunch hour, crowds filled the sidewalks and intersections. Except for the street vendors, jacarandas and mostly black pedestrians, Pretoria's traffic-choked center still, in 1998, looked like Any City U.S.A.

The second day of the Pretoria section of the trip, the tour was through Soweto, the enormous black township outside Johannesburg. We waved back, through the bus windows, at kids on narrow dirt streets and peered down at throngs of black people dressed in ragged, ill-matched clothes. We smelled meat, sold from street stalls, cooking over open fires and watched vendors parcelling out vegetables and fruit from piles on the dirt. There were no sidewalks. The roads were unpaved. Washing dried on thorn bushes and fences. As far as I could see, spirals of smoke curled upwards, hazing the air. We passed squatter settlements built of cardboard, tin, and scrap wood, rows of identical cement block matchboxes put up by the apartheid government, and a section of custom, luxury homes. Until the 1990s, rich or poor, if you were black you lived in the township.

Soweto stretched ahead to the horizon—vast, treeless and utterly grim, the home of two to three-and-a-half million black South Africans. In 1976, students had marched through these streets to protest a switch from teaching all subjects in English to Afrikaans. Police opened fire, killing many and triggering more, bigger and bloodier anti-government protests. By the end of that year, more than six hundred had died. Now two decades later, we had reservations for lunch at a restaurant in Soweto called Wandies.

I waved at some shoeless kids in ragged clothes and thought about the days to come: how different, I wondered, would be the lives of the women I had returned to talk to? Val Viljoen, who had been my neighbor in the South African coastal city of East London in the seventies, was a Member of Parliament. I remembered her as a hard working and dedicated volunteer at various welfare-type agencies. We had kept in touch. I knew she had married again, a high school principal whom I remembered as conservative. In South Africa, the terms conservative and liberal had more to do with views on segregation than on politics. Then there was Trudy Thomas, a doctor and former director of a mission hospital deep in the rural black homeland bordering East London. That was where I had interviewed her in 1972. In 1977, I did another story about Trudy. She had left the hospital by then and established a training center for health workers in Mdantsane, the black township adjacent to East London. She had divorced. Twenty years later, she was Minister of Health for the Eastern Cape Province.

In a few days, I would fly to East London to talk with Trudy and Val. Sylvia Hagerty had asked me to stay with her while I was there. We had worked together at the *Daily Dispatch*. During the violent 1980s, Sylvia's oldest son had lost his leg in a car bombing outside a Johannesburg sports stadium. A few days after this tour started, I had

3

met the current leader of Black Sash and later would talk with one of the founders. Black Sash was a national organization of white women dedicated to helping blacks. In the seventies, I had reported on speakers at their monthly meetings and sat in on their once-a-week Advice Office sessions.

Val had contacted Judy Chalmers, Member of Parliament from Port Elizabeth. She had agreed to talk with me. In the 1970s, Port Elizabeth had a reputation for a brutal police force and intense anti-apartheid activism. A notebook in my purse listed women I had contacted earlier by phone or letter: Mary Burton on the Truth and Reconciliation Commission; Ivy Gcina, a trade union activist; Virginia Engel, Nelson Mandela's private secretary; an Afrikans Member of Parliament for the ANC, married to the grandson of an assassinated former Prime Minister; the granddaughter of Mohandas K. Gandhi, also in Parliament; as well as another Member representing the major opposition party to the ANC. I would set up appointments with them when I returned to Cape Town at the end of the tour. In the days ahead, I expected to learn of other women relevant to South Africa's past and future that I would want to talk to.

But for now, I was still in Soweto and looking forward to getting out of the bus which had stopped in front of a small frame building. We walked past umbrella-shaded tables and followed Ella into the restaurant called Wandies. Quaint, maybe funky, seemed the right description. The ceiling was so low the tall men had to duck going through to the buffet tables. Walls and ceiling were papered with business cards of customers from all over the world. Our table was long, narrow and just fit in the main room, leaving barely enough space to get past either side. Photographs decorated the bar between the main room and buffet in the rear dining area. Among the smiling faces and scrawled names I spotted Quincy Jones, Johnnie Cochran, Hillary Rodham Clinton, and Evander Holyfield. So much for our American expeditionary force into Soweto. Through the open door, I could see locals filling up the tables outside. All white faces except for the restaurant staff. I walked along the buffet table, spooning out curry and rice, something with chicken, and sampling the salads. The food was great. For the first time, the country seemed topsy-turvy. Here I was, a white, eating in a black township restaurant, not only illegal but unimaginable before 1990, and couldn't leave the hotel in once-white-only Pretoria.

After lunch, we drove through more of Soweto and then got out of the bus at Point of No Return, a vacant-lot memorial to Hector Peterson, 10-year-old black schoolboy, first to die in the 1976 student riots. Black and white head shots of youngsters who died on these streets, enlarged to poster size, hung like wash on a line between two poles. Across the dirt was a row of ship containers, ends open. Pinned on the inside walls were photos of the riots that followed Hector Peterson's death: newspaper shots of distorted bodies, heads cradled in mothers' arms; police aiming automatic weapons from the tops of tanks; burning shacks; and mourning families.

What a contrast to the massive brick cenotaph on a hilltop in Pretoria which we had seen the day before. Behind it stood massive government buildings: in front, gardens bordered what looked like several acres of rolling, manicured lawns. Inside the memorial, serialized bas relief panels memorialized the Afrikaners' Great Trek and other less recognizable moments of their history.

A day or so later, we left Pretoria to visit the green and lush orange-growing valleys, descend into a diamond mine and spy on the wildlife that roamed Kruger National Park. We listened to lectures on history, nature and current events.

I like traveling alone, getting to know a new place at my own pace, exploring with my feet, getting acquainted with the person selling stamps at the post office and finding the bakery that makes the best bread. I had never taken a tour before and didn't think I would go on another. But this one gave me a speed read on the country's history, the main events between now and when I left South Africa, and took me to places I had not seen.

Then at the end of it all, an overnight stop in Pretoria once again. The next morning, outside the same hotel we had stayed in earlier, we bid goodbye to Ella, traded addresses and hopped on the bus for our last ride together. Most of the Elderhostelers were returning home. In an hour or so, I would catch a flight to East London.

As the bus headed toward the Johannesburg airport, I tuned in to the conversation around me. Everyone talked about the attack on the couple from New York City. He, over six-feet tall and proportionately big-bodied, his diminutive wife and two other women had left the hotel the previous afternoon to buy film. He had checked in at the desk first. The nearest store was two blocks away. The hotel provided an employee to go with them. On the way back, their escort shouted, "Run!" Four men, brandishing knives, caught up with them. They jumped on the American, knocked him to the sidewalk. His wife fell on top of him, trying to protect him. The thieves yanked her off, injuring her arm. They got away with about $50 in South African currency, but missed the airline tickets and a larger amount of money in another pocket.

Until Nelson Mandela emerged from prison, an immediate celebrity and a heroic presence recognized throughout the world, South Africa was a distant, little known land to many of us in the western world. A brief history of South Africa helps to make it clear why the country required a Mandela when it did. And, relevant to the stories ahead, such a synopsis provides a background to the women who are the subjects of this book, women who did an uncommon lot to change the course of that history.

In 1998, South Africa had an estimated population of 44 million occupying a land area the size of California and Texas combined. Seventy-seven percent of South Africans are black, descendants of the Sotho and Nuguni people who migrated southward many centuries ago. Eight and a half percent are termed colored, in South Africa *coloured*, an appropriately British spelling. Coloreds were the progeny of the earliest white settlers and the indigenous people, or of Malay slaves from Dutch West India. Seventy percent of the country's coloreds live in the Western Cape, the province of Cape Town. Two and a half percent of South Africans are Asian, the majority from India and first imported in 1860 as contract laborers for the sugar plantations in the province of Natal. Twelve percent of the population are white: 40 percent English-speaking, 60 percent Afrikaans-speaking. The history of the indigenous people of South Africa begins with the Bushmen or San, a race of hunter-gatherers believed to date back 25,000 years and the first black settlement from 200 A.D. White history began when Bartolomew Diaz came to South Africa in 1457, followed two years later by Vasco da Gama.

Events relevant to the country's contemporary social structure date from the arrival on the Cape of Capt. Jan van Riebeeck in April 1652. His Dutch ship landed whites whose mission was to establish a supply base for Dutch East India Company trading vessels passing to and from India. In 1657 some of the company's workers were released from their contract so that they could cultivate land and raise cattle. Replacing them as laborers were slaves imported from Angola and the East Indies. Dutch settlers followed, along with French Protestant Hugeuenots seeking religious freedom. Germans came later, the final element in the Dutch-French mix of whites known as Afrikaner.

A rapid and confusing series of land ownership claims began in 1795. That year Britain seized the Cape, taking away all Afrikaner rights to the ground so laboriously cleared and cultivated. In 1803, the British gave the land back. Three years later the English reclaimed it in order to protect sea routes to India during the renewed Napoleonic Wars. In 1835 the Dutch-descended Afrikans settlers, who called themselves Boers, or farmers, began a trek north to find new lands to farm, far away from the growing encroachment of British immigrants. Over the next eight years more than 12,000 Boers, known as Voortrekkers, traveling in ox wagons, pursued an uncharted course to the high velds, lands, of the Natal and Transvaal regions. This, the Great Trek, remains a revered chapter in Afrikaner history, regularly remembered with church services, proclamations and gatherings.

On their way north, the Boers often encountered hostile black tribes. In the bloodiest of these confrontations, the Battle of Blood River on December 16, 1838, 12,000 Zulu warriors attacked a laager, a protective circle of wagons, along the banks of the Ncome River. The tiny force of 500 Afrikaners triumphed. The date is a South African national holiday named Day of the Covenant.

Early in the 1850s, the Voortrekkers founded two independent republics, the Transvaal and the Orange Free State. After the discovery of diamonds in the Transvaal in 1867 and gold in 1886, English immigrants poured in. This incursion provoked two Anglo-Boer wars, in 1880-1881 and 1899-1902. In what Afrikaners called their Second War of Freedom, 480,000 British troops, later joined by 30,000 armed blacks, battled 88,000 Boers. Using guerrilla warfare tactics, the Boers held their own until the British instituted a scorched earth policy, cutting off their enemy's sources of supply. Thirty thousand farms were torched, wives and children on them rounded up and put into concentration camps. More than 20,000 died there, victims of starvation and disease. Losses of families and farms produced what guns could not. The Afrikaners surrendered. In May 1902, its leaders signed the Peace of Vereeniging. The Second War of Freedom came at great cost to both sides. In addition to the 20,000 Afrikaner deaths in camps, 6,000 fighters died. British casualties reached 22,000 dead and 150,000 wounded. It has been recorded in history as Africa's bloodiest conflict.

In 1910, the former Boer republics, the Orange Free State and Transvaal, and the two British-majority colonies of Natal and the Cape joined to form the Union of South Africa, a dominion of the British Empire. The union became a sovereign state within the empire in 1934. In 1961, South Africa, then governed by Afrikaners, declared itself a republic and left the British Commonwealth.

The system of apartheid, the legalized separation of races, is blamed on the Afrikaners. But the British system was not that different. Colonial-style race discrimination and exploitation existed in South Africa long before the Afrikaners' National Party trounced the ruling United Party, the political arm of the English, in the 1948 elections. Indicative of conditions was a demonstration in Cape Town in 1909; Mohandas K. Gandhi led a non-violent protest by coloreds against Britain's withdrawal of the right of "non-whites" to sit in South Africa's Parliament. The Native Lands Act of 1913 allocated 87 percent of the land to whites, 13 percent to blacks. But after Nationalists assumed power, apartheid became not just a practice but official government policy, increasingly complex and insidious. More and more legislation further reinforcing segregation was passed. This included the Group Areas Act of 1950 which determined where South Africans could live; established population registration by race; prohibited marriages between different races; and stipulated separate amenities based on race, i.e. toilets, drinking fountains, beaches, bus benches, schools, and entrances to public places.

Even under the slightly more relaxed British, blacks were excluded from the voting rolls. In 1956, the coloreds' right to vote disappeared in a flurry of ineffectual English rhetoric. Three years earlier, one of the earliest white champions of black rights, Helen Suzman, was elected to Parliament. She wrote in her memoir, *In No Uncertain Terms* (Alfred A. Knopf, 1993), that by the time of the disenfranchisement of coloreds, "the National Party government had already laid the foundation of what was to become the most racially defined society in the world, in which whites and blacks were segregated by laws covering every aspect of their lives ... By and large, the relationship between white and black was that between master and servant."

Little news from this land of entrenched, legal racism reached the outside world until two events during the 1960s: the massacres at Sharpeville and the assassination of a South African head of government. Sharpeville came first. In 1960, Robert Sobukwe, leader of the Pan Africanist Congress (PAC), called on blacks to burn their passbooks during country-wide demonstrations scheduled for March 21. Laws requiring them to carry these documents, including official entries of everything from birthplace and race to jobs and marriages, and produce them when called upon, dated back to laws adopted in

1922. Natives, as blacks were then called, could come to the cities to work but must leave when the job ended. Their only legal residences were the Native Reserves or "homelands," sections set aside for them by the Land Act of 1913.

Through the years, pass laws were added to and strengthened, eventually turning the need to carry these books into the very essence of apartheid, the most hated expression of white suppression. Blacks existed as migrant workers in the land in which they had been born, returning from jobs in the cities to families in their "homelands," traditionally for a month every year. It was even illegal for them to be in white areas—all cities were designated white areas—after sundown. Most dwelt in employers' hostels or squatted in the black townships outside the cities. The exceptions were servants who "slept in." And that specified somewhere on the property, not in the house. Police vans patrolled city streets constantly, randomly stopping blacks and demanding they produce their passes. Those who could not were picked up and imprisoned, having committed the crime of seeking work without a permit.

On March 21, 1960, the day of Sobukwe's planned pass law protests, violence first erupted between blacks and police at Langa, the black township outside of Cape Town. However, that date is remembered because of what happened at another township, Sharpeville, near Johannesburg. In what was intended to be a symbolic, non-violent statement, large numbers of unarmed blacks arrived at the police station to hand over their pass books. Though no order to shoot was apparently given, an officer fired into the crowd. Others then did the same. When the shooting stopped, sixty-nine blacks lay dead and 180 injured in what would be recorded in history as the Sharpeville Massacre. Just days later, the ANC and PAC were banned.

The second event that captured the world's attention was the assassination of Hendrick Verwoerd, Prime Minister of South Africa. On September 6, 1966, Parlimentarians were filing in and taking their seats in the wood-paneled chambers. At the opening of the afternoon session, the Prime Minister would address them. As Verwoerd came in and prepared to sit down, members watched in horror and amazement as he collapsed with a strangled cry. Some rushed forward to apprehend the attacker. An ambulance rushed the dying Verwoerd to the hospital. The assassin, a Greek-Portuguese immigrant by the name of Demetrio Tsafendas, had been hired as a messenger. Tried later in court, he was found insane and remained in prison for the rest of his life.

A period of relative racial calm ended with the schoolchildren's march in Soweto in June 1976. Trouble spread throughout the country. Hundreds of blacks were killed in confrontations with the police and military. Hundreds more fled the country, many to African National Congress camps across the border for guerrilla training.

In early September 1977, my husband, Fraser, a photographer at the *Daily Dispatch*, and I were packing to leave. A week or so earlier, his temporary residency had been revoked and he had been ordered to leave immediately. I had permanent residency status but little choice. Intervention by *Dispatch* lawyers gave us a short grace period. On September 12, 1977, Steve Biko, founder of the Black Consciousness movement of the late 1960s and 1970s, died in detention in a Port Elizabeth jail. Five weeks later all of the organizations that had sprung up through that movement were banned. Many individuals who spoke out against apartheid were banned or detained also. Among them was our editor, Donald Woods. On New Year's Eve 1977, Woods escaped across the South African border, joined up with his family there and eventually reached London. (That story was told in *Cry Freedom*, a 1988 film by Sir Richard Attenborough based on Woods' book, *Biko*. Woods died of cancer in London in August 2001).

In the years following Biko's death, the government became increasingly repressive, the country increasingly ungovernable. International sanctions had hurt the country economically. Black townships were virtually out of control. White privilege was eroding.

When F.W. de Klerk appeared before the South African Parliament on February 2, 1990, to open his first legislative session as president, South Africans expected some kind of reform concessions. But

De Klerk did not just advocate cosmetic changes. Journalist Allister Sparks in his book, *Tomorrow Is Another Country* (University of Chicago Press, 1995), described the event as ephochal: De Klerk unleashed "forces that within four years would sweep away the old South Africa and establish an altogether new and different country ... with another constitution and another flag and another national anthem. And above all another ethos."

De Klerk's opening sentence, "The general election of September 6, 1989, placed our country irrevocably on the road of drastic change," launched a half-hour speech that would end a half century of white domination and begin a new, black-led South Africa. Among the events following was the legalization of the whole range of black liberation organizations and their sympathizers, outlawed for three or more decades. These included the African National Congress, its guerrilla wing Umkhonto we Sizwe (MK, Spear of the Nation); the Pan Africanist Congress; and the South African Communist Party. Nine days after De Klerk's speech, on February 11, 1990, Nelson Mandela, imprisoned since 1963, was freed.

Initial talks between National Party and black leaders went nowhere. The apartheid thinkers first tried to prevent black participation at the political center, then to ensure the status quo by retaining veto rights to decisions other than their own. Finally, in January 1991, Mandela made a breakthrough. He called for an all-party congress to negotiate the route to a constituent assembly. Both the ANC and the Nationalists publicly promised citizens this would happen before the end of 1991. The weekend before Christmas, the Congress for a Democratic South Africa (CODESA) assembled at the World Trade Center, an exhibition hall near Johannesburg. Two hundred and twenty-eight delegates represented nineteen political parties. Absent were Zulu Chief Mangosuthu Buthelezi and his Inkatha Freedom Party and the Pan Africanist Congress (PAC) leadership, which boycotted the session.

When the council met again in May 1992, the major issue of contention concerned approval of clauses in the new constitution. The

ANC proposed a two-thirds majority vote for passage; the Nationalists insisted on a 75 percent majority. When talks broke down, the
ANC took a more militant stance. Boycotts, demonstrations and
strikes, organized and backed by the Congress of South African Trade
Unions (COSATU), followed. Violence was reported everywhere.
Thirty-eight blacks were massacred by Zulu supporters of Inkatha; a
crime the white government was suspected of abetting for the purpose of weakening the ANC. When De Klerk, in a gesture of sympathy, visited the site of the massacre, riots erupted. Police responded
with gunfire and twenty more died. The ANC withdrew from Congress negotiations and in June Mandela announced they would stay
away until fourteen of his party's demands were met.

In September 1992, twenty-eight marchers were killed and more
than 200 injured in demonstrations in the Ciskei homeland. A week
later, Mandela cut his demands to three: the release of 200 disputed
political prisoners; securing of eighteen Zulu migrant-worker hostels, identified as sites of violence; and a ban against the bearing of
cultural weapons, such as traditional tribal sticks and knives. Two
days afterward, De Klerk publicly invited Mandela to a summit meeting for the purpose of finding a way to end the violence. This session
ended with both parties signing a Record of Understanding that
negotiations would resume. Once again, Zulu leader Buthelezi
declined to participate.

Informal meetings between the leaders continued. In March
1993, a new negotiating council consisting of twenty-six parties,
minus the Zulu's Inkatha Freedom Party (IFP) once again, met in
Johannesburg.

After the murder of Chris Hani, a popular young black Communist Party leader, early in April and the deaths of six mourners at his
funeral, Mandela spoke to the nation on national television. He
appealed to whites and blacks to close ranks and prevent emotions
from destroying their joint future.

But more conflict lay ahead. In June, a raucus mob of 3,000
Afrikaner right-wingers marched on the World Trade Center in

Johannesburg, headquarters of negotiations. They overran the chambers and trashed whatever they came to, pouring juice on carpets and urinating on desks.

On July 25, five masked black men, armed with guns and hand grenades, burst into St. James Church in Cape Town. Inside were one thousand worshipers, all white, including one hundred and fifty Russian sailors. Twelve people were killed, fifty-six injured, many of them maimed for life. The attackers were suspected to be members of the Azanian People's Liberation Army (APLA), military wing of the PAC. Earlier the same group had been accused of strikes against whites in Grahamstown, Queenstown and Cape Town, as well as the murder of U.S. Fulbright scholar Amy Biehl as she drove three black friends to their homes in Cape Town's Guguletu township. More violence, this time from the South African Army, came in the Transkei capital of Umtata. Five 12- to 19-year-old students, wrongly identified as APLA guerillas, were gunned down by members of a commando unit. Once again black and white negotiations for a constitution acceptable to both miraculously survived.

Just before dawn on November 18, 1993, the final clause of the constitution was adopted. The agreement ended eight years of negotiating, Sparks wrote, which had begun in Nelson Mandela's hospital ward, continued through prison cells, through intelligence networks, secret channels, and underground communications systems and secret couriers and involved as many as twenty-six political parties and government bodies.

Much of the 142-page document was devoted to measures reassuring the country's white minority. Cabinet seats were promised to minority parties for the next five years; jobs and pensions of white soldiers, police and civil servants were protected; important powers were assigned to the nine provincial governments. A Bill of Fundamental Rights would be safeguarded by a powerful constitutional court. The bill guaranteed freedom of speech, of the press, of movement, the right to a fair trial and the right to life which meant that the state would never again be allowed to kill dissenters. Consensus was reached on a new flag and a new national anthem which combined the battle hymn of the liberation movement and the traditional Afrikaans anthem. A House of Assembly would be composed of four hundred members and the Senate would have ninety, ten from each province.

The compromise between power sharing and majority rule came in clauses stating that minority parties would share in executive power on the basis of proportional representation until the next general election in 1999. The country would be headed by a president and two deputy presidents, one for the party which came second in the election, the other from any third party which received more than 20 percent of the popular vote. If no party attained that, the office would also go to the winning party.

But despite the consensus at the top, dissension continued. Lucas Mangope, president of Bophuthatswana, an independent homeland since 1977, announced in March of 1994 that his people would not participate in the April elections. Earlier, on January 1 of that year, the South African Negotiating Council had agreed on restoration of South African citizenship to all residents of tribal homelands. Citizens of Bophuthatswana wanted their rights too. Strikes and looting spread throughout the homeland. Right wing factions dispatched troops to its border. The Bophuthatswana army mutinied; its police force lost control. After Mangope was deposed, Mandela sent emissaries to take charge. Elsewhere the president of the Ciskei homeland resigned. The Kwazulus still refused to be part of the coalition. But with just seven days to go until the election, the leader of its Inkatha Freedom Party announced it was ready to participate. That meant seven days to amend the printing on 80 million ballots. On the day before the April 26 election, a special session of Parliament passed legislation permitting late voter registration. A day earlier, a massive car bomb outside the ANC office in Johannesburg had killed nine and injured 92; another bomb killed ten. Six polling stations became bomb targets.

But the election went on as scheduled, with voting spread over three days. When the ballots were tallied, the ANC had won 62.65

percent of the national vote; the National Party 20.4; and Inkatha Freedom Party 10.5. The ANC carried seven of the nine provinces. The Nationalists captured the Western Cape and the IFP won KwaZulu Natal.

On May 10, 1994, Nelson Mandela was inaugurated as President; Thabo Mbeki, first deputy; and F.W. de Klerk, second deputy.

Going back over this, it still seems amazing that black majority rule in South Africa happened at all, even more so that it came about without a bloody, countrywide revolution. Violence and brutal deaths occurred from the day that Mandela's release was announced until he was inaugurated as president. Yet, somehow, the leaders, black and white, managed to contain the troubles, to put the peace process out of reach of those who sought to bring it down and to focus on resolutions of the issues that kept them apart.

I remember so vividly all-night talks in the '70s with friends, particularly those at *The Daily Dispatch*, about the country's future. Not one of them and no other South African, white or black, that I ever listened to suggested that anything short of a revolution, all-out war in the streets, would produce an end to apartheid, much less an election where all could vote, regardless of the color of their skin. That this happened truly is a miracle.

II
🌿 *Sue van der Merwe*

I've always thought of myself as working to change the country

A guard waved me through a grilled iron gate and I entered the grounds of Parliament. The president's offices were in the pillared building ahead, to the left of the main complex. In the week before sessions began there wasn't much going on, at least outside. A few people strolled along a broad, shady, pedestrian walkway. On one side lay the older, grander buildings, on the other, more modern structures that looked stark by comparison.

I had been here earlier, on the Elderhostel tour, and knew that extensive gardens, lawns and huge trees lay beyond the complex and all of this was right in the center of Cape Town.

I climbed broad steps to the classic Victorian, Corinthian-columned House of Parliament. The original wing had been completed in the mid-1880s, the newest extension in 1987. I took a narrow passage on one side of a towering entrance hall and ended in a cozy lobby. A half dozen colored men in white shirts, ties and dark pants watched cricket on TV. I told a desk attendant I had an appointment with Sue van der Merwe. He dialed her extension. Busy. I sat on one of the green leather couches and looked at the test match between Australia and South Africa. Five or ten minutes later, the man at the desk beckoned. I signed a visitors book, then followed him upstairs.

Van der Merwe was on the phone. Her office was surprisingly modest, small and spartan. If a secretary had come with the job, there

17

would have been nowhere to put her. A normal-sized desk, a couple of chairs and a tall cabinet for books and papers just about filled the room. A single, small dormer window framed a knobby peak next to the slab top of Table Mountain.

When Van der Merwe hung up, I asked how she came to be in Parliament.

In the weeks before the 1994 election, ANC leaders had called: Could her name be added to the list of ANC candidates? She agreed and became 141 of 200. That did not put her on the 1994 ballot, but a year and a half later, after several of those elected moved up to ambassadorships or to head government departments, Van der Merwe found herself in Parliament. She had arrived in January 1996, which meant she was just beginning her third year.

Other things about her position were different as well. While most MP's represented a single constituency, ANC leaders had asked Van der Merwe to take on two districts, one urban, the other rural. The reason was that, unlike all other provinces where the ANC won by large majorities, only 31 or 32 percent of the people in the Western Cape voted ANC. The consensus was that coloreds, who made up seventy percent of the population, voted for the enemy they knew, the National Party, rather than the one they didn't, the ANC.

Van der Merwe's constituencies were Malmesbury, approximately forty miles from Cape Town, and nearby Elsie's River where she shared responsibilities with another member of Parliament. "Elsie's River turned out to be a difficult place," she recalled, "filled with gangs and people living in urban squalor, high-rise flats, poverty and unemployment." She winced. "It is really gangland; a grim place."

The phone rang and she became involved with the call. Van der Merwe was strikingly handsome: tall, slender, with shining, shoulder-length, ash-blonde hair. Her voice was clear and strong. She impressed me as poised, articulate, self-confident, direct. Her tailored suit, in a beige-gray, added just that extra emphasis to her air of authority. On the other hand, a ready smile made her seem less of an important personage, more accessible. She looked healthy and fit.

Probably in her early 40s. Like many white South Africans, I thought, she could have passed for American, most likely because our ancestors shared the same national origins.

Malmesbury, continued Van der Merwe, turned out to be a problem, too. but quite a different one. The area, a Nationalist stronghold, had no ANC office and few ANC members. Those who did belong to the ANC were more involved in political infighting than in political action.

After a year at Elsie's River, Van der Merwe called it quits. She told party leaders she couldn't do both places and chose Malmesbury, the center of a district with an estimated population of 100,000. She opened an office there in August 1996 and had appointed an administrator to deal with daily concerns of the voters.

"I was on the phone to her when you came in," Van der Merwe said. "At the moment, it's mainly Advice Office stuff, but the idea is for us to act as a pipeline to Parliament from the community—so people understand what their rights are. When the constitution was launched, we took a week and went to all the schools, all the post offices and all the police stations in the whole constituency which is not only Malmesbury town but the seven surrounding towns."

"I keep in close contact with the town council and, while it did have a majority of National Party members, we now have equal numbers of ANC and ANC supporters and National Party."

As always, when I got into a conversation with a white South African, I was curious as to how he or she became politically aware.

"I came from a very political family," Van der Merwe said. "My father was involved in civic politics—he'd been mayor of Port Elizabeth for three terms—and my mother had an American view of life which was nonracial and nondiscriminatory. They instilled in us a sense of justice. My two brothers and I have all been very involved in politics—far to the left of our parents, of course."

Her American-born mother had been attached to the U.S. consulate in South Africa when her parents met. Van der Merwe's paternal grandfather came from England in the early 1900s, establishing a

19

timber and hardware business in Port Elizabeth.

"Growing up in Port Elizabeth—a community with quite a reactionary white community but what I would call a noble black community, strong and ANC-based—you couldn't help but think, 'This is wrong, what's going on.' And you read things. Then there was my mother's British friend who was told if she didn't cease with the Black Sash, she would be deported."

Van der Merwe said she hated high school from beginning to end, finding her country's educational system close-minded, narrow and discouraging of anything other than conventional beliefs. Midway through her first year at Rhodes University in Grahamstown, she received an American Field Service scholarship for a year of school in Redondo Beach, California.

"I remember being quite scared about the way I would be received in America, coming from this apartheid country," she said. "And I remember addressing groups of American school children, some of the groups mainly black, with some trepidation. I sometimes didn't have the answers to their questions and, at that point, I wasn't involved."

Back once again in South Africa, she studied sociology and political science at the University of Cape Town. After graduation and a series of jobs she took a year off, living briefly in Paris, London, Italy, and California.

"I toyed with emigrating," she said, "but watching South Africa from afar, I decided I wanted to be involved."

She moved to Johannesburg and joined Black Sash, putting in a couple of days each week at the Advice Office. Most of the problems that came to them involved pass laws, the laws which required all blacks to carry identity books, officially-issued records, called passes, that included place of birth, jobs, and designated homeland. Blacks were only permitted in cities if they had been born there or held a job there for a minimum of ten years. A woman could be in a city only if she lived with her husband who must be a legal resident.

Had Black Sash been her only anti-apartheid option? Van der

Merwe paused, looked out the window next to her, then said, "I've thought about this because many of my colleagues here, of all colors, were involved in the underground movement. When I came from that extended trip overseas, what I wanted was to *do* something, not just join, but do. And joining the underground would have meant leaving the country for military training and somehow I couldn't do that. Certainly Black Sash was the only legal organization that took a firm and courageous stand."

"I think the Black Sash women were seen as 'do-gooders'—but quite left wing do-gooders. There was the Institute of Race Relations and the Christian Institute but that was underground at that stage. Later, in the '80s, the UDF (United Democratic Front) emerged. UDF membershp was only through affiliation with other organizations. I was one of the proponents of Black Sash affiliation, but the organization decided to stay apolitical. And by that time I had babies and there was no chance of going into exile or anything like that."

Van der Merwe was a quintessential Afrikans name. I remembered that in the seventies, in predmoninantly English-language East London, Van der Merwe in the opening line was a clue the joke would be ethnic.

Her husband, Sebastian (Tian) van der Merwe was Afrikaner—a liberal, she said; "one of the courageous few in the tiny town of Williston in the northwest Karoo. His father was a teacher in a god-forsaken community of stones, pepper trees and a huge, monolithic Dutch Reformed Church. His father supported the old South African Party, the SAP, Jan Smuts party, which later became the United Party, and Tian started out in the United Party which was then the English-speakers political party. Later he broke away to join the Progressive Party, which in time became the Progressive Federal Party and then the Democratic Party."

As always when South African political parties came into a conversation my eyes, at least figuratively-speaking, glazed over. English-language politics thrived on revisions to party policies and every change apparently required a new name. When someone mentioned the Progressive Party, there usually was a reference, by name, to what it had been before and what it evolved into. By contrast, the Afrikaners stayed singular and simple—the National Party.

The Van der Merwes married in 1981, having met when she worked for the PFP in Johannesburg. For years that party, originally the Progressive Party, had one lone representative in Parliament, Helen Suzman. Eventually, white voters elected thirty-two PFP members to Parliament and in the eighties, the PFP replaced the United Party as the National Party's official opposition. Van der Merwe said while she had great respect for Suzman and the party's leader Colin Eglin, she left the party when a decision was taken to stay in a new tricameral Parliament.

"The question for me was: Should we participate in a white/mixed-race/Indian parliament from which blacks were excluded? My answer was 'no' and to end my involvement with the party." She joined the United Democratic Front, essentially the African National Congress, legal and with a name change, she said. Though the UDF was never banned, many of its members were terrorized and many locked up, including one of the organizers, Trevor Manuel. Anyone caught wearing the colors of the UDF flag—the same as those of the flag of the still-underground ANC—was arrested. The UDF had a strong women's faction. Women in factories covered T-shirts with UDF slogans with blouses, wore coats over the blouses and, Van der Merwe said, still got thrown in jail. Manuel was in prison two years. After serving as the Mandela government's Minister of Trade and Industry, he was then Minister of Finance.

Van der Merwe shook her head. It seemed impossible so much had changed in such a short time, she said.

Oh yes, she certainly did remember being afraid, especially after the birth of their first child at the end of 1982. "My husband represented the Green Point constituency and we lived then in Sea Point. There was always the threat of being teargassed by special police at a meeting. Occasionally we received bomb threats and Tian got a lot of hate mail."

"In '89," she continued, "we were on the streets every second week, marching—just fighting on, trying to erode the base of National Party power. They teargassed us, but with the organization of the UDF and the movement against South Africa abroad, the position for the government was quite rapidly becoming untenable. We did hope that eventually Mandela would be released, but the fear was always that no, he wouldn't be. I don't think any of us anticipated F.W. de Klerk's statement on the second of February 1990."

She paused and grinned: "In fact, Tian gave an interview to an international journalist the day before and said he didn't expect anything very dramatic out of that speech. He said to me afterward, 'As a politician, you should *never* predict anything because it's always wrong.' So that was the mood at that time—signs of strain in the governing party and a great deal of energy and power developing in the movement."

"I remember the day of that speech so well," she said. "It was hot and lovely. I went to work in Mowbray—I was coordinator of the Black Sash Advice Office there—and a number of us in the office decided to get on the train and come into town to participate in the protest against the government's opening an illegitimate Parliament. We got there and were mingling around, people were toyi-toying (a tribal jig), and then the word was out. Someone had seen the speech. The news spread like wildfire. Desmond Tutu was on the platform. He said 'We must keep calm' and 'The march will proceed' and 'We're going down Wales Street'—all of this. I saw my husband. He'd come out of Parliament to tell me. 'I already know,' I shouted. The whole day was a big march—from Green Market Square down past Parliament and back down to the Parade where there were lots of festivities. It was just euphoria."

"And then came a very difficult time. All the talk about talks. The negotiation process. It was difficult for groups like the Black Sash. Members became depressed: 'The country is open now, you're not needed.' International funding began to dry up."

Van der Merwe was elected to what turned out to be the final national executive committee of Black Sash. After two years of painful discussions, the decision was made to disband. The political wing of the organization disappeared. Advice Offices would continue.

In 1991, Van der Merwe joined the ANC. The Claremont section where she lived, bordering Newlands where I was staying, had the largest white ANC branch in the country, she added with pride.

It seemed a crazy world to her now, sitting in her office on the fifth floor of the Parliament building, an ANC Member of Parliament, a photo on her desk of her husband and Helen Suzman taken at Namibian Independence celebrations in 1990.

I knew her husband had been killed and kept putting off asking about something that could not fail to be painful. It was all right, she said. She could talk about it. Six and a half years had dulled the ache.

"He was killed in a car accident. It is one of the diabolical aspects of South African life—these appalling deaths on the roads. We have really bad enforcement of the rules, people don't have licenses, people drive drunk. We don't have an adequate public transport system so there are all these taxis with over-tired drivers carrying lots of people at great speeds."

"It was a very wet night when he was killed. He was coming home from the airport and someone just went straight into him. It was a great loss to me and I believe to the country as well. It was impossibly difficult—impossible to describe. You just eke out an existence. After a year you stop crying every day and then it gets easier. The responsibility is huge, but I had my two kids and I had to cope. You must make every decision. You've got to pay all the bills, earn all the money and so on."

Van der Merwe believed herself luckier than some widows in that she and her husband had always worked. They owned their house and had furnished it.

We went back to her work. Parliamentarians are asked to serve on two legislative committees. Political parties are represented proportionately: If a committee has 25 members, two-thirds must be ANC, roughly the same percentage as were voted into Parliament.

Van der Merwe's late arrival in Parliament limited her choices of committees and she ended up on tourism and environmental affairs and also on communications. The latter oversees broadcasting, postal service and telecommunications—three immense and complicated quasi-government services. Tourism especially interested her and she ended up heading that subcommittee. Tourism, she believed, could quickly and substantially increase employment as well as foreign revenue. Crime was a deterrent, she admitted, but the potential was there. At that time tourism accounted for four percent of the country's gross domestic product. She predicted that could rise to ten percent by the year 2000.

Van der Merwe leaned across the desk. She spoke with enthusiasm: "I believe that tourism has been treated in the past as a glamorous stepchild where it should be regarded as a major industry, particularly in view of the fact that global tourism has really taken off in the last ten years—to the extent it is megabusiness. It is a huge job creator at the service level and also because of spin-offs—more people selling more fish and so on. Cape Town is a hub and beyond we've got the bushveld, adventure tourism, everything."

I asked about the stability of the country's young government: She said, "After three and a half years of democracy, I think we are more or less on track. Nothing is as quick as we'd like it and I think we unrealistically felt that delivery would be faster. There are some major hiccups, the most of which are in education, welfare and housing. Our finance department has done an incredibly good job to steer us to a point where we are not bankrupt. They are constantly pressed to spend more and if they do, you get into a vicious cycle. We inherited this enormous debt which we're financing at great cost—a terribly difficult balance. We've currently got a two percent growth rate and we need about five or six percent to stimulate the economy to produce jobs. We need foreign investment. We need to modernize. But we need skilled people so we need the training and education side."

Van der Merwe shook her head: "It's going to be a balancing act for ten years and the decisions made by our ministers are going to be incredibly important because you can't get international investment without stability. I think this is a reality we've learned from Indonesia and Malaysia. Everyone said, 'Well, they've got economic development going and democracy will come later.' What has actually happened is the politicians in Asia, who unsuccessfully manipulated things, discovered they don't have the support of the people and it's all come crashing down around their ears. To keep a government here supported by the people, in view of the debt and the economy, is going to require a balancing act like Houdini never did."

I asked what role she expected to take in her country's development. She replied that she would like to become expert in some field—perhaps tourism. "I've always thought of myself as working to change the country, helping it develop. I have some advantages. Having come from a privileged background, in South African terms, I have a lot of connections and I think that is quite useful."

Did she want to serve another term in Parliament? "I would have to be nominated first," she replied with a smile, "*then* decide if I would stand, and that's a decision I haven't yet made."

I asked what members of Parliament earned. Quite a lot, she said, opening a desk drawer and rummanging through it. She brought out a slip: her salary was 13,000 rands ($1,444 US*) a month. With car and allowances, the total came to approximately 13,500 ($1,500 US) rands per month.

"That's quite a lot," she said again, "but for people who have been underground and have nothing, it's not enough. I think I earn it. I think a lot of my colleagues don't and I think a lot of my colleagues should earn more because they work extremely hard. For me it's ample."

"But I have to work. If not here, I'd have to find another job. And that's the way the cookie crumbles..."

Van der Merwe grinned: "That's an old saying from Redondo Beach."

As the time she had reserved came to an end, Van der Merwe said, "I love this country and am committed to it. And I'm very proud of

26

and in awe of people like Thabo Mbeki (Mandela's successor as president), Trevor Manuel, and the women, ordinary members of Parliament now, who acted with such integrity and decency in the face of great hardship. I'd like us to be tougher with those who didn't, but there's an African tradition of fairness and justice that often takes quite a circuituous route to the end goal of catching the bad guys and girls. I see these people in committee when difficult decisions are taken on a matter of principle and they make me very proud to be South African."

*Author's Note: The monetary amounts in South African rands were converted to US dollars at the time of the final editing in mid-November 2002. The rate of exchange then was approximately 9 rands per US dollar. In 1998, when the numbers were given to me, the exchange rate was 7.25 rands for each dollar.

III
🌿 *Trudy Thomas*
You've got to stand there, let the storms come and know who you are

Trudy Thomas had walked ahead, through a large room without partitions, between rows of beds and IVs hooked to silent, lethargic children with bellies swollen not by food but by starvation. Further on, in the adult wards, we passed patients suffering from tuberculosis, others with bodies covered by burns so horrible I looked away. Still others lacked arms or legs or hands or some of each. Thomas strode purposefully on, a small, straight-backed figure with head moving from side to side, explaining cases and situations over her shoulder as she went. We had been at St. Matthews, a mission hospital deep in the Eastern Cape frontier. To me St. Matthews looked like a chamber of death rather than a place of healing, a place from which there would be no escape.

I had met Thomas that day in 1972 and from that time on, no matter where she was, what she was involved with, my mind saw her right back there.

On a pleasant mid-summer January day in 1998, I again followed Trudy, this time into the living room of her house at Gonubie, a small, scattered coastal community a short distance from East London.

I had come to hear about Trudy's latest job: Minister of Health of the Eastern Province. Since I had seen her last in 1991, her life had changed as much as her country's. But she looked as I remembered. She was five feet one or two inches and still wore her light brown hair —now laced with gray—quite short. No white coat now, but a brightly patterned shirtwaist dress in a silky fabric. With her manner and her dress, she could have passed for a prosperous suburban matron. Her gaze was friendly, open and direct. Except there was, and had always been, that signature intensity of expression. Trudy came with a focus to her life that was obvious even before you knew what it was all about. I envied that and imagined others did too. Yet, once again, despite her welcoming words and smile, I experienced a sense that I was keeping her from responsibilities far more important than any words.

But, unexpectedly, words, words to get what she needed had become a large part of her job.

As Minister of Health, Thomas's domain included more than a hundred hospitals, over 600 health clinics and 38,000 staff. Six million people, likely more, lived in the Eastern Cape. The great majority were rural, uneducated and impoverished blacks. After practicing medicine under third world conditions for all of her professional career, Thomas had learned methods to alleviate environment-related health care problems. Along the way, she also had discovered that it took political action to get the resources required to do that. Now she was on the administering side of the equation and struggling for footing.

"I think all of us who have come into the government are, at this stage, trying to decide just what is politics?" Thomas said. "Three months after I was in this job, someone called me a politician and I felt insulted. Then I had to rethink this because if you are a minister, you are a politician. We've all had difficulty in seeing what politicians do: How do politics and administrators and administrations interface?"

"In this transitional phase, it is not a matter of taking over the existing offices and making modifications to established procedures and policies—shining them up. It is a total transformation and in this province, at least, has been totally unbelievable. We had the black homelands with white administrators and had to bring them all together."

Part of the transition involved the assimilation of employees of the former government. In the Eastern Cape, many worked in the areas set aside as black homelands. Between 1948 and 1959, in the hope of defusing the black population's increasing anger against apartheid, the government had established several black homelands in various parts of the country. Basically, what that meant was that blacks, denied South African citizenship and the rights that came with it, were decreed citizens of one of these homelands. Whether they ever lived there or not was, as near as I could understand, irrelevant. Two of these areas, the Ciskei and the Transkei, were in the Eastern Cape. There, the Nationalist government claimed, the black man could own land, work in his own economy and run his own government. Bureaucracy flourished. When Nelson Mandela's African National Congress party took over the reins of government from the National Party, it agreed to retain the former administration's civil servants. The homelands of the Eastern Cape came with more than their share.

I had hoped to talk with Trudy a day earlier but that had not worked out. She had been tied up at an all-day AIDS conference at Rhodes University in Grahamstown. That seemed a good place to start. She reported the rate of AIDS in the Eastern Cape at six percent in 1996 and eight percent in 1997, but believed it was probably at least twice that. Serious as that was, she considered AIDS relatively minor compared to other health issues she faced daily. Malnourishment, she said, constituted an enormous health problem throughout the Eastern Cape. While measles had been controlled in the Ciskei, it remained rampant throughout the homeland next door, the Transkei. The year before, Thomas had initiated a measles immunization program in the Transkei. Not much else looked positive. TB rates remained high. Typhoid and Hepatitis B were common throughout the region. Every one of the diseases she had brought up, she said, reflected socio-economic and environmental problems that could not be addressed by medicine. And these were only part of the depressing conditions she faced every day. She called the incidence of assaults "appalling." Motor vehicle accidents were epidemic; approximately 5,000 traffic deaths annually in the Eastern Cape alone.

"We have," she said, "terrible roads, drivers, vehicles and poor ambulance response." Roughly half the beds in long-term care wards held victims of trauma. The next highest category was tuberculosis.

What I was hearing sounded very much like the conditions that existed in 1972 at St. Matthews, the medical compound in Keiskammahoek, a vast rural section of the Eastern Cape with a desperately poor black population of between 30,000 and 40,000. Once a mission station, St. Matthews had evolved into the Anglican hospital run by Thomas and her husband, Ian Harris, also a doctor.

A driver from *The Dispatch* had delivered me to the mission, an hour or so ride from East London. I remembered taking a dirt path to the old frame house where Harris and Thomas and their daughters lived. It was hot. A dozen or so women sat on the porch stringing beads on stout thread. They sold that kind of "native" folk art in East London shops—dolls made of beads and wire, beaded hems and yokes on heavy cotton blouses and skirts, rows of beads strung together for bracelets, earrings, necklaces and pendants. The women would send off their work to be sold in the cities and holiday resorts. Thomas had organized the work sessions to bring in a bit of income to women and children struggling to survive on what they could raise on tiny plots of poor earth. Keiskammahoek, like much of rural South Africa, was a land without men. Able-bodied males disappeared at an early age. Some signed up to work in the mines. Others left to look for factory or service jobs in the cities. The best jobs came with an annual leave of several weeks so they could return to the families they left behind. Sometimes they sent money back, at least initially. All too often they simply disappeared, unable to find work or acquiring new families.

At some point during that first interview, I learned that Thomas and Harris had opened fifteen health clinics in outlying areas for patients who lived too far away to get treatment at the hospital. A few days earlier, she had said proudly, the many months she campaigned for government food supplements had finally paid off. As of that month, powdered milk and maize, ground corn, would be distributed by the hospital and clinics.

In 1991 I had interviewed Trudy again. Fraser and I, on our way back from a six months assignment in Namibia, had stopped for a month in East London and worked for *The Dispatch*. Again one of the editors suggested an interview with Trudy Thomas. No longer at St. Matthews, she had moved to East London. Most recently, she had initiated training programs for community health workers at Cecilia Makiwane, the hospital in the huge black township of Mdantsane.

As it turned out, Thomas had left St. Matthews a year after I'd talked with her there, twelve years after she and Harris had arrived. Harris's ill health was one reason—the nearest specialists were a couple of hours away in East London. They also wanted to avoid sending their daughters, then approaching high school age, to boarding schools. At that 1991 interview Thomas admitted the pace at St. Matthew's had brought her to burnout level: "That was at the end, when my husband was sick. Day after day, I'd see seventy to a hundred patients. After the wards, I'd go to the clinics and with four children ... well, I remember getting irritable."

In 1973, the year they came to East London from St. Matthews, Thomas had joined the pediatric out-patient clinic at the city's Frere Hospital. The hospital was for whites with the out-patient clinics open to blacks. Listening to Thomas then, I remembered on my morning walks from our house to work seeing the lines at the clinics snaking back and forth across the grounds. At the hospital, Thomas had organized nurse practitioner courses to alleviate case loads on too few doctors. Five years after that, Thomas set up six-week courses for nurse practitioners at the hospital in Mdantsane. Hundreds graduated, going out to work in outlying black communities and the growing squatter settlements around East London.

At one of these earlier interviews, I had learned of Trudy's background. Her father had been a miner in Cornwall in England. After emigrating to South Africa, he met and married an Afrikans woman. They lived in Krugersdrop, a small Transvaal town where Trudy was born in 1936. At five years of age, Trudy had decided to become a doctor.

Her medical career took the direction it did as a result of her childhood. She had witnessed the injustices suffered by blacks in the conservative, mostly Afrikans community, and heard her parents speak out against racism when they saw it.

Life must have been difficult for the family. In the more liberal, predominantly English-language populations of the Cape, Natal and Eastern Cape provinces, such views would not have been out of place. But the northern provinces of the Orange Free State and Transvaal were centers of Afrikanerdom and all that went with that society.

Now it was 1998 and Thomas worked out of government offices in Bisho, the new capital of the Eastern Province, a half hour drive from her Gonubie home.

My first impression of her house had been that it was like Trudy herself. Simple, honest, artistic, and at the same time functional. When she went off to the kitchen to make coffee, I strolled around. The floors were terra cotta tiles, the walls wood, brick and glass. The ceiling was open and beamed. Windows facing the rear of the house looked on an enclosed garden with small pool and palm trees. In the front, beyond a picket fence lay a narrow, little-traveled road, a strip of bush and then the Indian Ocean breaking noisily and rythmically on rocks, some of them the size of small buildings. Inside, bowls of shells sat near baskets of cactus. The furniture looked old, heavy and well-used. Open shelves held copper pots and kettles, a wine rack, books and fresh flowers. An eclectic assortment of art covered the brick wall of the entry and I walked over for a better look: a frame around a butterfly that appeared real; a pen and ink sketch of a room interior; a 12 by 24 inch portrait of a child; an editorial page cartoon from *The Dispatch* captioned: "In the memory of Steve Biko and scores of others who have died in detention in apartheid's prisons. Their spirit lives on."

Until I met Trudy Thomas, the only East London doctors I knew saw white patients in comfortable offices in the urban area. Over coffee I asked why, when she could have chosen a comfortable life and lucrative career treating whites, she had chosen to work in poor black communities.

"You could see results. You had this cause," she said, "and you were in the midst of apartheid. If you could fight apartheid, then there would be a way of correcting all these inequities. Working in this way, you could see what the reasons for the problems were, could do practical things at the time. We thought if we could change the political system, we could change that picture. You thought if you worked now and hard enough, the country would work out."

I asked how her new position had come about.

After the African National Congress was unbanned, she explained, she had joined that party and became chair of the health desk in the Border area of the Eastern Cape which included East London. In 1992 she and ANC health activists throughout the country began meeting locally, provincially and nationally. Putting in long hours after their regular jobs, they compiled what she described as "that lovely green book" which became the new government's guide to health services.

Many of these health professionals came from backgrounds such as Thomas's. Angry about apartheid, they had given a great deal of thought to the kind of health care that might work once the political situation changed. She said, "We'd gone through primary health care and community health workers and terrible fragmentation. We knew we needed a comprehensive service. But you didn't come into this blank territory where you could build your citadel. You met all sorts of resistances and existing troubles."

"We—the ANC—were elected on April 27, 1994," she continued. "And on the 13th of May the leaders announced the provincial ministers. I didn't even know I was on the list until I saw my name in the newspaper. I spoke to my daughters: 'I'm absolutely not sure of this.' They said, 'The people have spoken. Also you are a woman. Take it on.'"

Four years later, Thomas continued to work on exactly what the components of her office were. On a daily basis, she dealt with the tedious administrative duties that were a big part of her job. She met weekly with her top management and with the provincial cabinet composed of ten ministers and the premier of the province. Once a month she got together with other provincial health ministers. Keeping connected with party politics was a part of her job as well. She met weekly with the ANC caucus during legislative sessions and attended ANC political meetings. And of course there was paperwork, the prerequisite reports and documentation of everything.

Saturday, the day after our meeting, she would be with activists and members of the ANC executive council at a day-long session addressing the current crisis—a lack of money to pay legally entitled benefits to pensioners in the Eastern Cape.

Oh yes, Thomas said, she had almost forgotten to mention that in one seven-week period last year, she had attended openings of seventeen health clinics in the Eastern Cape.

She smiled, her first since she had begun talking about all the meetings and problems and responsibilities. "That took time, but it was exciting," she said. "The whole community comes together— you eat, you sing, you dance and make speeches."

Alas, she said, her smile disappearing, festive and friendly occasions came rarely. "Even within your own party, government is not a friendly environment. Politics is dirty and politicians have huge egos. They are very, very ambitious for their status and I think also very materialistic."

"This has been such a change for me because I've always been this community development activist where you get a huge amount of affirmation for saying the right thing and handing out milk. Now it's suddenly changed. In the beginning I got a mixture of what I think may have been a stroke and ulcers because I took everything personally. Then I realized people have their own agendas and you must keep very clear on what you want to do and not take remarks personally. People would say things about you, never having met you. You have to be pretty cool about it. Being older, being divorced and then finding yourself gives you a center that is very useful."

I had known about Trudy's divorce but not the reasons for it. I guess it always seemed too personal a question for our conversations.

Her husband had eventually become healthy, I knew. I had a faint memory of hearing something about his tiring of third world medicine. Had he emigrated or just moved elsewhere in the country? In South Africa, it was always tempting to blame everything bad that happened on apartheid and those who delivered it.

Trudy looked beyond me to the sea. "There's a rock there. It sometimes just stands, seemingly very calm and happy and holding court with the sea lapping around it. Sometimes storms bash it. Sometimes, at low tides, it is totally isolated. But it is always there and for me that is a marvelous analogy. You've just got to stand there, let the storms come and know who you are. You must recognize where the process is. When you're in a storm, you extrapolate the storm to the whole situation, whereas you must realize tomorrow there may be sunshine."

Thomas stopped talking, then smiled again, ruefully: "I think everyone had the idea we'd wake up the day after the government was in place and look outside and all the clinics would be built and everyone would have a house and a job. Certainly, if not then, we'd do it in three months. Possibly it might take a year."

Though that of course had not happened and she had no idea when it might, still she saw progress, within the country and her own area of responsibility. By the second year, Thomas had been given a budget. A health system had been initiated and sound future planning was underway. Eighty-six clinics had been built in the Eastern Cape. She believed another eighty would put one within walking distance of every "Eastern Cape mother with a baby on her back." Each clinic required proper staffing. Nurses had to be trained not only in health care but to be courteous, kind and friendly. To ensure that nurturing environment did indeed happen, Thomas had initiated a "culture of caring" which was promoted through festivals and celebrations. Unfortunately this came as a response to a 1995 strike which closed hospitals and clinics throughout the Transkei and left critically ill patients unattended.

Also on the positive side, she believed that she finally had gathered enough nurses. The next step would be reassigning many of them.

Fewer were needed some places, more in others, particularly in rural areas. She was then working on developing incentives to make redistribution more palatable to those affected. Unfortunately, doctors remained in very short supply. Cuban doctors had been recruited and the first of them had just arrived, specifically for duty in rural facilities. I'd read of this in recent issues of the *Dispatch* and in national papers. Communications between the Spanish-speaking doctors, administrators, staff and patients apparently caused some initial problems.

Thomas said the Cubans were a help but not an answer. Appeals also had gone out through the churches to doctors inside and outside the country asking for assistance, specifically in the remote, impoverished and desparately needy areas of the country. Proper management of pharmacies, getting drugs on their shelves, and upgrading hospital care were also being addressed.

"In the former black homelands, in the decade before the majority government, there were all sorts of perverse influences because of apartheid and misuse of the money that went there—not that there was all that much of it," Thomas said. "There was gross neglect in the hospitals. They'd truly fallen down. We're trying to build them up. And I think the human spirit had been damaged at least as much as the facilities."

She poured more coffee then talked about her personal health care priorities: "I have some special concerns, not in administrative or society's minds as yet. There's lots of depression, lots of anxiety, acting out, lots of substance abuse and practically no mental health services. And we've got violence and child abuse in horrific proportions. At festivals, people put on these little plays. In rural areas, where you think life must be idyllic, time and again, it's about fathers abusing their 13-year-old—or 8-year-old. And women too."

Thomas hoped to build a teaching hospital for health care workers in Umtata, the old capital of the Transkei. Plans had been drawn up and a ground-breaking scheduled. However, budget shortfalls had required this project to be put on hold.

In spite of what sounded to me like overwhelming difficulties,

Trudy at that point sounded positive, hopeful and enthusiastic. She was indeed optimistic, she acknowledged, about what could be done to improve health care: It was the lack of money to make these changes that worried her. For 1998, her allotted budget would cover salaries, fixed expenses, the security necessary to keep hospitals and some clinics open, not all of them. Some would have to be closed. There simply would not be enough money. The recent pension crisis in the Eastern Cape brought that reality home.

"Now we've got this huge problem and huge anger," Thomas said. "This province is a polecat because we didn't pay pensioners in December and this is a statutory entitlement. We warned them of these money shortages at the beginning of the financial year. This province is in fact the worst affected numerically and because of debt inherited from the old administrations. Computers bought by them can't be connected, just for instance, because of no electrical wiring. Some of our hospitals don't even have telephones."

Sufficient money for any kinds of public services was a problem that did not seem likely to have any immediate solution. The focus of the national leadership was on repaying, quickly, the hundreds of billions in debt inherited from the apartheid government, Thomas said. That meant budget shortages for schools, health care and everything else.

I asked what she thought the solution was. She replied without hesitation: "That we don't reduce the debt so fast."

Despite the country's financial difficulties during this transitional period, her own problems with running her office, Thomas remained optimistic about the future. She believed that the country's anticipated economic growth would bring additional jobs and income. She added that she hoped new enterprises would be concentrated in the impoverished homelands and the squatter areas "where crime starts."

I asked if she planned to remain in government after the 1999 elections. "I don't know that I will be among the candidates for this office," she replied. "I don't know actually if I want to be. I need time to reflect, to enjoy my grandchildren. I'll be 63 then. I'd like to sit in my top room and think a bit about what the next thing is."

What more could she say about these past years as minister of health?

"I can't say I've enjoyed it. There has to be another word. But I wouldn't have missed it for the world."

For the two nights I was in East London, I stayed with Sylvia Hagerty, friend and former colleague at the *Daily Dispatch*. On the last night, Sylvia's son Roger and his wife Morag came for dinner. Fraser and I had seen them in Johannesburg in 1991. They then owned a framing shop which also sold Morag's colorful art of bright, whimsical birds described in words that became part of her painting. Morag now worked in an East London nursing home. Roger was a manufacturer's representative. Roger always had been a sports enthusiast. These days, he said, he competed in bicycle races. He talked of the one coming up. I looked at a photo of him in such a race on the end table. When that was taken, he had both legs.

In 1988, Roger and a friend had attended a match between legendary rugby union rivals in the huge Johannesburg rugby stadium, Ellis Park. Game over, they were leaving the stadium when a car bomb just outside was detonated. Roger's left leg had been shattered and amputated. His friend lost his right leg. Sylvia said that their case had been filed with the Truth and Reconciliation Commission. Roger had not only lost his leg, she said, but as a result, his business and home in Johannesburg.

The next morning, on the way to the airport, we stopped for coffee with a retired *Dispatch* editor and his wife. Their eldest daughter and granddaughter were there as well. During the conversation, the daughter said she and her husband hoped to emigrate very soon to Australia. One of her two married sisters lived in Botswana; the other would move to New Zealand later that month. The latter and her husband had decided to leave the country after a friend who lived in the same walled and gated complex in Johannesburg had been attacked. Thugs jumped on the woman after she opened the gate.

They threw her to the ground and held a gun to the head of her 4-year-old daughter. Though she and her daughter got out of it without injury, a resident who tried to help them had been shot and seriously wounded.

Glyn Williams, the editor, and his wife Joan had come from Wales to South Africa in the 1960s. After this daughter left, they would have no family members in South Africa. Once again, it was clear that the problems of apartheid had not vanished with the old government nor been magically cured by the new one.

Cecily took a multi-laned highway from the Cape Town airport, an off ramp onto a main road lined with large trees through a residential area and then into an alley-like lane between walled houses. This section was Newlands, she said, a long-established neighborhood, about a ten-minute drive from the center of Cape Town. She turned her little blue car into a cul de sac with four double or triple garages and parked at the end in a vine-covered carport. I followed her through the gate of a white picket fence and up a walk bordered by lawn and exotic, tropical-looking plants and trees.

The house was white, small and one-storied, with plastered walls, shutters and a corrugated metal rool. A frangipani bloomed by the verandah. A metal plaque near the door read 1846. Cecily said the former slave residence had been restored by a succession of owners.

Putting my possessions in a small guestroom with a window on the garden. I joined Cecily on the deck in the back of the house. Over coffee and croissants we caught up with each other's lives. We had last seen each other six or eight months earlier in Leavenworth, Washington, where Fraser and I lived. Just about the same length of time before that, we had met in London. Both of us had come to visit mutual friends who had left South Africa and settled in London.

That had been the first time I had seen Cecily since the seventies when we lived around the corner from each other in East London. She then had been a stay-at-home mother of two boys, now, of course, grown. I had worked and we hadn't known each other well, meeting only at large gatherings. Since then she and her husband, Jan, had divorced. He had been an attorney and Progressive Party member of the Provincial Council. He now practiced law in Cape Town, not far from Cecily, but was out of politics.

Cecily had barely begun her year of round-the-world travel when I saw her in London. She explained that accepting early retirement from the library in Cape Town, where she then lived, had come with a bonus that made her dream trip possible. She promised when she got to the U.S., she would come to visit us.

The idea of this book had evolved then, on morning walks through the forests near Leavenworth. When Cecily returned to Cape Town, she had gathered addresses and phone numbers of the women we had talked about and suggested more possibilities.

Cecily told me she now had two jobs: mornings she drove to Houts Bay, an up-scale, English-speaking community about a half hour drive away. There she planned and directed preparation of the main midday meal at a retirement facility. After that, she drove an hour in the opposite direction to read manuscripts for a government-subsidized publisher of works by blacks and coloreds. Not an ideal job situation, she said, but she felt fortunate to earn enough money to support herself. In the new South Africa, whites had been moved to the back of the hiring line.

I listened and looked. The setting of her house was magical. Figs ripened on the tree next to the railing. Fern fronds and leaves the size of elephant ears—which turned out to be their name—covered the steep bank opposite. Between the banks an invisible creek made its presence known as it bubbled along, skipping over and around rocks. Around the deck and across the way grew tall willows, frangipani and bougainvillaea in bloom and palm trees. The only signs of neighbors were bits of roofs behind the greenery.

IV
☙ *Val Viljoen*

You didn't think the situation would change. You were so used to it. You just battled on

Val Viljoen had been off on some official mission when I had been in East London, but a week or two later we got together in Cape Town where she was back and forth between workshops and information sessions in the week before Parliament opened. We sat around the table in Cecily's dining room. Sun slanted through the wavy old glass and onto the scarred top of the long farmhouse table. We started out with coffee and catching-up talk. When she had lived around the corner from us all those years ago, she had been Val Sullivan, a single mother with two daughters. Not long after we left East London, she married Tony Viljoen, a principal at a local high school. Now—and I had not been all that surprised, since I remembered her as committed and energetic—she was a Member of Parliament.

Val is a medium-size woman, attractive with even features, short and gray-streaked hair. She looks British in a hard-to-define way, perhaps a precision of nose and chin. In a country where sub-tropical sun ages women prematurely, her skin was clear, fair and, since she was in her mid-fifties, remarkably unlined. I had forgotten Val's wonderful, unusual voice—almost a whisper, soothing yet enthusiastic. Because her voice is soft, one becomes only gradually aware that she speaks with authority and without hesitation, leaving little room or reason for interruption.

She was born in England, in Surrey. After completing high

school she went on to a two-year French school in London where she learned secretarial skills in French, English and Russian. She took a job for a London firm, married an engineer whose name was Colin Sullivan, and soon became pregnant.

"We wanted to travel," Val recalled. "We had a choice between Canada and New Zealand, though he had also been offered a job in South Africa. I told him I could never live in an apartheid society. I knew about this because we were a very political family, though this was ordinary party politics—Liberal—in England. One of the things I had always liked about the Liberal Party was its proportional representation in government. We have that here now and it's quite interesting that we've come full circle."

"I've always been fascinated by politics and always loved the whole sort of election fever. In England I had been involved to a certain extent in anti-apartheid movements, but in an informal way. Then Colin was offered a job in Zambia and it sounded very good. I was quite happy to go to Zambia. And at the last minute, when we were about to leave, they said, 'Sorry. But that's changed. It's not Zambia, it's Salisbury, Rhodesia.'"

"And I wasn't terribly happy, but it was a bit late by then so off we went. That was 1966. I had one child. She was six weeks. We stayed three years in Rhodesia before his company opened an office down in South Africa and he was transferred. We came straight to East London. It was quite by accident, my coming here, and it was not where I wanted to be at all, but I've remained in East London ever since."

"I'd had my second daughter in Rhodesia, as it was then, and we didn't have much money. We only had one car in East London so I was stuck in the house. I read an article in the *Daily Dispatch* about the Black Sash and I thought, 'This sounds really interesting.' A neighbor took me along to my first meeting and I realized that this was where I belonged." Val smiled. "They were very hesitant to accept me because they thought I was an informer. I think I was a bit too good out of the blue. I said, 'Black Sash sounds like something I'd like to be involved with. What can I do? I have time on my hands.' I said, 'Of course I'll help with the minutes,' and 'Yes, I'll do that.' They said, 'Uh, uh. There's something funny here,' so they were very skeptical for quite a long while."

Black Sash, a national organization of white women, had operated Advice Offices and now and then gathered for quiet stand-ins. In East London, Sash volunteers turned up weekly to staff its Advice Office, held on the second floor of an old hall used for local theater productions. There they listened to a steady stream of blacks with problems related to poverty and racism. The women wrote letters to employers and to government officials for them, told them about various welfare-type agencies and helped individuals when possible. When Black Sash members determined that some piece of legislation, or act of government, eroded human rights in their country further, they stood in silence on city center corners, holding up signs of what they were protesting, black sashes knotted at their waists, symbolic of the death of yet another freedom.

I wondered about other anti-apartheid organizations Val could have joined. "There was Institute of Race Relations," she replied. "It became more research-orientated in later years, but in those days it was activist. I don't know about the larger centers, but in East London we had only those two organizations. And those were the two everyone came to for help. I then started working for the Institute of Race Relations because that was when my husband left."

No, she said, after her divorce she never considered going back to England to live. When Fraser and I left in the increasingly turbulent seventies, many whites we knew had emigrated, fearing for their families' futures and even their lives. Others confided that they were seriously considering getting out, too. It was more problematic for South Africans looking at Australia, New Zealand or Canada, but simpler for the first-generation English immigrants. They retained British citizenship even when they became South African citizens.

Val had paused to think about the question. "I don't know that it was ever a conscious decision not to return to England. My mother had died a couple of years earlier so there wasn't that sort of tie. And also since my daughters' father was in South Africa, would it be fair to take them back to England? So I stayed. But it was necessary for me to work. My children were young. I had to support them. I found a mornings-only job as administrative secretary at Race Relations and it suited me perfectly. And from then on my involvement just grew."

Years after I had left East London, someone who knew Val well told me how poor she had been after her husband left, and that she had difficulty just getting enough money together to buy food for her daughters and herself. She had never indicated this in any way and I never guessed. She had been no complainer and she wasn't now. Her manner, which I would describe as up-beat, positive and optimistic, was exactly as I remembered.

"When the regional secretary of Race Relations—or director as they call him now—retired I took over there. That was when I became more involved in bursary work and in the African Art Center and the craft work and the employment opportunities. That was for the Institute of Race Relations, but Black Sash and Race Relations were very intertwined. In a small center like East London, it's really the same people doing everything. It was a very ordinary life, really. I stayed with the Institute of Race Relations until 1984, or maybe '85, when they had a new national director. He was not happy with the project work and wanted to make it a research-based organization, which wasn't my idea at all. I dropped out. I remained associated with Black Sash until about the 1990s."

"With Black Sash I worked in the Advice Office. There was really no over-arching campaign we were involved with. We didn't have the influx-control problems the bigger centers did because, being adjacent to the Transkei, we were where they were sent back to. We did quite a bit of work with returning political prisoners. A lot of welfare type work, a lot of bursary work, so it was really your day-to-day, common garden problems—helping wherever we could with detainees, with families of detainees, with people in prisons."

"I remarried in 1980. Tony was principal of Cambridge High School. He did not have the same political views. It was more ignorance. He'd never had the opportunities I'd had to get involved. He had always voted UP (United Party). His was that sort of involvement." Val shifted in her chair, sat back and smiled. "I remember in Black Sash, whenever there was to be any sort of public protest or lobbying, the minute one of the women said, 'Let me just ask my husband,' you could cross her name *right* off the list. The wife of a businessman was terrified of being seen to be involved politically in any way because it would affect their business, and I know that my involvement cost Tony at least one promotion. That was the way life was in those days. People were scared. I thought it very, very generous of him—and very unusual—to accept my involvement."

I asked if she had ever feared police reprisals for her activism. "No," she replied, then thought about it. "Actually, I think we were incredibly naive. We were white, middle-class women and we'd grown up in a society where you were privileged and you thought privilege gave you protection. Which it did, of course. We didn't think what we were doing was dangerous. We actually laughed at the idea. I always found it very strange that the more the security police tried to hassle us in various ways—the midnight phone calls, the letting down of your tires at meetings... Obviously, compared to other centers, these were very minimal. But the more that happened, you thought: 'Oh. Isn't that marvelous? We must be quite relevant. If they're this worried about us, we must be doing something right.' We were not that important. We just did what we thought had to be done, in a very minimal way."

After sitting silently for a moment, she said, "I don't think I ever really had an idea how this was going to turn out for South Africa. Every new year, I remember saying, 'Next year can't be as bad as last year. It cannot be.' You just sort of battled on. I remember being brought up short once. An ex-pupil of my husband, from Cambridge, was MK—Umkhonto weSizwe, Spear of the Nation, the ANC's military wing. She was sent to jail, tried and sentenced to twenty-four years. Tony was asked if he would give her a character reference for her trial, which he was more than happy to do because she was a super person. I remember being very upset by this and saying to my middle daughter, Julie, 'This is just a terrible thing to happen. When she gets out, she will be old. She will never, ever, be able to have a child.' And Julie said, 'Mom, do you actually think that in twenty-four years the situation won't have changed?' And you know at this stage, we didn't actually think the situation would change. You were just so used to it. You just battled on. You didn't know how it would change."

"Only on the 2nd of February 1990 did I hold some hope it might change. That took us totally by surprise. Don't forget East London is right out of it. You know, they say the good thing about living in East London is that when the end of the world comes, you'll still have twenty years to go. And on that day I was home. I was in the kitchen, but I wasn't listening to the radio when Stephanie phoned through from Johannesburg. She said, 'Have you heard? It's just been on the news.' She told me about De Klerk's speech and I thought she was joking. I just couldn't believe it had actually happened. It was the most amazing thing and you couldn't credit it for a long time."

"I was still involved in Black Sash at that stage. And they could have said, 'We have done a marvelous job. We have played our part and we are now disbanding.' But I think what they should have said is, 'There is a need for a human rights organization in South Africa, but it cannot be one that is perceived as being for white women only'— because Sash members until only recently had been white women. Therefore Sash must launch itself as a new organization aimed at encompassing all women, free of this perception, or indeed encompassing everyone, men and women. But they didn't do that either. So I resigned in 1990, 1991, and joined the ANC. I worked for them in the informal settlements (squatter camps)."

"In our branch there were two informal settlements, in Gonubie and Beacon Bay, and that was where there was the greatest need. And they are still there. Those were previously all-white areas, but they were different and the authorities did totally different things. In Gonubie there were domestics working and gardeners and they set up house on farmland. The municipality then said, 'We acknowledge that we have working people who will need low-cost housing and where are we going to put them?' And they began looking. They identified a suitable site and laid it out and the people moved on to it. Even now it's a really good settlement. In Beacon Bay they took exactly the other stand. People started moving on to excess farm land and the Beacon Bay municipality said, 'No. We don't want low-cost, informal housing here. We are not accepting this at all' and they did nothing. And of course the people didn't go away so that squatter camp is actually a disaster. It is so higgledy, piggledy, it's impossible to get water and other services in properly because it was never laid out. We worked in these settlements with the women who were there, looking at setting up pre-schools, creches, getting water, funding for water tanks, arranging with the municipality for water to be delivered, just the day-to-day activities—not political activism, more welfare work."

"Next thing was the election coming up," Val said. "The ANC called. 'We want an administrator for the elections.' Next thing I knew I was running the ANC election office. Working in voter education. We went into the Quigney. It had been white but had become a non-racial area. We had our pamphlets and before we knocked at the first house, we worked it out. 'Now. Do we know what we're going to do? If it's a white person who opens the door, I will speak. If it's a black person, you've got it.' So we knocked at the door and it was a colored woman. We both stood there and looked at one another. But it was great fun and we'll never have that time again, you know. It was very, very special. We worked blooming hard though. We did a lot of setting up tables at shopping centers, walked the streets looking for donations, going shop to shop, particularly targeting those that had a large black business. We opened an election office and asked for monthly donations to run it. I remember driving down Deveraux Avenue and seeing ANC flags waving. It was *just so exciting*.

"And," she continued, back to her taking-care-of-business voice, "I had all the rallies. One of the most amazing experiences I ever had and which I shall never forget: thousands and thousands of people;

suddenly the word comes that Mandela is on his way. The tension builds. In the distance you hear the cavalcade coming and you can hear a pin drop. Then out of the loudspeakers come the freedom songs, and then '*Nel—son Man—del—a, Nel—son Man—del—a.*' Then he would appear, usually on the back of a bakkie (small pick-up truck) and people would just go crazy. But that moment before he actually arrived was just amazing, incredible, and everyone was exactly that way."

"We did other rallies without big guns and a lot of house meetings as well. Our goal the whole time was to get to white voters. We didn't expect them to vote ANC. What we did say is, 'You may not vote ANC, but in the end they are going to get in, so you'll have to work with them.' We had to show them they were not something to be scared of. I don't think anyone knew how terrified the white community as a whole was. You've read about the stockpiling—candles and baked beans. It was real because no one quite knew what the ANC was. I remember at one stage thinking, I'm actually the only person here looking forward to this election."

"So election day came. And there were three election days, don't forget. The first day they dealt with the mobiles (polling places), going to hospitals, to the points where the disabled and the elderly voted. And then there were two days of actually proper elections and it was absolutely exhausting. We had a number of polling stations within the area I was responsible for. Each station had ANC people on duty as election monitors, to make sure everything was OK. But there were problems. If you had white ANC members as monitors, I'd get a call saying, 'There's no ANC representation at Cambridge Town Hall.' Black voters didn't realize those white guys were actually ANC. So you'd switch them and put blacks on and then you'd get a call from black members saying, 'The election officials won't pay any attention to us because we're black.' We were running around like mad things, going from one to another to another to another to another. Just to make sure everything was OK and doing the basics, making certain coffee and cool drinks and sandwiches were sent through to our people."

"I was then put in charge of the technical college vote-counting station, and that was an experience I will never ever repeat, I'm sure. Absolutely amazing. I think it was probably one of the best of the counting stations because it was run mainly by women. It ran like clockwork. They were using students as counters. Again we had our people in and if you went in, you had to stay for twelve hours. We would be there for twenty-four hours so we had two teams. I would be there the whole time, so I had all my food supplies, my sleeping bag and everything. People were at each table, just to make sure there was no skullduggery. We were doing Duncan Village (an old, mixed-race area within East London that had been razed and evolved into a squatter community). You can image what it was like. You'd hear the ballots opened and these young student voices: 'ANC.' 'ANC.' 'ANC.' About twelve tables and every single table, 'ANC, ANC, ANC.' I still couldn't believe it was happening."

"In the run-up to the election, we'd done a tremendous amount of working with people, doing mock ballots and mock voting days. One example was domestic workers. All ANC. A friend of mine was in the jails and she said, 'You'd expect here there'd be some PAC (Pan Africanist Congress), but it was all ANC.' The results began coming in and it was clear we were going to have a hell of a big ANC vote. And yet you still were scared. In the end, at Duncan Village, the station where I was, it was 96 percent ANC."

I asked if she had any idea of how East London whites voted.

Val nodded, "Because they voted in their own neighborhoods, it seemed clear they voted mainly (English) Democratic Party, (Afrikans) National Party, and, surprisingly, for the Inkatha Freedom Party (ANC opposition based in the Zulu province of Natal)."

I was curious as to how she had come to be a Member of Parliament. She obviously enjoyed remembering: "My ANC branch first phoned and said, 'We'd like to nominate your name as a Member of Parliament.' I just laughed and said, 'You've got to be crazy. Out of the question.' And the guy who phoned me said, 'We know you've got a difficult husband, but just go and ask him and see what he says.' So I did that. I said, 'Look, this is absolutely crazy, but they've asked me if they can put my name forward to stand for the ANC in the election.' And Tony said, 'Well, why don't you? You know that you love elections; you've always enjoyed them. You're going to be involved. You'll find it great fun. Just make damned sure you don't get in.' So OK. But also I thought, 'Well, it would be doing them a good turn because in me they've got two minorities in one.' In other words there was a formal quota for women in that a third of all nominees must be women and an informal quota for minority racial groups, such as coloreds, Indians and whites."

"So I phoned back and said, 'OK. Put my name forward. But let's be quite clear about this. I'm only doing it because I want the fun of the election. I don't want to get in, so you make damn sure I'm at the bottom of the list.' So they did. They put me right at the bottom. And we had this thought that we would get about an 80 percent poll which left me right under that (votes proportionate to party representation). Never in my wildest dreams did I think I'd get in. I remember going to one rally with Andre de Wet who was standing for the ANC for the provincial legislature and he said, 'Who is going to care for your family when you go to Cape Town?' I said, 'Don't be crazy. I'm not going to Cape Town.' He said, 'But of course you are.' I said, 'No, I'm not.' Andre is a pharmacist with a good grasp of math and he said, 'You've got so much percentage whites in the Eastern Cape and so much percentage Indians, so much percentage coloreds. And if all the whites vote this way and half the blacks . . .' And he said again, 'You know, you are going to get in.' I said again, 'You're crazy.' And I didn't actually believe him. So then the election was over. The results started coming in and Duncan Village was 96 percent (ANC), another area 98 percent and I started thinking, 'My god. This is *not funny.*'"

"It took about a week because they weren't absolutely sure how to calculate the proportional representation and it is quite complicated. For example, I think we got 84.6 percent and no one knew if they were going to take it up to 85 or down to 84. If they took it down I wouldn't be in. If they took it up, I would be. Was I going to be in or wasn't I? For about a week I didn't know. It was a terrible week. Tony was absolutely shattered. He didn't know what to expect. No one knew what to expect. I don't know if Trudy (Thomas) told you, but none of us knew what was really involved. I remember her saying to me, because she'd been asked to be a minister, 'Do you think it's a paying position?' Then it was time to be sworn in and still no one knew whether I was in or not. Pretty, the ANC secretary, called and said, 'You'd better get down to Cape Town.' And I said, 'Am I in?' She said, 'I don't know. Just get on that plane'—they'd chartered a plane to take the MP's down—'go to Cape Town and see what happens.'"

"I got on the plane and we were taken from the airport to the House of Parliament in a bus. The first I knew for sure was when I went in and saw a friend. I said, 'Janie, am I or aren't I?' and he looked through these papers and said, 'Ummmmm: V. Viljoen . . . Yes. You're a Member of Parliament.' Until that very moment I thought, 'Hey, this is fun. I've got a free trip to Cape Town. I can see my daughter who lives here. Then I'll go back home and life will resume.' Suddenly I realized that life wasn't going to resume. My whole life had been changed around. That was in May 1994. I still can't quite believe that it's true. But it is, isn't it?"

Val serves on three committees: environment and tourism; education; and her favorite, art, culture, language, science and technology. As a longtime volunteer at the East London Museum, she understands its structure and staffing. That committee is her major focus and within it, she has concentrated on heritage.

Family responsibilties had not proved a problem. Her husband took early retirement and assumed family duties in East London. Though Val only sees their 13-year-old daughter on weekends, she rationalizes that parents of boarding school students have that situation as well. There is also compensation for her in that her two older daughters and two grandchildren now live in Cape Town.

"But," she added, "if Tony had not retired early, I don't know what I would have done because women I serve with have appalling problems. Do you leave your children in your constituency, in school there? See them weekends? Do you bring them to Cape Town where you are during the week, but you've got to get back to your constituency weekends? Then comes a recess and they're still in school here. For women particularly, it's a total mess. I'm luckier than someone like Sue (van der Merwe), who has her family here. I remember sitting with a group at lunch one day: (MP) Judy Chalmers and a male member of Parliament. And he was going on about how he missed his wife, how lonely he was. How depressed he was. And he said, 'But you, Judy, you, Val, you must feel exactly the same.' And we said, 'Oh, no. We're quite happy.' If I had my family here I don't know how I'd cope. You have evening meetings and if your family is here, it is always in the back of your mind: What are they having for supper? Have you got enough toilet rolls? Has she got school shoes? With them not here, you can be single-minded. A lot of women won't come back, but you see the ANC has a quota—a third—so they'll have to find others."

Whether Val runs for reelection or not is not up to her, she said. That depends on whether or not ANC leaders nominate her: "If I am nominated, I'd love to serve and I think it would be very sad not to let us because it's taken quite a long time for us to get the hang of exactly how things work, to get our contacts going. I think not to have that continuity would be bad. I do think I probably have a pretty good chance of being asked to run again because I am a minority." She laughed. "Whenever they want a delegation to go somewhere and I don't want to go, I sit in the back of the room and try to pretend I'm not there. And then they say, 'Of course, the delegation must be representative.' And I think, '*Oh, god.* That's me.' But even if I serve again, there will never be another Parliament as amazing as the present one."

I asked about the pluses and minuses of her job. "Well, I love working on legislation," she began. "I've got that nitty, picky mind. I like studying foreign legislation, comparing it. Meeting people is a plus. To go to a museum or a library and be taken behind the scenes is wonderful. The constituency work is fascinating, but possibly the most difficult part of it all. In Cape Town dealing with the legislation, you're very focused. When you're in your constituency, every problem that comes to you is totally different."

I was curious if, when she returned home, she listened to the same problems that she once did when she worked at the Advice Office?

She nodded and sighed. "Housing, water, pensions, pensions, pensions, schools, jobs. But schools and education is for me the big one. I'd been associated with the Institute (of Race Relations) bursary fund for so long, I thought I knew black schools. But I really only knew the township schools which were't that bad. You go out to the rural areas which were the old Cape Education Department—black education. I went to a report-back meeting to the community being held in a school classroom. The school was so bad, when one of the other people was speaking, I just started crying. The windows were broken. There were no doors, goat droppings on the floor, no teaching aids. There were no blackboards. It was just a shell. And then you get angry. You think nothing can be worse than this. And the next weekend, you'd go somewhere else and it was worse. You'd sit in a classroom which didn't have a roof. The conditions were unbelievable and, gradually, I now see them being put right. Emergency classrooms are going up like mushrooms in our area. There's never enough because there's never enough money because the need is so great in the informal and rural areas, but things are definitely changing."

"The good thing is that our education department is working hand and hand with the NGOs (privately-funded, non-governmental organizations). Whereas in the past they worked against one another because the white government saw the NGOs as a threat. And I'm very positive about the future of this country—though it's easy to be positive in Cape Town. We're not always with the nitty gritty of what's on the ground. We see the longer term, the plan, and I think this will be good, though we're in for a bad period. I know Trudy (Thomas, Minister of Health Eastern Cape) has very bad problems. And while I do agree perhaps it (debt payback) could go a bit more slowly, I think the fact that they (the government) are not giving into popular pressure, for jobs, for housing, and all of that, is good."

"Crime is a major problem, certainly. But I consider our big problem is to keep the involvement of the people. Democracy in America and in England, as far as I can see, means voting every few years. What we want democracy to mean here is that people are aware and abreast of what is happening every step of the way. We've got several ways to keep people involved: report-back meetings, discussion papers and draft legislation. We're in the process of setting areas in libraries in all the big centers where we'll have all of the official government publications that come out so people can read them easily and be able to comment on them."

"And if you talk to the Black Sash ladies now, they'll tell you it has been a phenomenal experience to be welcomed into the legislature and listened to. Input has been welcomed at all levels. I think this happened because we're so new and we didn't actually know if we were capable. We wanted people to help us, we needed their input. We asked for it and this has now become an ongoing thing. For example, there was a green paper on higher education. So I went to the public hearings in the Eastern Cape where it was being presented and the people there were absolutely anti. In one particular area the minister of education had the power to appoint what he called an assessor if there was a crisis at a university. This assessor would go in to the university, size up the situation and report back with possible solutions. The university said, 'You are attacking our autonomy. We will not accept this.' The professor doing the presenting said, 'Look. Don't attack me. This isn't set in stone. Let's look at the problem. Please acknowledge that we have a problem. We have crises in our universities. How are we going to attack these? At the moment the minister must appoint a commisison. This is time-consuming. It's expensive. And it's not the best way of doing it. The assessor system is something that's worked in Australia. We think it could work here. Please help us come to a solution.'"

"OK. So they went away. And we had public hearings at national level and the same people, the university representatives, came. They said, 'We acknowledge that we need an assessor, but we would like to see higher education nominating three or four people as assessors to form a panel. Then if there's a crisis at a university, the minister will appoint someone from that panel to go to that university.' And we said, 'What a good idea.' So it was written in and it came to the actual bill in Parliament and none of the universities mentioned it. They were absolutely happy and that is how I see it working out. At that level."

Val paused, collected her thoughts then said, "I think one of the most difficult things for us is the lack of resources in Parliament—secretarial help, research help. When we arrived, we were just shown into empty offices. I had this manual typewriter which I set up and this is what I used. At that stage we had one secretary for about twenty-two people. Now I share a secretary with twelve others. Obviously she can't cope. Also she's the hell and gone, way at the end of a lo—o—o—ng corridor. So most of us do our own filing, our own typing. Actually, your secretary is not worth worrying about because she just doesn't have time. The European Union gave us a certain amount of money so some of us have been issued with laptop computers. To get one, you had to write why you wanted it. I was lucky enough to be allocated one. But Sue (van der Merwe) doesn't have one and a lot of people still have nothing at all. The ANC appointed a certain number of researchers, but not nearly enough. The EU has also put money into researchers but again, the researcher is allocated one, two, or three committees and the researchers are taken by the chair, which means ordinary members have no access to them. Plus a lot of what you want researched is not altogether your portfolio work. It's work that comes out of your constituency. What I've done is employ my own researcher and that has made an amazing amount of difference to the way I perform. You see, we're never in our offices. I get in about quarter to seven in the morning. The first meeting starts at about half-eight. You go through to lunch. You're sitting in the house from quarter past two on through the afternoon. There's never time to do your administrative work."

And, she said, stopping abruptly, looking at her watch, that's what she must go back to at that very moment. Parliament would open in a few days and that afternoon, she had another in the series of pre-session workshops. She would call back. Make arrangements for dinner together.

After Val left, I wandered out to the back deck of Cecily's house, where I was living. It was especially nice there in late afternoon, a shaded getaway, peaceful, with a babbling brook as background music, a shelter of unfamiliar and exotic green. Val and I went back a long time and I would always be grateful to her for giving our young black lab a home when we had to leave the country in 1977. She did a tour of the U.S. in 1980, on a U.S. State Department-sponsored, fact-finding tour of cottage industries in impoverished areas. The purpose was to pick up new ideas on how and what black women in South Africa could successfully produce at home, or through a cooperative, to bring in money. She stopped with us then for a weekend. We met again in East London in 1991, when Fraser and I were on our way home after working for a newspaper in Namibia. We got to know her husband, Tony, a bit better then and to pat our old dog. Now it was 1998 and she had become a Member of Parliament. The details of the election and the days and weeks before had all been new to me and highly interesting. I remembered being dismissive of white opposition efforts, welfare work rather than revolution, during my early days in South Africa. But women like Val had produced an absolutely amazing change, slowly and in the only ways open to them.

I admired Val. A single mother, she had worked to support her family—and found a job that implemented the causes she believed in. Her husband Tony didn't sound like a docile, "Yes dear" type. And now she filled a demanding new role as a lawmaker in a government without a history. Val remained upbeat, enthusiastic, and positive. Exactly as I remembered her.

V
⚜ *Ivy Gcina*
No, I was not afraid. I was prepared to die actually

Inside the Parliament building, a white-shirted attendant at the information desk called Ivy Gcina's office; from there I passed through security and signed the visitors book. When I had come to see Sue van der Merwe, like Gcina a Member of Parliament, the information person took me upstairs to her office. This time I was on my own in a rabbit warren of corridors, anxiously lost until I finally spotted somebody in one of the mostly empty offices. Gcina was room 304.

Eric, Ivy Gcina's driver, was inside. We waited in a comfortable silence. I checked out the room. Two photographs of Nelson Mandela, one on her desk and the other on the wall; the rest appeared to be family photos. Like Van der Merwe's office, this one was small. A desk, three chairs against the opposite wall, a coat rack and a bookcase with cupboards below filled it. A cup on the desk held pencils and the new South African flag at the end of a stick. The phone rang and Eric picked it up. He spoke in Xhosa. I inspected the Christmas cards lined up along the top of the heating and cooling system box next to my chair. Among them was one from the Trauma Centre for Victims of Violence and Terror.

The door flew open, followed by a breathless Ivy Gcina, plastic bags swinging from each hand: "I bought groceries," she told us. "I had nothing in the house. Then I ran straight to the bank."

She dropped the bags behind her desk and handed Eric a check. She had arrived speaking English but switched to Xhosa. Gcina was short, about five feet, stout and wore glasses. Her hair, black with graying roots, was styled in a modified Afro. She wore a silky, sleeveless, tank top above an accordion-pleated skirt. Eric left and Gcina hoisted her skirt to sort out an unruly petticoat which she muttered at. Yes, the photos were of her family: three sons, one daughter.

Gcina's hard life began in 1937 in Richmond, a suburb of Port Elizabeth where, before apartheid, both blacks and whites lived. After her parents divorced, the children remained with their father. Their mother remarried and went to Peddy. The year after her father's death, the children moved to Veerblaas, where they lived with relatives and attended schools. In those days, churches provided English-language schools for black children. Gcina lived in a house with other Xhosa and English-speaking students. This had been arranged by members of the ANC Women's League.

In 1953, Minister of Native Affairs H.F. Verwoerd introduced the Bantu Education Act. Grants were removed from the mission schools and black education came under state control.

Gcina continued her story:

"Then there was this campaign against Bantu Education and we boycott the schools. One then another of the ANC Women's League are taken by police. But if this lady is arrested, another takes over; then she is arrested, we move to another house. And then the students have been assaulted by the police, and a girl—I've forgotten her name because it is quite long ago—went to hospital. And we said, 'No one go back to school until this Bantu Education is abolished.'"

"And then it was '55. I was 17. I started to work because my grandmother was very strict. She said, 'If you don't go to school, you must do something.' At the same time, I was busy with the campaigns of the ANC. I was in the ANC Youth League for fourteen years. We used to do the job of taking the pamphlets to New Brighton, to Veerblaas. So I was busy, but I obeyed my grandmother and said, 'OK. Let me go and work.' So I worked at London Cafe. It was fish and chips."

"In 1956, in March, I get married. I was eighteen years, my nineteenth coming 13th of July. The marriage was not my choice. I married because, in the custom of our black people, if there is a person who wants to marry you and you say no—the first one, the second one—the third one you must marry. And then I went to Adelaide where is my in-laws. I stayed there '56: '57 I came back to Port Elizabeth. Why? I was very young. I had been staying nightly with my sister-in-law. They were nice to me. There was nothing wrong, but things I didn't like. I decided to go away. I started to work at a bottle store of Mrs. Robeson's. Then I did have the money, so I just take the train myself. My husband was working in Port Elizabeth. He and his brothers take me back with them to New Brighton."

"So in late '57, I expect a child now." Gcina stood up, rearranged her skirt, sat down again behind her desk and continued. "I get my son, my baby, 22 June 1958. July '59 I get the house where I am still living now. Then there was a campaign of the ANC Women's League for the uprising (raising) of bus fares. In the campaigns of staying home, no one must go to work. I used to go out each day and see that people were not going to work. I did that from childhood. I was always there with them. Then in 1960—April—the ANC was banned and now we have the meetings in my house."

"In 1976 come the uprising of the students. We were there, giving the children (ANC) information because they come up with the Black Consciousness of which it is not good. The Freedom Charter of the ANC says everyone belongs in this land. I started with my own children saying to them the Black Consciousness is not the right route. This is the right route, of the Freedom Charter which is the ANC."

"Then my brother was on Robben Island, our father's brother, but in our custom he is my brother. He was just released from Robben Island after ten years. I went to him. He must write a Freedom Charter then I can hand it to the students. Now they have to know what is right and which is wrong. If they say Black Consciousness is best, that is a mistake."

"Then my oldest son was harrassed, then he was arrested. He was eighteen years and he get eight lashes with some others, all young.

The eldest ones, they come to Robben Island for five years. The parents were not informed of this and they were sentenced at night. You won't know where is your child. You will be worried. You had just heard the knock when they came. In early hours."

Gcina's voice was husky, her tone even, uninflected. I had the sense that she had told her story many times.

"In 1977, after we went to Biko's funeral in King Williamstown, my son didn't turn up. We were together at the funeral. The last time I saw him it was in King. When I came home, he was not at home. It was just me, his younger brother and my husband. Early hours on the third of October, 1977, Security Branch came looking for him. And the Security Branch, Mr. Rolefsson, was saying to me, 'If you die in this house, how your son will know?' I said, 'I can never answer that question because it will be him who is alive.' He said 'You will die in this house.' I said, 'No problem. The people surrounding me and my family will bury me.'"

"That was the third. On the 18th, they came to take me at work. I was working at a high school in Port Elizabeth. Mr. Blackburn, the headmaster of the school was asking, Where are they taking me to? They say they want to question me about my son. And Mr. Blackburn said, 'She doesn't have any scars. Do you see? She must come back as she is.' They took me to the New Brighton Police Station and I find my husband is there as well. When I was talking to him, they separated us. But no one is questioning me about my son. They locked me up. And there was another lady there. They were looking for her son also. We stay there 18th, 19th; 20th, about 5 o'clock we are released. When I arrived at home, my husband was saying he took our children away because the Security Branch came, get my eleven-year-old son. They beat him. He was blue—head, everywhere. My husband took the two sons away to his brother's girlfriend's home. He was saying to them, 'You don't know anything except me and your mother.'"

Gcina became silent for a few moments, then said, "I missed a place. I missed to say after Mr. Rolefsson said I am going to die there, on the 27th of September the petrol bomb came in my kitchen. We don't have electricity then. I've got a fridge of paraffin (kerosene). I've got gas stove as well. I went out to call my neighbors to help with the fire and I watched the Security Branch car start up at my gate and move away. All the people came and helped. The fire was out. It was just my kitchen and things were damaged, but it didn't go further."

"Now it is 1978, 8th of February. Monday. My husband he works shifts, he was in night shift. When I come from work Mondays I always change my bedding. My windows and my doors, front door and back door, were all open. I was just going to have a bath then change my bedding and my neighbor came. She say two black men, one of them tall with a hat on top of his head, came there, saying 'Hahahaha. We've got you. Hahaha.' Then somebody came and say to my neighbor, 'Mama, someone call you in the house.' She went. It was after nine o'clock. I was left with my sons. My oldest was gone out of the country already. When I entered to my room, I see something. My sons were coming after me. My second boy said to me, 'Yes, there is something.' When I look at my bedding, it is like a sugar. Fortunately for me, I am working at school so I know this. I was cleaning labs there. So I said, 'Don't touch it. Please will you bring me the yellow duster?' I put it on top. The yellow duster, it was like you had cut it into small pieces. I said to them, 'Look, this is acid. Don't touch it.' I put it and the bedding and my gown outside. Then my husband's sister's son came. We turned the bed with three guys, washed my floor, put the polish on, clean up—even the letter box at the door. It was hard labor until 1 AM. On my way back to work, I met a gentleman from the township who was shivering and biting his teeth, looking at me. He was scaring me. I said, 'Tell the Special Branch to give you a gun and shoot me, then you'll be satisfied. Otherwise, you won't do me nothing.' That was the 8th of February."

"It was the 10th of February when someone came to me and say, 'Hey, she's crying, that boy's mom. Will you please go and see this woman?'" Gcina leaned forward and explained: "The Security Branch was at the house of my son's friend and this woman always cry when she sees the police. When I arrived at that house the police were gone so I came back home. I was passing a small lane, somebody grabbed me from behind. He wore a cap. I just twist his arm and I ran. But he was saying, 'Wait Mama, wait Mama.' But I didn't wait. On the 11th the police come and pick me up, swearing, talking all they want to say. That was 1979 and I had started to organize the women again."

"No, I was not afraid. I was prepared to die actually. I mobilized the women, to make a women's organization, a non-racial one. I was going up and down in town. I get support from women in the white suburbs. The first secretary was in the Black Sash. Her husband divorced her because she was involved."

"We went to the factories. We organized there and we get the women for our women's organization and I think about fifteen women for the trade union. Because when I was organizing, I was organizing for the trade unions, for the students, for women, whatever. We elect an interim committee. And we had this committee until December 1980, PEWO, Port Elizabeth Women's Organization. I was in and out of prison then. If there were two days I was not picked up, I would think, 'What did I miss? What have I not done today?' "

Two of Gcina's sons, the eldest and second born, had been across the border in Lesotho for some time. The latter went into exile in 1980 after being arrested at a student meeting and assaulted in prison. Some weeks later, he had phoned his mother to tell her he was still alive. He didn't know why. Those arrested with him were all dead. Gcina's youngest son had fled the country in 1983, joining his brothers in Maseru, capital of Lesotho, a tiny nation surrounded by South Africa. In December Gcina traveled to Maseru.

She explained, "My second one phoned me and said one is not well. The third. So I went up. It was me, my sisters, my brother's wife and my neighbor, and my other son. The police at the border keep me there, asking where am I going? I said I am going to get my son because I am taking him home. This gentleman is saying to me, OK. They will protect me when I bring him home. They give us the go-ahead and then we cross the river. I meet my son there. He said he had wanted to tell me but didn't want to tell me over the phone: 'If I die tomorrow, you mustn't be worried.' It is because of apartheid they leave their homes and loved ones. If there was not apartheid, they would be with us. They have been harrassed, arrested, assaulted, so they are tired of that. He want to see me for that.'"

It was still December 1983 when the ANC sent one of its representatives to tell Gcina about her son. He had been working for the ANC in the Transkei while based in Maseru. In the Transkei town of Aliwal North, the police attempted to search his bag. He fought them off, then fled onto a train. Gcina was told she must not say anything about him when the police came to question her.

"When I come home, I tell my husband. Eighth of August 1984: Security Branch come to my house. I was preparing for Women's Day which was the 9th of August. Denis, the name of the security, came with two police to my house. Three white men. They took me to Sanlam and when I arrived there, he was putting these pictures in front of me: 'Who is this?' I said, 'I don't know.' And he would throw another one. Another one. I could see when it is my son. 'Who's this?' he said. I said, 'It is my son.' He asked me where he is. I say, 'I don't know. In Maseru.' And he said, 'Don't you know that we know the ANC called and informed you that he is dead?' I said, 'If this is true, where is his grave?' He said, 'We know everything you are doing. Before he left Maseru, we have been informed by the senior of the ANC we must wait for him (in Aliwal North). We waited. We saw him getting out of the car, coming to the station. We have knowledge of that. And when he arrived, we gripped him and he fly into the train when the train was pulling away.'"

"I said to him, 'Of course. This is a revolution. You've got the senior of the ANC. We've also got the people from your police. There's nothing wrong to that.' He was swearing. He went out with another one. Left one inside. This one says to me: 'Mrs. Gcina, your son died six October. His grave is in Barastoke township. Not to the old cemetery, the new cemetery. His grave is 437.' I keep this in my mind. I was released. I went home, informed my husband, go to do this job with the Women's League. Then I went to the lawyer to apply for my son's corpse. They deny and deny and deny."

As happened often, Gcina eyes moved away from me and she addressed a place or person beyond my shoulder.

"Then '85, we were arrested, state of emergency. It was 24th of July. After the funeral of Matthew Goniwe and others in Cradock. I was taken with three girls. Then on 30th of July, the Security Branch get me from the prison. And I could see today there is something wrong. There is no seat in this kombi (van). Just the driver and his partner who had the seat. I was standing. When the kombi moved, I swayed. When the kombi swerved, I swerved. When I arrived at the prison in town, the white Security Branch is saying they are very worried: 'I wonder where he is.' They were talking Afrikaans. They were in and out in Mr. Coetzee's office. I know him. He always interrogates me."

"Then they all went out. Eventually, here come a black man, Security Branch. He was saying, 'I know your husband. He was working with my brother.' When the white men entered, he changed the subject. He was saying, 'Mrs. Gcina, we know everything about you. We don't want any lies here. You must tell us the truth.' I said, 'What truth it is you want?' He said, 'We know that you are taking the children outside the country . . .' and so on."

"When I was starting to say, 'Since when do you know that?' he hit me on my ear. He hit me to early hours in the morning—that black one. I don't know for how long. I could feel something going down my throat. It smelled like blood. Then my eye sunk in. Then another Security Branch say in Afrikaans I am stubborn. They stop that black one and he went out. The others they say to me, 'We're going to talk here. We're going to hit you until you talk.' This one hits me with something like a pipe that is hard. On my back, my legs, elsewhere. Until very late. Until he gets tired. My whole body is pitch black. They say they know the whole thing, but they want me to confess with my own mouth, to say that I took the children out of the country (to join ANC forces) and when they come into the country, I keep them. I said, 'If you have the knowledge of this, why don't you arrest me and charge me?' They said, 'No. You are too clever.' I said, 'No. I'm not clever. I am working here in your presence.' Then they took me to another room. There is a big machine there. They turn it on. This machine is not working. They kick it, kick it, kick it, kick it. But the machine is not working . . . "

When the door to Gcina's office opened, I jumped, instantly transported from the horrors of the scene from the past to the safe now. Gcina turned from the visitor to me: "This is Beauty. Beauty, this is Barbara. You can go now and do your telephone." Beauty nodded and left again.

Gcina turned back to me and continued as if there had been no interruption: "It is a choking machine I think. It was very late now. I couldn't breathe. I wanted to faint. But I think I must stay strong. While this white policeman is beating me, another came, shocked my neck. Another came to shock my leg. I fell down. When I stood up, another one takes my head and hits it on the wall." She leaned forward and spoke confidentially. "When they hit me, I always bite my teeth together. Then I do not bite my tongue."

She sat back in her chair. "After that, Mr. Van Wyck, he took the tall tear gas tube out of his briefcase and say, 'Let's throw the tear gas on her. She will talk.' They then all got towels and twist around their noses with these towels. They took me to the main toilet, to the men's cloakroom. And they put me in and opened this tear gas and threw it on me. I got dizzy. But I managed to grip the door because they wanted to close that door while I am inside. I managed to pull the door and I was also out. They also are dizzy. I am much better than them. But it was hard to breathe. Then the black man comes and he says, 'What are you doing? Why are you using the tear gas here?' And Mr. Coetzee said, 'Did it go upstairs?' He said, 'Yes. Of course. What do you think? And what are you trying to do now?' Then he went inside Coetzee's office. The one was beating me with the pipe, he came with a towel to squeeze my neck. Mr. Coetzee said, 'No. Tomorrow. We go now. It is very late.' "

"We go to the kombi. They take me back to the North End prison. It was night now. These were the night shift people. I said to Miss Lewis, she's a warder there, 'I want you to check me because I want you to see I am not like I was when I left here.' She was worried. She was really worried. I was swelling up. I was pitchblack. I was in pain. She writes down everything. They take me to the cell. Those three girls that were there, they were also shocked when they see me."

"The following day, the girls were all released. In the morning, they take me to the doctor. Fortunately, it was Wendy Orr (a young district surgeon who voluntarily treated prisoners). When she see me, she could not believe she is seeing a human being. I did not know that young girl, pretending to be a doctor. I could not believe that. But she said, 'No, I am a doctor. I will help you.' She wrote down everything. She gave me very good treatment. It was nine o'clock when I was at the doctor and she write down the prescription. But to my surprise the medicine never came. There was no medicine for one day."

"There was a warder, Mrs. Krause. She was a white lady. She came to my cell. She got my medicine. She rubbed me all over my back. Gave me something to gargle with. There was something coming out of my throat, like when you grate a beetroot. She put me to bed. She gave me more blankets. On the following day, she came early to check how I am. I could not bathe because it was painful. She told me, when she saw the prescription still lying there when it was time for her to go home, she take it. She went to the chemist and she brought it back here. That treatment of Wendy Orr helped me. At least my eye. Now I could see. They break my ear drum and I can't now sleep on my left side. I've got bad smell with my nose to now."

Gcina shifted in her chair, rested her forearms on the desk top.

"Coetzee send his people to pick me up, but they did not assault me again."

"We get no newspapers in the northern prison. You can not crochet. You cannot knit. Wendy Orr took this to the parents, and the parents took this up as a cause. Then I stay four-and-a-half-months in the single cell (solitary confinement). No visitors for me. A small, small place. This table (desk) we sit at is very big. That was small. There is a bucket with a lid for your toilet. A pot for your water. A small one. It is just one mat and one blanket. One blanket on top. In the morning when you wake up, all those are soaking wet. Water runs down the wall and comes under your bedding. If you ask to take these outside to dry, you are not allowed. You must sleep on it, wet as it is. Eleven of November, they release us. Before they release us, they say we must go to the township and talk to the people, tell them they must spy. I said, 'I cannot do that. Because before I have been arrested, I said to them, "You must not spy." So I would not know who to go to when I am released here.' "

Gcina stopped and we sat in silence for a few moments. "But I think now I have forgotten something again: '85, the 30th of April, there was an AZAPO (Azanian People's Organization) and UDF (United Democratic Front) conflict." AZAPO she explained, was begun by students and based on the Black Consciousness principles of black self-determination. "One of the AZAPO's wanted to stab my daughter. My daughter was a member of COSAS, that is the student movement of the UDF. The taps were still outside then and she had gone with a pail to fetch water. And she fight with this pail. When I heard and went out, this one ran. But on that same night, here come the AZAPO in my door. When those (AZAPO) students come, they shoot and then they run away. From then there were the AZAPO and they break my door and my windows. And they were with the police. In public—and this is not a secret—the white police they came to my house. They were wearing gray tracksuits and balaclavas (a hood covering head and face). And they were smashing all my windows. I had a glass door. They smashed that door, petrol bombed my house. Everything burned. That is why you see this."

Gcina twisted her body in her chair so that much of her upper back faced me. She pulled the shirt strap from her shoulder. Thick white scar tissue covered her upper arm, shoulder and the part of her back that was visible. Turning around again she shook her clothes back into shape.

"Then we were arrested in that state of emergency. After we were released, in and out: day of questioning, back again, night of questioning, back out again and so on. '86. Second state of emergency. Again we were arrested. But I was fortunate in this time. We were not assaulted. Even though one year I could not get any visit, second year I get a visit. My sister. I saw my husband third year, when I was in Grahamstown prison. It was his first visit to see me. Fortunately, I was with people (other prisoners) that time. I was not alone. We had a hunger strike. We wanted to be charged or released. So we were released 11 of May 1989. We were on restrictions (house arrest) when we were let out. We must sign at the police station twice a day: morning and evening. No visitors, no gatherings."

"There came a national march in all provinces. Someone said, 'We must not go to that march because we will be shot.' I said, 'They will do their duty because they are the police. I will do my duty: I am a politician.' So we went to that march. I and some others who had been in detention. We were in the front line, holding our ANC flags. The day they were taking all these restrictions away, they say to me, 'You. Mrs. Gcina. You defy us and I can show you a video...' And I said, 'OK. Put it on.' But he left it. He did not bring it back. Yes. I did defy. Of course. Another time when I was in restrictions, a friend in Cape Town phoned me and said I must go organize in Transkei. I went. I signed at the police twice on a Friday. I left with my cousin's car with two ladies. I sleep in the back (trunk) of the car when they show their passports."

"Then one piece I have forgotten. It was the 3rd of October 1984 when the petrol bomb came to my house. There was the tear gas, chemicals. They cut the windows out and put all the chemicals into the bedroom. It was the small bedroom. After that they went to my husband's and my bedroom and they throw the petrol bomb. We get up and try to put the fire out. We go to our neighbors. When I came back to my dining room, that room was finished. My wardrobe, my television, all was gone. So I've got also those wounds of apartheid."

"My third son, he came back inside the country. I do not know when because I was already in prison. He died here in Cape Town, 27th September 1988. My son was an MK (ANC military wing) member. They saw him and they were with the Security Branch. They could not turn their car because lots of cars, I believe. My son went to the cafe where he bought the papers and he said, 'I'm going to die now. This is my home number and this is a lawyer's number. Inform them.' And he went out. There was a fight with the police and he died. I did not know until there was a visitor for a fellow prisoner. He informed her my son had died in Cape Town. Then my husband also came to tell me. I think it was a really bad funeral. The police did not want the people there so they stayed until he was buried."

"When I was released, we went to put a stone on his grave: the baby of my boys. Then I went to the Human Rights and requested they buy me a ticket because my children are dying. The two that are left, I want to see them. They bought me a ticket to Lusaka (in Zambia). I met my eldest son and this one, the younger, he was an instructor (ANC military). I went in December '89. I came back in January. Then on the 10th of October 1990, on his birthday, he got an accident. My youngest now. Three days later, he died. I went up to Dar es Salaam, Tanzania. The state did not give me permission to bury him here so they cremate him in Tanzania. I bring the ashes here and we bury the ashes here."

Security Police had told Gcina a detailed story of her oldest son's death. However, in 1985, she had received a letter stating that Grave 437 in Barastoke township, which she had been told was his, was in fact, that of an unknown male. At the time we talked, her only living son was a member of the new government's security forces.

It was absolutely unimaginable to me what she had gone through. Why had she not given up, told them whatever they wanted to hear? Without hesitation, Gcina said, her voice firm, "It is because, firstly, from the childhood we knew the constitution of the ANC. This country belongs to everyone. That was great and we grew up with that spirit. On my mind, all along I have got that. The Freedom

Charter is for everybody. We will win. So to be afraid, I won't do what I want. I will not achieve anything. If I am not afraid, I will achieve something. If I die, my blood will water the tree of freedom for everyone. This was just on my mind."

On my walk the next morning, I thought a lot about Ivy Gcina. The combination of tragedy and courage she carried with her was as difficult to come to terms with the day after as it had been at the time. Not that I doubted her. On the contrary, what she told me remained all too real.

As usual, I headed toward the Liesbeek River Trail which Cecily had recommended. I chose the route with a minimum number of street crossings because of rush hour traffic and took a graffiti-decorated underpass below Main. Since my last time through, someone had scrawled "White SA Repent" in big blue letters.

The path on the other side wound about a mile along a shallow and narrow waterway with the occasional sign: "River Floods Occasionally." This part of the walk, without the distraction of traffic, provided space to think of the women whom I had met and would meet. The path was shaded and bordered by the same jungle-lushness as Cecily's back yard: wild ginger, elephant ears, ferns, vines dangling from tree limbs, out-of-control morning glories loaded with jewel-blue blooms. Runners, walkers and dog-walkers shared the trail.

On the way home I dodged knots of uniformed kids with backpacks and turned right on Palmboom Lane to join a procession of maids on their way to work. We walked alongside white masonry walls, five to eight feet high, some topped with spikes or concertina wire. Above the walls rose tile roofs. Through the barred gates, I glimpsed entries, gardens and handsome houses. Pink, lavender, and red impatiens bloomed below metal signs on the walls: "24-hour-a-day armed response."

Near Cecily's, a large bird with a squawk to match waddled out a garden gate, followed by a string of chicks and a woman shooing them along with her apron. "Guinea hens," she announced. "They live in the neighborhood."

That night and many nights in the small back bedroom, I lay awake, vaguely apprehensive of what lay beyond in the darkness. This country was such a paradox: of beauty and ugliness, of courage and brutality, hardship and luxury, evil and saintliness. I listened to the relentless bombardment of acorns on the tin roof and, for a very long time, Ivy Gcina's story chased away sleep.

VI
🌿 *Judy Chalmers*
We both felt a part of the struggle in a way we never stepped away from

Judy Chalmers was elected to Parliament in the country's first democratic election in 1994. In the years leading up to that, Chalmers had been a prominent anti-apartheid activist in her hometown of Port Elizabeth, a city notorious for violence and brutality both in behalf of and against the apartheid government.

The week before Parliament opened she had made time between committee sessions to tell her story. We sat at the old farm table in Cecily's dining room. Chalmers was tall and willowy, had graying hair cut short and wore a well-cut dark gray tailored suit, white blouse and black pumps. She was a good-looking woman with regular features and a pleasant, intelligent face.

Her parents, a grandfather and both grandmothers had been born in Port Elizabeth as she was in 1932. "My father was a very good attorney in a firm founded by his father and which is still going strong," Chalmers said. "I'm deeply rooted in the Eastern Cape and I love it." After attending local schools, she learned social graces and good citizenship along with secretarial skills at a private girls school in Hertfordshire, England.

When she finished school, she worked in her father's legal offices until her marriage to Des Chalmers. Chalmers came from an Irish-Catholic family, also Port Elizabeth residents. Like other women of that era, Judy stayed home to raise their children. One of her four daughters had been born severely brain-damaged and her care had totally absorbed her until the child was institutionalized at eight years of age.

One of her adult daughters had emigrated to Australia. Another had married a dairy farmer and lived near Port Elizabeth. The youngest worked as a journalist in Johannesburg.

Chalmers grew up with politics. She obviously enjoyed telling of her father returning home one day and saying to her mother: " 'I met the most amazing young man today'—and this would have been about 1952, '53—and she said, 'Oh yes? Who?' And he said, 'His name is Nelson Mandela and I'm sure we're going to hear more about him in the future.' "

"Even as kids we worked in elections. Though this was very much white politics, it was not on the National Party side. Sir de Villiers Graaff, an anglicized Afrikaner by birth and head of the opposition United Party (UP), had been a close friend of my father for many years. I remember he and my father having a whingding (*sic*) argument: 'Dev,' my father said, 'you've got to move the United Party into a different sphere, take cognizance of black rights. Justice has to happen in this country. We cannot continue being almost a party to the apartheid regime.' And de Villiers said, 'I can't do it, it's too soon . . ..' And he had a huge following, de Villiers Graaff, because he'd been in World War II, spent time in a prisoner of war camp. He had the whole white male society on his side and he remained head of the UP from the end of the war until it disappeared."

Since its beginnings in 1933, the United Party had been the political voice of South Africa's English-speaking white population and the official opposition to the National Party of the Afrikaners.

In the mid-1950's, Chalmer's father, "Buller" Pagden, joined Helen Suzman, sole woman member of Parliament, in the United Party breakaway group that formed the Progressive Party. As Chalmers recalled, her parents' guestbook records not only the names of Graaff and Suzman, but a wide range of other well-known South Africans including Alan Paton, author of *Cry the Beloved Coun-*

try, and Jan Hofmeyr, Member of Parliament and Cabinet member of the Jan Smuts government. Smuts' United Party lost the 1948 election to the National Party and never regained power. In 1977, the UP ceased to exist.

Like other white South African women sympathetic to the injustices they witnessed daily, Chalmers protested in the only way open to her. She joined Black Sash. She recalled the circumstances that led to that.

Chalmers said: "It wasn't until the late 1970s that I joined Black Sash. I was a late starter in the activist field—though I had always worked against the Nats (National Party). I think now that I stayed in white politics for a surprisingly long time. One of the things that sparked me into becoming more active, my sister Molly Blackburn and I went with Helen Suzman to the funeral of Robert Sobukwe."

On March 12, 1978, Chalmers and her older sister, Molly Blackburn, drove to the town of Graaff Reinet for the funeral of black leader Robert Sobukwe. Sobukwe had been the leader of the banned Pan Africanist Congress (PAC), formed in 1958 by a more radical element of the African National Congress party. In March of 1960, the PAC launched non-violent mass protests against the pass laws that required all blacks at all times to carry with them a record of their lives from birth. After sixty-nine deaths following confrontations between police and blacks at Sharpeville, a black township near Johannesburg, violence and mob demonstrations swept the country. Sobukwe was arrested and the ANC and PAC banned. Sobukwe was imprisoned on Robben Island, though the PAC continued to operate outside the country and underground. When Sobukwe was diagnosed with cancer in 1972, he was released but immediately banned and restricted to the northern city of Kimberly. He died there. His funeral took place in Graaff Reinett, the small Eastern Cape town where he was born. Chalmers and her sister were among three to four thousand mourners.

"The funeral was in the showgrounds and the crowd was 99 percent black," Chalmers recalled. "It was a very orderly funeral compared to some I went to in the '80s, but there was a strong police presence. We sat with the black community and that was a real eye-opener because, in South Africa, one could live from birth to death and never have a black friend. You were in a separate part of the hospital, a separate school, separate church, separate city and led a separate social life. Apartheid was extremely well engineered and unless you made a very strong attempt to move across the divide, you could live very comfortably, very successfully, in your own ghetto."

"At the funeral, in the midde of the showground, was this little dais for special friends and leaders. Among those on it were Helen (Suzman) and Mangosuthu Buthelezi (Zulu chief). This was a token of respect for Sobukwe. Even though he came from a different party and had a different philosophy, he was widely respected."

"It was a remarkable occasion for several reasons, one that it occurred at all. People stood and spoke and it was all going very smoothly. Then, when Buthelezi stood up, a murmur began in the crowd and young people started heading toward the stage."

Buthelezi had always been considered a sell-out by black—and white—opponents of apartheid. Buthelezi had remained within the system, heading up the puppet government in the Zulu homeland which the National Party established. His Inkatha Freedom Party (IFP) was the only black political group which had not been banned. The apartheid government nurtured Buthelezi. The black community regarded him, because of his own ambitions and because he was not ANC or PAC, as someone who must be on the side of the whites.

"These youngsters began to surge forward," Chalmers continued. "They wouldn't let him speak. Now Gatsha (the chief) is a very, very proud man and he became extremely upset. The protestors ordered him to get out of the stadium and it soon got quite ugly. Stones were thrown. Though we didn't really feel threatened, I remember Molly—it was also her first occasion at such a meeting—worrying because a number of youngsters had climbed on the roof and we could see and hear that it was buckling. She went around to women near us and said, 'Let's sing.' They began singing hymns and this was picked up all the way around. And it was really the women who calmed down that whole situation. We both felt the vibrancy, the excitement and felt a part of the struggle in a way we never stepped away from. For me, that day was a point of no return."

Chalmers and her sister Molly Blackburn started moving within black circles. Blackburn ran for election to the Eastern Cape Provincial Council on the Progressive Party slate and was elected. She joined Jan van Gend, Cecily's former husband, also PP, on the Council.

"Almost immediately Molly became tuned in to what was happening in the schools—in the Eastern Cape and all over the country," Chalmers said. "It was the beginning, really, of the black children of South Africa rising up. They said their parents were doing nothing, allowing the Boer (Afrikaner) to walk over them. The children, as young as primary school, were now going to the streets to become the militant force in South Africa. We started listening to what these youngsters were saying."

"We met Siphiwo Mtimkulu who was, at that time, national head of COSAS (Congress of South African Students), an absolutely remarkable young fellow from PE (Port Elizabeth). We heard what their aspirations were, what they were thinking and how they saw themselves taking forward a campaign."

"Molly did what she could by raising issues in Provincial Council. She and Di Bishop. The two Progressive Party women stood together, very articulate, very courageous. They were hated by the National Party."

Chalmers, meanwhile, worked with Black Sash. By the late '70s, membership in Port Elizabeth had dwindled to about eleven paid-up members, most elderly and inactive. There was then no Advice Office. Chalmers recruited friends and they opened a Saturday morning Advice Office. Inevitably, the police paid attention. The Eastern Cape, as Chalmers said and I remembered, was in many ways the most militant section of the country with security forces that reflected that.

At about this time, the Security Police started a campaign of harrassment of Siphiwo Mtimkulu, the young black student leader. He ended in prison. There, Chalmers recalled, "he became extremely ill then paralyzed. His hair fell out. The realization we came to was that something funny was going on. When he was released from prison, he was in a wheelchair. He could no longer walk. We found a doctor at UCT (University of Cape Town) to look at him. He said, 'This boy's been poisoned.' And he treated what he said was thalium poisoning. Gradually Siphiwo's hair grew back and he regained the use of his legs. He remained at the head of COSAS until 1982 when he suddenly disappeared. His body was never found, but it has come out since that they (the security police) killed him and threw his body in the river. For years we battled to get the truth about him and it's only come out now. He's been one of the major cases with the Truth and Reconciliation Commission."

As I gathered from letters to the editors in newspapers, not everyone in South Africa approved of the Truth and Reconciliation Commission. Chalmers was not among the opponents. "You often hear from the white society, 'Why must we hark back to the past? What is the point of it? We must move forward.'" To answer that, she said, she need only look at Siphiwo's mother who told her "Though I don't have the bones of my son, I now can sleep at night because I know what happened, who did it, and why they did it."

Though Chalmers was unsure if she could ever forgive the dead boy's murderers, at least, she said, his mother knew her son's fate.

The whole of the '80s were what Chalmers called a torrid time. Many fellow activists were picked up and imprisoned, particularly during the 1986-1989 government decreed States of Emergency. Meetings or any gatherings of more than three individuals were then banned. Those arrested and imprisoned were denied recourse to courts or lawyers, even their families.

Chalmer's sister Molly questioned whether to remain in white politics. Chalmers had already bowed out of the Progressive Party—by then the Progressive Federal Party—and moved her loyalties to Black Sash which she believed far more relevant to the struggle. Black Sash somehow survived, becoming the only unbanned, activist, opposition organization.

Both women combined their work with gathering testimony in the rural Eastern Cape where police harassment had increased in viciousness. They talked to victims, compiled clear written records and made certain police were aware of exactly what they were doing: being monitored might slow their persecutions.

"The 28th of December 1985 Molly and I drove up to Oudtshoorn to take statements," Chalmers recalled. "Di Bishop and her husband Brian had flown up from Cape Town and we met them in Oudtshoorn. We talked to people through the day—in fact there is a little booklet, *The Last Affidavit*, done that day. We had finished up and were driving back to Port Elizabeth. It was night. On this dark country road just outside Humansdorp, about an hour from PE, suddenly in the blackness in front of us lights appeared. We hit the car head on."

Brian Bishop had been driving. He lived for half an hour. Di Bishop was seriously injured. Chalmers, in the back seat alongside her sister, suffered fractured ribs, cuts and bruises. Molly's neck was broken and she died instantly as did the driver of the other car.

"We just sat," Chalmers said. "After awhile a car came along with a little family. A couple of them stayed with us. The others went on to call for an ambulance."

An inquest found a high alcohol content in the blood of the driver, a youth from a nearby village. Molly's husband and her brother, a lawyer in Australia who had been home at the time, visited the young man's family. His grieving parents described him as a church-goer and teetotaler. Many of those familiar with the details of the case believed the accident had been no accident.

A decade later, the Truth and Reconciliation Commission was asked to investigate. No evidence had been produced to prove conclusively one way or the other.

Blackburn had been a mother of seven, the youngest about 13. "It was hard for that little family," Chalmers said. "My life went on."

But before long, her life changed as well. Within the year, her husband Des had lost his retail business. "I met the man afterward

81

who had done this," Chalmers said. "He was in the South African Defence Force and in charge of the dirty tricks department. He sent a letter to all the builders in the district saying 'Boycott this paint firm.'"

"We sold our house and lost our car. I started working for Black Sash as a field worker. At the same time our phones were tapped, our mail interfered with and our house quite often searched for activists they said we might be hiding. One learned to be careful. You told people where you were going. If we went to the country, we made sure someone knew when we left and we phoned them after we arrived. It became a part of our lives."

Judy Chalmers looked no different to me than the average middle-aged woman shopping for groceries in the supermarket in Cecily's neighborhod. She appeared moderately prosperous, friendly and open. Nothing bold about her, certainly no advertisement for brave crusading. Yet what she had chosen to confront time after time demanded more courage than I thought that I, or any other American woman I knew, possessed.

"We—Black Sash members—were arrested many times because we'd go into the townships without the permits they required." Chalmers grinned: "We used to give them a hard time. They would arrest us and cart us off to the New Brighton Police Station and we would make *such* a fuss. We'd say, 'We've got to phone our children because we're not going to be there to pick them up from school.' And we really went into this white, middle-class mode which these cops used to hate. And their phone might not be working and we'd say, 'Well? Where *are* we going to phone then? What are we going to do about our children?'"

"And there was a part of them that identified with that. Picking us up wasn't like arresting black activists where they could just give them a clap and tell them, 'You sit here until we tell you what to do.' This was probably also why the Black Sash wasn't banned—because we were white, middle-class and very often, middle-aged like their mothers."

"They used to say to me, 'Mrs. Chalmers, we've got *such* a file on you.' And I'd say, 'Good. Hang on to it.'"

She looked back on these tumultuous years as a scary but exciting time. Colleagues were arrested. Would that be the day she would be also? Black Sash activists moved into new areas. They worked with prisoners: trying to get items to them to make their lives more bearable, keeping track of where they were being held and passing along that information to their families.

Early in 1986, between states of emergency, violence erupted somewhere in the country every week, and every weekend funerals were held for those who died. Chalmers and her group attended many. She recalled one in particular.

"An organization called PEWO—Port Elizabeth Women's Organization, a black group—sent a letter to Black Sash and it said: 'We, the women, are going to be the ones who will manage the funeral next weekend. We are going to preach. We are going to carry the coffin. We're going to mourn at the graveside and we're going to march. We want you to be with us.'"

"Now it was absolutely illegal for us to go and we knew that. And we knew there would be shooting and trouble because there always was. But we thought, 'Maybe if there are women ....' And we must be seen to be there, because for us it's the bottom line. We must go. So six of us did. We caught a taxi and found a way into the township. They had barbed wire around it. We met the women—there were hundreds of them in their church uniforms—coming down the street."

"We joined them in the front row, linked arms with them and started marching. In no time at all, the police arrived and blocked our way. We stopped just for a second then went around them. With that, they stood up in these huge yellow caspirs (tank-like military vehicles) and fired down into us with thunder flashes and tear gas. Thunder flashes are stunningly noisy and can do damage if they hit you. Women ran. The air was blue with smoke. We started to run with the others. There were rocks everywhere under our feet and the going was very difficult. I tripped and I thought, 'I'm not going to do a somersault in front of these guys.' Three of us said, 'OK. Let's just keep going.'"

"And a man, a dear little tiny man with a Bible in his hands, came out of a house and he joined us. Eventually everyone reassembled and we continued on to the church. Then they surrounded the church and fired tear gas into it."

Chalmers paused and shook her head: "April 26, only eleven years ago. Not long at all."

After the ANC was declared unbanned early in 1990, she became a member. However, the party's subsequent invitation to stand for office was unexpected.

"When the lists came out the beginning of '94, I was quite far down so I thought I was fairly safe," she said. "I could see that to be elected would disrupt my life considerably. And then, suddenly, they pushed me up to number eleven out of twenty five on the regional list. It became clear at that point that even if we got fifty or fifty-one percent of the vote, I would be in Parliament."

Chalmers explained that she, like several other women elected to Parliament, had made the roster of candidates because the ANC wanted to recognize activists in their struggle for equal rights. She also heard that "apparently this guy stood up and said, 'If you don't give Judy a place on the list where she's going to be able to make a difference, you go to the country people and explain why not.'"

Chalmers served on three Parliamentary committees, Welfare, Health and the Environment, and Tourism. "Welfare was fine because I'd worked in the Advice Office," she said. "And Environment. I'm actually passionate about that. It's where I think I'm doing the most meaningful work. There was never a proper monitoring in place for sensitive environmental areas and now we have legislation for environmental impact assessments. Health was completely new. There also good things are happening. I have a great admiration for our Minister of Health (Nkosazana Dlamini Zuma). She's spot on in fundamentals. There was nothing in the Transkei and what's happening there is wonderfully exciting."

"On delivery and at the provincial level," Chalmers continued, "it is very chaotic to create nine provinces where there were five before. There wasn't an administrative support system, no capacity to make new policies happen and there still isn't. While we have a wonderful constitution, it has created problems. We can't sack people and are stuck with non-deliverers from the former regimes and this is hugely problematic. Transkei has so many employees who won't move and there's no work there so this is difficult. Everyone wants something and there are critical needs. Money is tricky. We inherited a huge debt from apartheid policies. Just paying interest is crippling, let alone coming to terms with the debt itself."

"Crime is scary. There are new hijackings (of armored cars carrying cash) daily and just coming here I was listening on my car radio to another. There seems to be an international factor. Crime is affecting our ability to impact world tourism. It's worse in the Johannesburg area because the money is there. The international mafia seems to be doing its contracting in that province. But crime is here in Cape Town and in other centers as well. I believe that there is such unemployment people turn to crime."

"At the national level, we are putting relevant and wonderful policies in place, but making them happen is the huge challenge."

I asked what, if anything, an individual could do to help the country move ahead.

"I would like to see every citizen playing a role," Chalmers said. "People tell me, 'We don't watch TV news any longer because the crime is so depressing.' And they just build higher walls, buy rottweilers, contract with security firms. I want to tell them they must stop wringing their hands and get involved, find out what's happening."

But getting involved isn't easy either, she admitted. In Port Elizabeth there is an exclusive group of businessmen in an organization called the Pyramid Club. They had a speaker from the ANC recently, Chalmers recalled. One of the members of the club said to him, "We'd like to get involved, but you don't call on us." But they are white. The fear is that they would take over and that, she said, is indeed likely.

The conversation ended abruptly when Noel Robb's driver appeared at the half-open door and returned to bring Robb up the brick path. Robb walked slowly, leaned heavily on her cane: he steadied her with a hand on her elbow.

Though they lived in different cities, Chalmers and Robb knew each other well from Black Sash. Robb took advantage of their chance meeting to do some politicking. She didn't bother with small talk, just started in. She was highly annoyed at the recent purchase of a fleet of top-of-the-line BMWs for government officials.

Said Robb, "I honestly think that Parliament has got to take a cut in salaries and drive little, cheap cars before you can expect the people in the townships to believe what you say about no funds available for services. What do you want a BMW for? Why not a little car that would sit well in traffic? If you look at my son—a pediatrician and with Red Cross and so forth—he was told that his car had to be between 90,000 and 120,000 rands (approximately $10,000, $13,333 US) and he bought a nippy little thing for about 50,000 ($5,555 US)."

"Well," said Chalmers, "I drive a...."

"I don't think," Robb interrupted, "that you can expect people to believe there is no money for education when they hear you are having BMWs, trips overseas—all those things that have been going on forever throughout Africa. It would look so good if you people took a cut in your salaries. Not a raise."

Said Chalmers, "You know, Trudy (Thomas) said something very like that at cabinet level in the province and they nearly killed her."

". . . And the other thing," Robb thumped her cane on the wood floor, "all these commissions, particularly that youth commission with all those huge salaries ..."

"I know."

"Some of these commissions are doing something. Most are doing very little."

"I think," said Chalmers, "the ..."

"They should be paid enough to live on, but that's all. We've got to spread the money ..."

"... I know. I know now. I will do my best."

They both laughed.

VII
🌾 *Noel Robb*
We decided to carry on fighting for human rights under the name of the Black Sash

I pulled out a chair at the long table Cecily used for company dinners. Noel Robb leaned her walking stick against her chair and sat down heavily. Robb obviously disliked her lessened mobility but also ignored it. After hovering to make certain she was settled, her driver disappeared out the door.

Robb was a legendary figure among Black Sash women. Every one I talked with mentioned her somewhere in the telling of their own stories.

Robb's father was a British naval officer, her mother South African. They met in the latter's hometown of Simonstown, a picturesque seaside village on the western cape. Noel had been born in Plymouth, England, on Christmas day, 1913. She grew up and went to school in England.

In 1936, the year Robb graduated from college, Britain was in an economic slump. She had looked futilely for work. When a cable arrived from her former science teacher, then in South Africa, with the offer of a teaching position at a private school in Cape Town, Robb accepted immediately.

"I loved it here from the start," she said. "I came for a year, but I recall driving around not long after I arrived and thinking, 'I'm never going back.'"

In December 1939, she married Francis Charles Robb. He was a lawyer who later moved to the financial field. Her husband was old-fashioned, she said, and Robb left teaching to remain at home to raise their five children.

When World War I created a teacher shortage, she filled in at St. Cypriot's, where she had taught before her marriage. But when the war ended, her life returned to its familiar pattern.

Since teaching was not an option, she chose to become involved at another level. She joined the St. Cypriot school committee and also the committee of the social center in District Six, the largely colored, mixed-race community in central Cape Town. There the committee established and directed sewing and dancing classes, a nursery school and a group for retirees.

In 1955, Robb took another step beyond her traditional role: "The last thing I wanted to do was to get involved in politics," she recalled, "but I came in when the government wanted to double the size of the Parliament. I realized that was to get enough Nats (National Party members) to make the majority necessary to change the constitution and the idea behind that was so they could take the vote away from the coloreds."

She discovered a group of women who thought as she did.

"One time, when the Parliament met all night, we stood all night outside of Parliament, in pouring rain. I remember the head of the ANC—it had not been banned then—came and shook our hands and thanked us."

"When we determined the battle had been lost, members of what was then the Women's Defense of Constitution League met in Stellenbosch. There we decided to carry on fighting for human rights for all under the name of the Black Sash, which is what we wore when protesting and what people had been calling us."

Robb paused at a personal memory: "For the next thirty years, since we met every single Monday morning, I had to do the washing on Sunday. "

As I had already learned, when someone began to talk of Black Sash, Noel Robb's name followed. Chalmers had called her Granny Black Sash. Robb was impressive. With a total lack of self-consciousness she conveyed, by bearing and appearance, a queen mother image. A halo of pure white hair, styled in soft waves, framed a strong-featured face with pale, cared-for skin. Her dress, of deep blue silk, draped across the bosom and fell in folds from the waist. My mother would have described it as an "afternoon dress." In spite of the softness of skin, hair and dress, Robb projected authority and purpose. To emphasize a point, she reached for her cane and firmly rapped the end on the wood floor. Her voice was strong, her pronouncements unqualified.

Robb's focus had been the Advice Office. She ran the Cape Town office for years. While some of the women who spoke with me gave up on Black Sash in the turbulent 1980s, Robb never did. Though Black Sash now has paid staff and a minimum of volunteers, she continues to give a day each week. I was curious as to what she dealt with there: "housing, work situtations, disabilities; but the largest part of it is still poverty, dreadful poverty."

In the ANC government, Robb serves on one committee that monitors legislation and another that keeps track of bills being written. Both meet a day a week and require extensive research and analysis.

She remains on the board at St. Cypriot's school and on the District Six community center committee. Though the District Six houses have been leveled, the center runs two nursery schools for almost two hundred youngsters, one in the District and another in the area where residents were relocated.

Robb is also with the Institute of Race Relations which operates a Saturday school for high school students needing help with English, mathematics, or science. The object is to raise their skills to college-entrance level.

I asked about her own children.

It turned out that, like their mother, all five had involved themselves in their country's future. The eldest, a social worker, is also a volunteer with programs for the physically and mentally disabled; the second, at Natal University, researches income possibilities for the rural poor of Zululand; the third works in a land restoration program;

the fourth runs workshops in gender and culture, how to integrate other races into schools and workplaces; the youngest, formerly administrator of a black township hospital, is chief director of the Northwest province health department.

At 85 years of age, Robb appeared to be as deeply involved in South African politics and as outspoken as she undoubtedly had been for the past half century. Up until 1990, she had taken the National Party to task. Now it was the ANC's turn.

"I realized there would be a lot of pitfalls and we are getting into the pitfalls now," she said.

"When this government came to power, it promised free education for everyone for the first nine standards (grades). Now all schools are having to find money to keep teachers, cleaners—all levels of staff."

"Hospitals, same thing. They're closing them, cutting staff." Her tone grew increasingly indignant, the cane hit the floor. "Pensions aren't being paid. There are shortages everywhere and we're running out of money. The government has cut child support. It used to be 400 rands ($44.44 US) monthly to the mother, 180 rands ($20 US) each child up to age 18. Payment is being cut in stages to nothing at all for mothers, 100 rands ($11.10 US) for each child and only up to the age of seven. The cut-off was set at seven because children then can come in for the schools' feeding programs. But that doesn't work all that well. At best, children in the Western Cape are given a couple of slices of bread with peanut butter and a cup of soup. And there are no meals on holidays and weekends."

"They do have medical care for pregnant women and children under six. That's a good thing. But financing these new free clinics has made it impossible to keep the standards of the hospitals up."

"I reckon we should leave the debt payments for the moment. All the white businessmen are delighted with the debt pay-off. The Sash is not. We feel that by not paying people, not keeping the teachers on, not being able to run the hospitals properly and so on, the average voter will not vote for the government and that will bring chaos to the country."

"Democracy is very dicey and hasn't basically reached the man in the street. So far, it's just nice places open to all."

"What worries me most is the youth, particularly the black youth who are very anarchistic, out of control. From 1976 on, they were largely out of schools where they had to be on time and had their days structured. Thousands are now too old for schools and have no skills except in stealing and holding up cars. They have no culture of learning. It worries me and I can see this being so for years and years and years."

When the interview ended, I walked from the house to the carport with Robb. Her car and driver waited under the trellis, shaded from the hot summer sun by the thick tangled vines and pink blossoms of what Cecily called a Zimbabwe creeper.

The driver opened her door and as Robb prepared to step in, she paused. "The nice thing is, the government is trying to do the right thing. It is very approachable and nice to Black Sash. Even though they're making every mistake imaginable, for the first time the country is going the right way."

When she left, I thought again of things she had said, in particular of that rainy night when the ANC leader shook the hands of each silent Black Sash protestor. My theory was that incidents like that one had accrued to make possible the amazing good will among the races that I witnessed daily. But thinking back to my time in South Africa, I realized that good will had been as apparent in the apartheid era, at least in everyday dealings, as it was among the leadership now. Given the brutality and injustice of the oppressors, that depth of forgiveness seemed beyond our human natures.

After Noel Robb drove off, I walked from Cecily's house to the office of her ex-husband, Jan van Gend, to send a FAX. He was an attorney and his office was a half mile or so from the house. On the way back, I bought lunch at the Woolworth store in the big Claremont shopping mall. Unlike the Woolworths I remembered from childhood—we called them five and dime stores—those in South

Africa, as in England, carried not only department-store type goods but top-of-the-line foods. On the walk home, I crossed the street to avoid passing three young black men loitering ahead. Sometimes people wanted money. Other times they just stared. I cowardly avoided them when I could.

After lunch on the deck and finishing a letter to Fraser, I locked all doors, checked figures on the digital read-out of the security system panel and made sure the right numbers came up. These told which doors and windows had been locked, which ones overlooked. This whole routine would have to be reversed after the post office run. I nearly always had trouble, but that time all went OK: code punched in; door closed to set the alarm; stayed out of line of the electric eye; opened door; shut it quickly before the alarm sounded at security offices.

I pulled the door shut behind me, simultaneously realizing not only the letter but the house key lay on the table by the door. My worst nightmare from the very day I arrived. I recalled Cecily telling about once locking herself out. She had to break the glass in the doors off the back deck to get in.

After squashing panic enough to think, I walked to the cul de sac where neighbors parked the overflow from their garages. It was 1:45. Cecily would be at her afternoon job at the publisher in Cape Town. There was nothing beyond the tops of the cars but walls, tree tops and roofs. The widower who liked opera and lived next door had a grilled gate. I peered through. His usually open front door was shut. A Land Rover arrived and parked by a garage. The man who got out listened to my problem. He was noncommittal. I followed him through garages and gates and introductions to a pit bull, an English bulldog and a basset in the kitchen.

Thank goodness, Kwela Books was listed in the phone book and I had remembered the name. Cecily said there was no way I could find the key she had hid in the garden. She would come home and open the house. Fifteen minutes later, a colored man from her office showed up with a house key. Chagrined and shaken, I walked to the post office and bought some dental floss at a shop across the street. I looked at post cards and sunglasses. Nice ordinary things.

The usual, early evening routine at Cecily's was a rerun of the day over a pre-dinner glass of wine. We sat in the room adjoining the deck, French doors open to the late afternoon coolness—the jungle beyond the deck shining green and gold in the late day sun, the badminton bonks of a pair of frogs above the burble of the brook running at the bottom of the bank.

Talk of the Chalmers and Robb interviews reminded Cecily of Molly Blackburn, Judy Chalmer's sister. Cecily's ex-husband Jan, like Molly, had been a Progressive Party provincial counselor. The two had been close friends.

"It was late December when Molly was killed," Cecily said. "We were at our holiday house in Knysna, the whole family, brothers, sisters and all their families. My mother was coming from Queenstown which was five hours to PE (Port Elizabeth) and another four hours from PE to Knysna. Jan flew to PE to meet my mother and drive her down. He was early and had the morning so he spent it with Molly."

"When he arrived back at our house, he collapsed in a chair and said, 'Boy, I've just had a day in the life of Molly Blackburn.' He proceeded to tell me what they'd packed in after she met him at the airport at 7 AM. They had visited a hospital and gone to authorities to make inquiries about someone's child who was in jail. And this was just a tiny part of a day of normal activities for Molly. She had said, 'Next week, we'll go to Oudtshoorn to visit all the children in jail.' This was a time when they were arresting very young school children and throwing them into adult jails."

"Jan told her he didn't plan to go: 'It's now my holiday time and I don't want to do that.'"

"Our holiday house doesn't have a phone," Cecily continued, "and two days later, one of the neighbors came to tell Jan he must call his sister."

"He returned weeping. When he could talk he said, 'Molly and

Brian Bishop have been killed in an accident.'"

"We were going to drive my mother home and we stopped at PE to attend Molly's funeral. We had to park several blocks away from the church because of the crowd. Mother said, 'I'll be fine. I'll just read my book until you come back.'"

"I didn't expect it to be what it turned out to be. It was an hour before the funeral and it was packed in the church. They had saved seats for us."

"The funeral had been taken out of the family's hands by the UDF (United Democratic Front). The ANC was banned and the UDF became its legitimate wing. Things had been well-organized and the crowd controlled. Hundreds of buses brought people from all over the country. Most stood outside—just to be there."

"The wife of one of the members of the Provincial Council said to me, 'I don't think the family was prepared for this.' She told me that after the news of Molly's death spread, groups of blacks would arrive at her house, just to sit with the family. They called her 'Mother Molly.' Fifteen thousand people attended Molly's funeral."

"Even though Jan knew her well, that day with her had been an eye opener."

"The funeral went on for several hours," Cecily said. "This was an early funeral and from then on, these became political rallying points. The state of emergency meant meetings were forbidden, but they couldn't ban funerals. This was the first one I'd been to. For the family, it was not their wife or mother or daughter or sister, Molly was a political icon."

"Mother was absolutely amazed. I was afraid she would be terrified at the crowds, but they were amazingly well behaved. I think she was amazed at the power of Molly."

Molly's great power, Cecily recalled, "was making you feel important. Nobody was small. The police loathed her—but I think even they had enormous respect for her."

Later, I checked back with Judy Chalmers to clarify a couple of points.

Toward the end of our conversation, she said in spite of the problems, present and future, facing her country, she had no wish to be anywhere else. "South Africa is full of challenges," she said, "and an exciting place to be."

She wanted to know how Noel Robb and I had gotten along. She listened to a brief recap, then laughed. "Noel is wonderful. She takes no shit from anybody."

VIII
✺ *Sheena Duncan*
I saw a need for women to work for justice in this country

Sheena Duncan, the head of Black Sash, lived in Johannesburg. When the Elderhostel group had arrived there, I called her. We compared calendars and arranged to meet at Gold Reef City, a gold rush theme park on the Elderhostel tour schedule.

I left the other Americans at the gate and queried my way to the Gold Reef City Hotel. It was early, about nine, and the park gates had just opened. I waited for Duncan at one of the small tables outside the hotel. A machine watered down the dirt street, moving slowly and noisily back and forth. A woman in a sunbonnet, wearing a white pinafore over an ankle-length cotton dress, swept the sidewalks. Flimsy frame buildings along the deserted street looked like those at Knotts Berry Farm and Disneyland.

When Duncan arrived, we ordered coffee from a waitress in a dance hall hostess outfit: black stockings and a pink, very short, satin dress with a draped bustle. It was already hot and we adjusted the umbrella for shade.

Duncan explained that Black Sash began in Johannesburg in 1955 when six women, one of them her mother, mobilized friends to protest the government's proposed removal of coloreds from the voters rolls. Though their efforts proved futile, the women decided to continue as an organization to fight against human rights abuses. The form of protest they decided upon was to appear as a group in a public, heavily traveled area, usually a city center street corner. They stood together in silence, placards held up, explaining their stand on some new racist ruling. They took their name from the black sashes they knotted around their waists, symbolic of the death of yet another freedom in their country.

In addition to occasional stand-ins, members began staffing facilities they called Black Sash Advice Offices. The first opened in Cape Town in 1958. There, and eventually elsewhere in the country, volunteers with the help of interpreters tried to assist those who came to them in endless streams, seeking work, housing, food, legal aid, word of imprisoned family members, help with passes, race classification and a hundred other black-only problems.

Duncan was a straight-talking individual who spoke sparely in a deep voice. She answered questions with authority and without hesitation. Her hair was straight and short with shades of gray; her features strong and square. She wore a cool-looking, well-cut skirt and blouse in a silky fabric, not particularly stylish but tasteful and expensive.

She had been born in Johannesburg in 1932. Her mother was South African. Her father had emigrated from Scotland following World War I. Duncan grew up exposed to her mother's political activism and said she could not remember a time when politics did not interest her. After attending a private school in Johannesburg, she studied domestic science at the University of Edinburgh. She came back home to marry an English-speaking architect. The couple lived in Harare, Zimbabwe (then Rhodesia), from 1956 until 1963. When they returned to Johannesburg, she connected with Black Sash because, she said, "I saw a need for women to work for justice in this country."

I asked why Black Sash rather than some other activist group.

"Because in 1963," Duncan said, "there was nothing else to join. There was NUSAS (National Union of South African Students) and I wasn't a student; the Institute of Race Relations which was very useful and I belonged, but it wasn't an activist group; and the Christian Institute which started in 1963, but that worked within the churches."

Black Sash was it until the end of the sixties. Political activity began then at black universities where there was a large Christian involvement.

Steve Biko's Black Consciousness movement suddenly appeared. That organization and its spin-offs preached a new style of black self-reliance, as the Black Panthers had done in the U.S. in the '60s.

After Soweto blew up in mid-1976, anti-apartheid groups sprang up almost overnight. But within months, all protest ended abruptly. In 1977, Steve Biko died in prison at the hands of his captors. Black Consciousness organizations and others like it were banned along with hundreds of activists. Among them was Beyers Naude, an Afrikaner, former Dutch Reformed minister, then head of the Christian Institute. That was declared an affected organization which amounted to the same thing as banning.

"If you were declared affected," Duncan explained, "you were not allowed to receive any money from overseas and that was one way of putting organizations out of action."

Black Sash survived as the sole legal and active anti-apartheid group in the country. The fact that Black Sash had not been shut down with the others had always puzzled me.

Duncan said, "I think, actually, that our rulers in those days—they were very Calvinist—didn't take women very seriously. And we were mainly middle-class white women. Some of us, like Noel Robb, with husbands in powerful places and we'd become very well-known overseas. I think it probably wasn't worth the hassle of banning us, particularly since it would have been very difficult to label us as Communist, which was the reason they usually gave for banning an organization."

Some cynical voices, I recalled, had suggested that the existence of the Sash actually served the apartheid government's purposes since it could point to that very visible opposition as proof that South Africa was indeed a functioning democracy.

Duncan went from chairman of the Transvaal region of Black Sash to its national president in 1976 and she was reelected in 1982. Her activities with Black Sash remained much the same until 1990 and President de Klerk's speech. From then until 1994 had been extremely busy for Sash members, she said. They had provided input to the country's new leaders and kept a watchful eye on the progress of the interim constitution, the drafting of the new constitution and preparations for the elections.

"We—Black Sash—worked very closely with other organizations, particularly the churches, on voter education," Duncan said. "We had a huge network of contacts around the country and people trusted Black Sash. Of course, until 1994 we had De Klerk as president, so there were those battles (on immediate issues) as well."

"Now that human rights are protected by a Bill of Rights, we don't have to go on the streets to influence what will be done. In the new South Africa, we have the tools you need—though they don't always work."

Soon after the Mandela-led government took over, Black Sash changed its structure to become a trust. The privately-funded trust, chaired by Duncan, operates eight Advice Offices in cities throughout the country. Each employs a paid director.

The cases that come to these offices remain much the same, Duncan said, mainly welfare and justice for the poor: "Problems, as always, arise out of poverty."

At the same time, Black Sash continues to keep a watchful eye on the establishment. A recent protest filed by the organization concerned harsh conditions for inmates of a newly-opened, high security prison facility.

"Since they're talking about putting the same high security prisons in other places in the country," Duncan said, "what I've done is take these problems up with the government department involved so as to influence what is done in the future."

"And you've been here since the pension crisis in the Eastern Cape (no pension payments for December 1997)," she continued. "That should not have happened. You can do cash flow projections by the month and know that if you have been given this much pension money at the beginning of the year, you're going to run out by the end of the year."

Pension-related problems deluged the Eastern Cape Advice Offices, she said. The province, traditionally poorer than the others, had to integrate the Transkei and Ciskei. Thousands of civil servants in these homelands, their jobs protected by the new constitution, had to be absorbed.

"For example," Duncan said, "more than 30,000 policemen in the Eastern Cape are illiterate—they can't read nor write and they can't drive and these are almost entirely homeland people. They have somehow made more of a mess of it there than the Northern Transvaal, for instance. This had Venda and Bophuthatswana, all those non-independent homelands, who nevertheless retained full control of their own police."

"For some time, one gave government a lot of leeway because you understand they couldn't do everything at once. But now you feel they have to be criticized sometimes. The awful thing is the global economy and the trends. We are trapped in that. You can't isolate yourself any longer. When the government tries to reduce its debt, for example."

South Africa's national debt, Duncan explained, is mostly internal and inherited from the National Party government which spent enormous sums to maintain the structure of apartheid. Servicing of the debt heads the budget of the new government. Money is owed mainly to the nation's financial institutions and pension funds. Banks recently announced they would not increase overdrafts for any provinces so as not to be trapped like institutions in Asia which over-lent.

"You can't have banks collapsing because we're not repaying the debt," she said. "But it does mean, as government cuts expenditures, these cutbacks—and you see governments all over the world doing just that—tend to come in welfare and housing."

Duncan's smile was wry: "We're all having to learn a lot about economics."

Central government controls the funds on which the nine provincial governments operate. When cutbacks come, the lump sums they are handed are cut as well. That puts all in crisis. Duncan would like to see more control of spending in the hands of provincial governments.

"The money problem, in turn, is fueling the high crime rate," she continued. "If you look at the papers, up here in this region you're starting to see these heists of money which is being carted from one place to another in those armored vehicles they use to do that. The type of attacks now is much more like a military operation. The one yesterday involved fifteen men with AK-47s."

"You begin to worry that perhaps the old units of the liberation forces, because they haven't got jobs and haven't all been integrated into the Defense Force or the police, aren't regrouping. And as crime goes up, you feel a bit insecure."

The rate of violent crime in South Africa is the highest in the world, with Johannesburg recording the highest incidence of any of its cities. Twenty percent of crime victims in Johannesburg are white and, as Duncan put it, "experiencing now what blacks have lived with for ages."

Unemployment, particularly among youth, is a leading contributor to the crime rate, she believed. In the Eastern Cape, for instance, unemployment had reached 56 percent.

Duncan said she has no fears for her personal safety beyond what is "rational." I asked if she had increased security at her home. She thought about this for a moment and said, "Our cars now sit in open carports. I believe you're safer if you're exposed to the street because people in the neighborhood look out for one another."

On a political level, she was more optimistic. She talked about a recent ANC party session. After Parliament adjourned in December 1997, three thousand delegates gathered for the annual congress. There had been fears, she said, that the national leadership of the ANC would appoint from its ranks, resulting in insufficient representation of Asians, coloreds and whites. But of the top ten ANC leaders elected, only three were blacks.

"This proved to us that the democratic process was actually working," Duncan said. "Racism fears disappeared."

I asked about her other involvements. In addition to chairing the

Black Sash Trust, Duncan was a member of the executive committee of the South African Council of Churches.

Speaking as chairman of a Gun-Free South Africa, she said, "I was very pleased when I arrived here to see that notice at the entrance: 'Strictly no firearms allowed on the grounds.' That's my major work at the moment. It's a tiny little organization, but doing extremely well."

In 1997 Sydney Mufamadi, Minister of Safety and Security, had appointed Duncan to lead a committee of inquiry into the central firearms register. After the committee's report in April, he named her to a team of police and army personnel seeking to retrieve all state-owned firearms.

"These include the guns brought back from the years of struggle by the ANC and APLA (Azanian People's Liberation Army, military wing of the Pan-Africanist Congress party) and," she added, "they're all over the place."

I asked how guns could be controlled.

"It looks like we'll get new legislation later this year which will tighten up the licensing system, making it much more difficult to get a license," she said. "At the moment all people have to do is ask for a license. One of the things we found out is that these are given so carelessly. A lot of criminals, people convicted of serious offenses, have gun licenses. We're weeding them out now, but it is a lengthy kind of task given the shortage of police."

Adding to the problems her committee faces is the alarming statistic that 1,700 guns are stolen every month.

"We don't waste time with formal meetings," Duncan continued, "but I do meet with the superintendent of police, who leads the team, and work closely with him and with some of the Army people as well." She grinned, "—going swooping around the country in a police Mercedes."

Yes, she agreed, times indeed had changed for activists.

I asked about her family. The Duncans are the parents of two daughters. Both married foreigners and live overseas.

"I would never advise them to return. At this moment that would be a bad move, particularly if you're white, because job preferences are given to blacks. Which is right, of course, but that is one of the things that is difficult."

Would she leave the country? "No. No. No. But my answer might not be the same if I were much younger."

A couple of weeks later, a national newspaper verified Duncan's hunch. The paper reported that many robberies of armored trucks had been linked to dissidents of Umkhonto weSizwe, the ANC military wing. The official quoted by the paper suspected "a well-organized, counter revolutionary force."

After the interview ended, I walked over to another part of the park to meet my fellow tour members. They had been down a gold mine, one of the park's major attractions. Next up was tribal dancing in a small outdoor theater, which was where I found them. After that we would walk across a few streets to watch a demonstration of the processing of gold from ore to bars.

For some unknown reason, sitting on the bleachers among the Americans and vaguely aware of drum beats and the thump of bare feet, thinking about what Duncan had told me, evoked a vivid, remembered time, totally unrelated to what was happening now. It was 1972, near the end of my first stay which had been three months. An English-born couple, who lived in a beautiful home overlooking the Indian Ocean, had invited me for a weekend. The house with its windowed, sliding walls opening onto decks and terraces with lush tropical growth, looked like a place I knew from a Somerset Maugham book. Across the lawn, large red blooms hung from the twisted branches of a great kaffir boom tree. We sat in filtered sunlight around their pool, making languid recoveries from the late party the night before. Friends had driven out from East London. The talk had ranged from international politics to books. I was impressed by what interested South Africans, all they knew and how well they expressed themselves. Conversation here approached art. I wondered if this was because the government had banned television.*

I took a tall Pimm's Cup from a tray brought by a black man, listened to talk of yesterday's cricket match and got lost in the beauty of the place.

South Africa was shameful, racist and unjust, and yet I wanted to live there forever.

*The government did not permit television in South Africa until 1976.

IX
✺ *Jean Pease*
If you teach literacy about people's real interests, they learn far quicker

I'd been lucky so far. The women either had come to the house or picked me up, or Cecily had taken me where they were. But my luck ran out. Jean Pease would be free: that afternoon, her office. My problem was how to get there. She suggested a taxi. This sounded easy, but Cecily had said taxis were dangerous: incompetent drivers; passengers robbed or charged exorbitant sums; cabs hijacked.

Taxi companies filled several yellow pages of the Cape Town phone book. All size ads. One did not look any safer than another. Where were they? Where was I in relation to them? I went back to a small, low-key block for Western Cape Taxi Information.

I asked the man who answered what the fare should be, Newlands to Athlone-Rylands, round trip? He said 100 rands (then approximatly $14, now $11.10 US) which sounded OK. Could he recommend a reliable company? Why not his, he asked.

I waited under the carport by the drive, in the shade of the Zimbabwe creeper. The four-door, medium-blue sedan that turned into the cul-de-sac had no lettering on the door, no sign on the top. The driver jumped out and came around to open the passenger door. He was stocky, maybe mid-thirties, with black hair, a black moustache and an engaging smile. He had answered the phone when I called, he said. His name was Aldino.

Inside the car, a taped female voice, flat, mid-west American after the soft-spoken South Africans I had been hearing, pitched Amway. Aldino talked above her as he drove. That empty land to the left of the freeway, between Table Mountain and the city center, had been District Six. He had been born in District Six, "heart and soul of the colored culture." Also multi-cultural. Not only coloreds lived there, but East Indians, Portuguese, Jews and whites.

In between narrative, he asked questions: Why was I in South Africa? What interested me here? Where did I come from?

A little further on, he pointed to one of the early resettlement areas for coloreds ejected from District Six.

"The first thing they had to do was destroy the culture of the people," Aldino said. "At the end of the day, to the benefit of the elite white minority."

The elite soon were left behind as the taxi crossed a bridge and headed along a bleak street, wide and treeless, of factories and strip malls.

"It's basically a colored area the minute you go over the bridge," Aldino said. We passed an "informal" fish market where a white fish called snook was sold off the beds of trucks.

Non-governmental organizations, NGOs, tagged with acronyms, were rampant throughout South Africa. POLP, Primary Open Learning Pathway, was involved in primary level education. Jean Pease was its director.

POLP offfices were on the third level of the Rycom Center in Rylands. The Taj Radio Shop, metal bars across windows and door, was on the ground floor. A dozen men and boys lounged around the entrance leading to the stairs. They watched in silence as the car stopped. Aldino said he would check to see if this was the right place. He came back, took me to the door, and waited at the bottom of the stairs until I waved from the top. He said he would be out front.

Inside, six or seven women in a large room worked on computers or talked on phones. Some looked East Indian and wore saris, others were black or colored. After being announced by the receptionist, I looked around. Steel shelves held books and files. Brightly-colored covers of booklets and brochures filled magazine-like racks. A closer look revealed material for beginning and intermediate readers. Boxes of papers covered most of the floor.

Jean Pease led the way into a large back room with folding chairs below curriculums and organizational charts written in felt pen on newsprint taped to the walls. A bank of windows on the outside wall overlooked a cemetery. Women in Indian dress strolled through the paths between markers.

"These southeasters leave dust all over everything," Pease said, whisking a cloth across the table top.

Pease was tall, slender and straight-backed. Born in 1940, I learned later. Her hair was dark with gray strands. Cut short, it curled loosely around a face with even features made beautiful by high, elegant cheekbones. Her skin was the color of coffee with milk. A ready smile revealed even white teeth.

"POLP goes back almost eleven years, I would think." Pease said. She had a light tone but spoke firmly. "I left teaching at the end of 1986 and joined SACHED trust—South African Council for Higher Education—one of the large NGOs consisting of many different projects. Funding came from the Rockefeller and Ford foundations, among others. SACHED was a national organization and I joined the Cape Town branch."

"It came into being in about 1959 as the result of what I think they called the Universities Extension Act. You know how apartheid used to be—they really weren't extending education, they were actually restricting it."

One of SACHED's first projects had been preparing African students for universities overseas. It went on to respond to various needs of the community, Pease said.

"If teachers wanted alternative history resources, maybe a teachers resource center would be set up. Labor unions were just beginning. They needed training for shop stewards."

"SACHED attracted a number of activists because there were resources, and it gave people a space to do anti-apartheid as well as educational work; gave access into the community so you could be doing empowerment stuff."

"Beginning of 1987, I went into a teachers resource center with a staff of one which was me. You gave yourself a job description; you wrote a proposal. If the funders bought into the idea, then you would have to deliver on that. This center was aimed at high school teachers who wanted alternate resources—many apartheid textbooks were terrible—to use in their classrooms."

Pease knew what schools lacked. She had arrived at SACHED Trust after twenty-two years of teaching high school science.

"I wasn't quite sure what to do to take the project forward," she continued. "No one had left anything to carry forward, except some workshops for children leaving primary school for high school."

"But before getting into that, we have to go back to June 1986. The whole Cape Town area had been really shocked by attempts of the South African Defense Force to move people from Crossroads and a little informal settlement called KTC. They had been resisting being moved for fifteen, maybe twenty years."

"June, July, August is mid-winter and it rains in Cape Town. And what government had been doing over several years, when it came to June they would go in and raid houses for passes, particularly targeting women because men would be at work. Women had no right to come into the city under apartheid, only men if they had jobs. What they would do is raid, then bulldoze the homes. Every winter this would happen and they'd put people into buses and dump them in the Ciskei or Transkei and say, 'This is where they're coming from.'"

"Actually, the large number of people in those areas were born and bred in Cape Town. But because the Western Cape was a colored preferential labor area, under the Group Areas and other apartheid laws, it meant employers had to take so-called colored people before they could take Africans. For fifteen years prior to 1987 when they created Khayelitsha, they had not built a single home for African people in Cape Town. So there was this natural expansion of people. If they went to the council and said they needed homes, they were told,

'Oh, go to the bush.' And this is exactly what they did, because on the outskirts of the city it was bush. People cleared that bush and that's where they lived."

"The name KTC," explained Pease, "comes from a trading company right on the border of the bush and the only landmark when people, about 18,000 eventually, settled there."

"The government worked with a segment in Crossroads and one man was virtually a warlord. He ruled the people in Crossroads and KTC because it was such fragile tenure for them. He and his henchmen had such a hold on the area that, when new people came in, they would allocate where they could live. In return, they had to pay. If these bandits didn't get paid, they'd break down the house and terrorize residents out of the area. This gang was allowed to operate by the police because it was in their interest to get people out."

In June 1986, mid-winter, armed members of the South African Defense Force poured in with tanks and caspirs. Residents fled, returning to find KTC burned to the ground. Pease and others in religious, political, and community organizations arranged temporary housing in church halls for the victims. Pease added that SADF involvement was later proved. KTC residents received compensation for their homes in a court decision in their favor.

"When I came into SACHED the following year," she recalled, "delegations of KTC people came to ask the NGOs, including SACHED, if they would help them put up a school in KTC to demonstrate their determination to remain there. I got involved almost from day one. After a couple of meetings, SACHED said to me, 'Well, perhaps your project could collaborate with these people.'"

KTC people wanted their own school, Pease said, not one registered with the government, and women from their community to teach in it. Under the Bantu Education, or Bantu Affairs Act of the '50s, this was illegal. Even church schools had been taken over by government. Privately-run schools had a reputation for turning out activists, community leaders. Not, Pease explained, because students had been indoctrinated, but simply because they were literate and had been taught to think independently.

Pease acquired a Xhosa-speaking assistant. The two of them worked with a KTC committee through 1987 and 1988, a nervous time because of spot states of emergency and continuing violence in the schools.

While a school was put together from ship containers—they would not burn—Pease and SACHED trained KTC women to teach.

"When we were putting the classrooms down," Pease recalled, "we had to build a road in because these people lived on sand dunes. Residents provided labor and safety. I could walk in any time of the day or night."

"At one point, there was friction between various sections of the community, a lot of fighting, burning of homes and so on, so much so that the government declared a state of emergency, putting barbed wire around the perimeter. Non-residents were not allowed and we had to go in and out illegally as well."

In February 1988, KTC's school opened. "What struck me was, of the three hundred children who came, many ten years or older had never been to school," Pease said. "We all knew about this theoretically, but practically we had never come across the problem. Now, the community had decided children should be in age-specific classrooms—six-year-olds would be in grade one, twelve-year-olds in grade four, and so on. Here you had these inadequately trained, inexperienced teachers, some had not completed high school, and amongst their twelve- and thirteen-year-olds, perhaps half the class was illiterate. But teachers were expected to teach at the grade four level, or whatever, because parents wanted their children in as normal a school as possible."

Before very long, on-going help to teachers with over-age students became impossible for her because of other obligations, Pease said. But what had been learned formed the basis of their work. Though rundown and smaller, the KTC school still exists: not because the new education department won't build a public school, but because residents want to retain total control.

"Because of our work in KTC," Pease said, "probably by word of mouth, other informal settlements throughout South Africa got to know about us and we got flooded with calls. The communities we dealt with is a fascinating story of its own. There was Peelton, a little village near King Williamstown, in the Eastern Cape. This was at the time of the homelands and at least half of the community of Peelton refused to become Ciskeian citizens. As a result, government simply sent in troops and demolished the homes of the people who resisted. And these were their own homes. They had cattle, horses, all sorts of things."

"The government said, 'Right. You want to be South African citizens? Good.' They simply dumped them on the South African side of King Williamstown."

"The people walked back and there began a process of the Ciskeian police dumping them in South Africa and the South African police taking them back again. After a couple of these, the Peelton community was dumped back on the South African side, probably in '89, and the South Africans dispersed them into the region. These people then walked from village to village, collecting their community until they were all together again."

"We had a call from the Trust for Christian Outreach, also an NGO, and they said, 'Look. There's this community which is squatting in tents'—the South African Council of Churches had provided tents—'and they're just outside King Williamstown. All these children are just in the streets. Isn't there something we can do?'"

"We're two people in this project. And we got calls from as far afield as Namibia. 'Can't you do something? Here's also this informal settlement; no school; is it possible to train someone?' I'd be in my office and in would walk a nun from Guguletu and she'd say, 'You know, I don't know what to do or who to turn to. We run preschools'—or creches—'in Guguletu and we get these older children coming in there, eight or nine years old, who want to join us because we do educational sorts of activity. Is there anything you're doing we could do also?'"

Pease said while they knew of classes for adult literacy, there were none for children.

In February 1990, the project staff expanded to five. They traveled to places in and outside of Cape Town that had contacted Pease, including Grahamstown, Peelton, a site in the Transkei.

In a large settlement in what is now Gauteng province, volunteers, residents, taught in a farm school for two thousand children. Staff varied from high school dropouts to a couple of unemployed teachers.

"When we met them," Pease recalled, "they didn't even have a building. People taught under the trees and students sat on bricks."

Later that year, 1990, fifteen individuals began a five-month course designed by Pease and her staff. This was not simply a teaching program. Those in it learned how to organize their communities, how to bring out-of-school children into the classroom.

In special classes for over-age children, teachers worked from a literacy program developed in Latin America. Pease used it first at the KTC school.

"We said to the kids, 'Tell us what you really feel strongly about.' And the KTC kids couldn't talk about anything but the fires that had burned their homes. Every time we asked them to talk about something, it would end up with this fire."

"So we wrote their first little reader around the fire at KTC. And they learned very, very quickly and it seemed to give them a sense of," Pease paused, "empowerment is such an overused word, yet it's all one can use, because suddenly these kids had so much confidence. Of course, they wanted to read more and there were no books in their mother tongue. We took the *Three Little Pigs* and sort of Africanized it. It has such resonance because of their homes being burned and they loved it, so that was very useful."

"Much of what we experienced at KTC, we incorporated into this training program. The underlying principle was that if you teach literacy about what people's real interests are, actually use their own language about what they feel passionate, they learn far quicker because, unlike in school, literacy is relevant."

Teachers in Pease's course on literacy for older children came from throughout South Africa: two from the Johannesburg area, six from the Eastern Cape, one from Transkei, and four from the Western Cape. Two were from Namibia. The first two months they learned community organization, how to use a camera and a tape recorder. They returned to their homes to research the interests of the children. A month later, they came back with photographs and a story.

"They used these to generate lessons," Pease said. "That's the story in a nutshell. After about five months, they went back. They had to raise their own funds, start their classes, and resource themselves—and these were all absolutely impoverished communities. At least twelve classes operated for awhile. One or two are still going. They're not needed, but residents want them."

Though the government has changed and "Bantu" education no longer exists, Langa hangs onto its school, mainly to prepare over-age children for conventional schools. These youngsters usually come from squatter camps, Pease said, or have drifted in from rural areas.

"Our interests obviously grew in this whole problem of out-of-school children. By then, we'd started advocating the issue of what appeared to be hundreds, maybe thousands, maybe millions, of children who should be in school and were out."

Seeing the beginnings of change which she and her staff helped bring about, they saw the importance of helping develop or shape educational policies of the new government.

"If the ANC," said Pease, "kept to its pre-election promises, government would provide free and compulsory schooling for all children. Then classes for over-age students would cease to exist because even though kids would come until they were literate, parents would then put them into primary schools."

"In 1994, which was quite coincidental actually, SACHED was also reorganizing. This was a huge NGO and with all the changes and because there were so many activists in SACHED, many would be leaving to go into government."

For a year or so discussion in SACHED circles had concerned future focus. Without the necessity of hundreds of different projects to meet community needs, SACHED opted to concentrate on adult education.

In 1994, POLP, then with a staff of six, chose independence from SACHED: POLP would work with out-of-school children. Right from the beginning, recalled Pease, there was much to learn.

"We had never raised funds before because the SACHED parent body had done that. No one had any skills in fund raising or project management at that level," she said.

"It was also a very scary time because with all the political and structural changes in the education department, NGOs didn't know where they would fit in the new South Africa. Funders were starting to withhold monies; for example, the Swedish development agency had funded adult education through NGOs because they wouldn't work with the apartheid government."

"Because of the uncertainty, it was a very frightening time to go independent, but in retrospect, it was the best move because large NGOs, like SACHED, started to crumble. Their people began moving into government positions and funding was drying up. Helping us was that no other organization in the country focused on out-of-school children. There were the street children projects, but that was a very specific focus, street children and shelters. We were concerned with the education of these children."

"As I said, it proved to be a good move. We then did a lot of advocacy work, on a platform of 'You can't forget these children. If you're talking about educational redress, more than anybody else, they need to be looked at.' We kept arguing that if you don't address these children, they will join the unemployed, illiterate youth and this will become a real social problem. By about the year 2000, I think about sixty percent of our population will be under the age of eighteen and if we don't resolve the problem of our youth, what will we be saying about the future of South Africa?"

"So we did things like push ANC policy makers, at public meetings, to include out-of-school children, not only youths, in education policy. When research was done on out-of-school youth, it was sixteen to twenty-five-year-olds. We wanted children younger than sixteen years to be included in policy."

"The government would simply say, 'We're opening the schools and the kids are free to come in.' But unless something was done they were not going to come in. And if they did, they would simply drop out, because teachers had not been trained to work with children older than the norm."

From 1994 on, POLP campaigned the country's teacher training colleges to add a course developed for their first year students.

"Nobody was interested," Pease remembered. "They were interested in what we were doing, but they argued that this was a specialist focus for teachers and should be done as a fourth year. So we were doing advocacy in the colleges and at the same time, lobbying to get the national education policy to read 'children and youth.'"

"We also worked with the Center for Education Policy Development, the ANC think tank on education. What they did was get as many players in education together as possible to think through what they called the national qualifications framework. Education and training and even peoples' skills would all be brought into the system of accrediting."

"So we were a part of all that. We knew exactly in which direction the policies were going and we could intervene and so on."

For the past three years, POLP had worked with Cape Town College of Education where a fourth-year course deals with teaching over-age children. A requirement for those in it is that they come from classrooms with over-age students.

"This is an in-service course," Pease said, "and we've trained about a hundred teachers, of whom fifty have already graduated. Others will complete this year."

I asked about funding. Current operating expenses came from Independent Development Trust, World University Service, the Rockefeller Foundation, and the Joint Education Trust funded by

South African corporations.

I was curious as to whether she had any figures on the numbers of over-age students?

Pease nodded, "The ANC government white paper on education, the first one that came out, acknowledged 1.6 million children out of school. We use that as a sort of official figure, but we suspect there are more. The first proper census was in October last year and we haven't yet seen statistics from that. So far, by the way, figures indicate that total population numbers are lower than people thought."

In January, a pilot program for the Western Cape Education Department had begun: Open learning classes in primary schools would take children three years or more over grade level.

"Over the next three years," said Pease, "we'll be running this research project in twelve classrooms. These will be in about eight or nine schools with teachers trained by us. And it's all very fortuitious because Curriculum 2005 has just been implemented. Classes with these children will be able to accelerate their learning. We felt that if they are ten-year-olds or twelve-year-olds, they don't need the same amount of repetition as six- or seven-year-olds."

One snag is likely to be remedial students added to over-age classes since no special education classes existed in black schools during the apartheid era.

"We will be working with teachers," Pease continued, "to develop a learning program and look at factors which prevent learning, or make learning easier, so we can make recommendations to government: 'This is what works and this is what doesn't work.' And possibly whatever the lessons are from this pilot could be implemented provincially."

The aim of over-age classes is to get a child into a traditional classroom as soon as possible so he or she will not feel stigmatized by being in a special class.

POLP also tracks what is being done elsewhere, she added: Gauteng's back-to-the-fast-track pilot project; Fort Hare University's first year in-service, multi-grade—all farm schools are multi-grade—teacher education.

"We're trying to bring these programs together," Pease said. "If we can pool expertise and information gathered over the years, we're not reinventing the wheel and can get things going faster in the country."

She sat back in her chair, opened her arms and held her hands palms up. "And this," she said with a smile, "has been the story of my life since 1987."

Pease was born in Kimberley in 1940 of South African parents. Her father reached Standard Four, (US grade six) in school then dropped out to work. Her mother, a dressmaker, went to Standard Six.

"We were seven children," Pease said. "I had an elder brother; I'm the eldest daughter. I completed my schooling in Kimberley. It was a very small town. There was only one high school I could attend. I intended being a doctor. But my parents said, 'There's no money for going to medical school.'

"I ended up going to Fort Hare University which was obviously something that has shaped my life. Fort Hare was ... Well, the apartheid government said they were turning out black Englishmen. It was regarded as a kind of hot bed of politics."

"I came out of sleep little Kimberley where politics hardly was mentioned and got dumped in at the deep end."

"Of course, one got involved in all the discussions at the college, and you suddenly realized there was another part of South Africa you didn't know at all. That you'd grown up in a bit of a cocoon. And I think it also gave me insight into how whites grew up in this country, too, because many people said at the end, 'But we didn't know.'"

"And it was actually possible, certainly in the days when I was a child, to grow up without knowing. I mean after that, things exploded in the newspapers and television and so on. But there was no television in those days and you could grow up in a very isolated way."

Pease paused. "I remember as a child of eight or nine, seeing armed police in Kimberley for the first time. I looked at them and wondered, 'What on earth do they need guns for?' Thinking back on that now, it was a time of bus fare increases and probably people in the African townships on Kimberley's outskirts had been protesting."

"Our high school teachers certainly didn't try to politicize us. It was Fort Hare that changed my whole outlook. I was there with some interesting people—Chris Hani (Communist Party general secretary) was a student when I was; Stella Sigau (Minister of Public Enterprises); Ivy Matsepe-Cassaburi, premier of the Free State."

"Many of them left the country and formed the ANC in exile." Pease shook her head. "No, I never thought of leaving the country. During the years I was at Fort Hare the ANC politics was quite racial. People thought of Africa for the Africans. I think there was then an Indian Congress and there was a Congress of Democrats which was colored people, things like that."

"At Fort Hare, you listened because if you were not classified as African and you said something, they said, 'That's not really your concern.'" Pease's classification had been colored.

"I completed a Bachelor of Science degree in three years," she continued, "and then the fourth year we were the last non-Xhosa speaking students allowed at Fort Hare, which had been designated a Xhosa college. University of the Western Cape was to be for coloreds; Westville was for Indians. By then the government had taken over the college, so I had two years under the old university and two years under the new."

She came to Cape Town where she taught from 1962 until 1965. She married in 1964. In 1965 she and her husband went to newly-independent Zambia to work. Her two sons were born there. She returned in 1972 because she wanted her children educated in South Africa. After a year with her parents in Kimberley, she resumed teaching in Cape Town. She divorced in 1981.

In 1985, during the school unrest, Pease was arrested. She had addressed student and teacher groups and was among the organizers of the Western Cape Teachers Union (WECTU), now the South

African Democratic Teachers Union.

"It was," she said, "the first of the teachers' unions to align itself with the students. We had just been going about three months when they began picking up all the executive members. They were then able to detain people without trial and I was in detention about eight weeks. Some people stayed for months. I had one son at home. My mother happened to be visiting and stayed with him."

"Hundreds of people were being picked up, I wasn't unusual. I knew they were going to pick me up because I was on the WECTU executive. I stayed at home about two days to get the minutes up to date and out of my house. Friday morning I went back to school and Saturday morning they picked me up at home."

"This was the beginning of October. They continued to pay us, which was a good thing. One of the sad things was that the same weekend I was picked up, my ex-husband died. So it was a sort of double tragedy for the children and they wouldn't let me out for the funeral. So I came out eight weeks later to traumatized children."

Pease shook her head as if to erase bad memories: "1985 was an extremely difficult year to even be in South Africa. The schools were an absolute battlefield. We would go to student meetings and try to protect the children if they went to other schools for mass meetings. The cops would come and whip and teargas the children."

"I realized in 1986 there was no way I could stay in the schools. In a sense, once you had been in prison, you were marked. And I thought also there was very little else I could still do in the schools. I looked around and was offered a job at SACHED trust. And I thought this might give me scope for a different kind of involvement."

"My sons were then fourteen and seventeen. If I was going to make a move, I needed to make it before I was much older."

"I've found these last ten, eleven years very exciting. I direct this organization and we now have a staff of ten."

I asked her about her sons. Both were pilots. Her eldest had just begun working for a national airline in the U.S. He had married an American woman and would probably settle there unless offered a comparable job in South Africa. Her youngest son completed the commercial course for pilots as well, then earned an advanced diploma in computers. He lived in South Africa.

"I never tried to politicize them," Pease said. "I always felt they had a right to their own lives, to come into things their own way."

As always when I talked with South African women, I was interested in her perspective on the future of South Africa?

"I suppose I've worked with the poor so much I have a kind of socialist outlook on political matters," Pease began. "Yes, there's been a lot of change and in some cases very little change. One realizes that the macro changes had to take precedent over micro changes. Certainly for people in informal settlements and in black schools, very little has actually changed."

"But in informal settlements, there is no harassment of people. They can go where they like. The government is trying to build houses. They are little matchboxes, but better than the shacks they had before, and they've been given the land on which to build these places so, in one sense, I suppose they are doing the maximum they can given the kinds of resources they have. We did inherit a terrible debt so that constrains a lot of developmental work."

"But it's an exciting period to be in because one can be a part and parcel of actually shaping what happens. There's so much scope for development. What is exciting about our work is that this is a problem endemic in Africa. So one also feels that what one develops here, might also extend to other parts."

When the interview began running long, I had fidgeted. Would the taxi wait? How much more than the agreed upon one hundred rands would the fare be?

I was very glad to come out of the building and see the blue car and Aldino jump out to open the door. Inside, Frank Sinatra's voice had replaced the Amway promotional tape.

On the drive home, I told him a bit about the interview and Aldino told me his mother had been a runner-up in the Miss South

Africa beauty pageant. But because she was "non-white," she could not advance to the more prestigious white competition.

After parking in front of Cecily's carport, Aldino opened my door, then went back to open the trunk, reappearing with an arrangement of pink and white flowers and interesting foliage overflowing the top of a basket a foot and a half wide, pink bow on the handle. He handed this to me.

"This is for you," he said, "because you like South Africa."

I didn't know what to say and probably muttered something stupid, like "you shouldn't have done this." He waved away whatever it was that spilled out. No charge for the extra wait, he said. Eighty rands would do it. He had said a hundred and that is what I gave him.

X
🌿 *Maureen Jacobs*
I began teaching in 1984 in the squatter camps

"Townships always have only a single road in and out," Aldino said over his shoulder. "This was for the convenience of police when they wanted to close off the area."

We were on the broad road leading into Langa, the black township closest to Cape Town and one of the first in the Western Cape, according to Aldino. Langa looked like Soweto. Shacks and dust and people in ragged clothes. In a vacant lot, three cows, ribs showing, ate their way into a pile of cabbages.

"People in one township didn't mix with those in another," he said. "As coloreds, we were too white to go into a black area, too black to go into a white area."

Aldino's father was white. He had married a colored woman. Aldino proudly recounted the details. If as a white man his father could not marry the woman he loved, he declared he would become colored. "White Man Becomes Black for Love," read the headline above his story in a Cape Town newspaper.

"His nickname was Blackie," continued Aldino, "and he was persecuted for years after he married my mother."

The first time I rode in Aldino's cab, a taped American voice enthusiastically urged on Amway dealers. Aldino hoped to make a great deal of money with Amway. At that moment, volume cranked up, Nat King Cole crooned about something light years from the munching cows shivering off flies.

A mile or so further along, Aldino turned off the main road. He drove up one narrow dirt lane and down another, scattering shabbily dressed pedestrians and leaving behind clouds of dust. We passed "PAC" spray-painted on a wall: Pan Africanist Congress, the militant ANC opposition.

Contrary to directions from Jean Pease, the Chris Hani School was not behind the Langa Police Station. I wanted not to see what I was looking at—squalor illustrated by plastic, paper and every other kind of transient litter humans generate, blown into corners, against the sides of shacks, flattened against fences and scattered across fields of dusty and trampled-to-death weeds. People everywhere: men in old clothes, women with white plastic bags, children kicking a ball. The head of a bony dog hid in a bag of garbage.

I felt not only vulnerable but an intruder. Looking down on high from the Elderhostel bus had established a more comfortable distance between poverty and privilege. The car came to a stop. Aldino got out and walked across the dirt to a metal building. I considered locking the car doors. A strong summer wind kicked up dust and trash. Aldino came back with a young man who looked about 20. He knew the school. We turned more corners, passed more unrelieved grimness.

Aldino turned into a large lot where kids chased each other in the dirt. Beyond, Chris Hani Community School was lettered across the side of a ship container. Jean Pease and Hani had been classmates at the University of Fort Hare in the Eastern Cape. Hani, charismatic leader of the South African Communist Party, had been a hero of radical black youth during the apartheid years. On April 10, 1993, Hani had been shot as he pulled his car into the driveway of his home. He died instantly. The Polish immigrant charged with the murder was linked to South Africa's far right.

The youth who had showed Aldino the school began walking across the play yard to the street before I woke up. I grabbed coins and handed these to Aldino who called to him. Trotting back to the cab, he cupped his hands in front of his chest. I knew he wanted and needed money. But I hated the feeling of playing Lady Bountiful. We both had uncomfortable, unwanted roles.

Behind the container, decorated with the school's name and bright and primitive paintings of children, lay the main building. In the dirt yard in front of it, mothers with babies tied to their backs kept watch over the toddlers on the ground. A woman hung clothes on a row of wash lines.

The school director, Maureen Jacobs, came out. We exchanged greetings and I followed her back inside. School desks and chairs filled a single room, large and without partitions, at that moment empty of students. Institutional-green paint flaked off concrete walls.

Two fair-skinned young women who looked about eighteen sat at two of the desks. One had spiky magenta hair and the other was blonde and blue eyed. Jacobs didn't introduce them. We eyed each other curiously.

"This year, so far," Jacobs said, "we have eighty-five in this classroom, last year 201. We're waiting for children from the Transkei. They'll come later."

Students ranged in age from five to nineteen years, she said. They studied English, Afrikaans, Xhosa, arithmetic, geography and history. She showed me a text. A single page. Each page of a beginning reader had been pasted on a piece of cardboard to accommodate a maximum number of students.

We went from the school to another steel container, blue, at one end of the washing lines. Inside, Jacobs sat at a desk and I in a plastic dinette chair opposite. The only light came through the opened end of the container. Jacobs was a short woman with rounded edges and very dark, smooth and gleaming skin. A cotton scarf, knotted at the nape of her neck, hid her hair. The scarf was blue, a medium blue, and matched her uniform-like cotton dress that buttoned down the front. She wore slip-on sandals. Her expression was serious and serene as was the tone of her voice. She spoke quietly, her words heavily accented.

"Parents send their children to us because they don't want them in the other schools," Jacobs said. "I started this school in 1991. I was

127

trained by Jean Pease. I began teaching in 1984 in the squatter camps at the place they called KTC. In the squatter camps there was just the open space, no building at all. I used black plastic bags to make a shelter for the children. I got the plastic from the Council of Churches. The white policeman used to burn the plastic every time. He did not want a school established there. They didn't like the KTC set up."

"I made the shelter several times, until the KTC people built their building. The parents did that. So I teach in this building in KTC in '84 and '85. In '86 there was a big fire. The school and houses of KTC burned. It was very sad for me."

The laughter and shouting of the children came closer and I leaned forward so I could hear Jacobs' soft voice.

"Then I just stayed at home. The children, they were in the churches because they had no houses. Then the children they said to me, 'Miss Maureen, we want a school. We want to go to school because other children are at school.' So I started a school again. 1987. Then I met Jean Pease. Another lady told her about me. Jean Pease said, 'I can help you.' And she met the KTC community. After that Jean Pease said I must collect all the girls that had passed Standard Ten and they are going to train them. For KTC school. So we did that."

A siren wound up somewhere nearby. Jacobs shooed curious children away from the open door. She stopped talking until the noise lessened.

Jacobs was patient with me when I asked her to repeat what she said. I had trouble with her accented English, which would have been her third language after Xhosa and Afrikaans. During the forty-plus years of apartheid, year after year classes in Afrikaans had been required for all South African students, whether they spoke English or a tribal language.

"We put the school in containers," Jacobs continued. "Jean Pease got them for us." She waited when the siren began its cycle once again. "I think about seven containers. We had a lot of children. Three hundred. Parents wanted the community school, not the government school. In those days there was apartheid. Sometimes the children that are coming from the Transkei just walked bare footed. They had plastic on their feet so they don't go to the government schools. And some of these children were older than twelve years. But they can't study Standard Eight in the government schools."

"In 1990, Jean Pease made a national training. It was for (township) teachers in Namibia, PE (Port Elizabeth), from Umtata in Transkei, East London, Jo'burg, and Cape Town. I led the other teachers in KTC. And after 1991, I come to work with hostel dwellers."

During apartheid, she explained, hostels in the cities had been for male contract workers only. After apartheid ended, these hostels were opened to their families. Chris Hani students came from the hostels nearby.

"These were children who were loitering outside, doing nothing," Jacobs said. "Nombaliso was the school before. I changed the name after Chris Hani died. The parents said they liked that name because Chris Hani was a hero and he liked children and poor people."

I asked why she had chosen the work she did. "Because I was born like that," she said.

Jacobs was born in the Transkei in 1947 and grew up there. Her mother was Xhosa, her father from Zanzibar. She said she had always enjoyed children. "I used to collect the children and make the children happy. Even now at home they meet me and say, now I must come back to the Transkei and make a school there. My own children are in Transkei. I've got two, they are 22 and 16 and they are living with my mother."

"I came to Cape Town in 1975 because there are no jobs in Transkei. I found a job. I was working in Seven Guys Jewelers. After that I went to work in a squash court. After that I said, 'No. I'll try to work with the children.' I felt they needed help. In those days I was living here in Langa. I went to KTC in 1984."

Recess over, children began tumbling into one another, piling up at the container opening, curious about what was going on inside.

"Sorry. " Jacobs left to deal with children and school matters.

When she returned she said, "UK golfers once come, then just give us this container. From the UK (United Kingdom). This container was full of equipment." Some of its contents remained, stacked against the end and around the edges: nesting plastic chairs, filing cabinets with stuffed animals on top, a table. "The only thing we were unlucky, this container had no stationery. The children have nothing in their hands."

"Some children from other schools come here," Jacobs continued. "From the government, mainstream schools. They beg their parents to come here because the children are enjoying it. They are doing everything—drama, music, poems. And we're lucky. I have people that come from overseas to teach."

Aha. That was the answer to the mystery of the school room. The girls inside were from Denmark, volunteers, Jacobs explained, who would stay three months then be replaced by others. They taught English and math. In addition the school had four local teachers.

A school bell rang and children streamed by. In a mix of English and Xhosa, she scolded the children who interrupted.

"Ooooh, children ... "

Jacobs shook an index finger at the animated little faces, then turned back to me. "Education is very important," she said. "Since the end of apartheid most students stay in this school two to three years and go on to government schools. They get confidence here with us."

Jacobs left, returning a moment later with Thozama. Thozama was 15.

"She came here late last year," Jacobs said. "She could not even hold a pencil. This is her book. She can do everything now."

They spoke to each other in Xhosa. I opened the book. The language in it was Afrikaans.

"She came from a poor family," Jacobs explained, "from a family that didn't care about school. I told them about the importance of school."

I turned the pages of Thozama's book. The exercises and drawings inside looked to be about a one to three grade level. Thozama chewed the end of her pencil and watched with obvious pride.

After Thozama returned to the school room, I asked about the costs to parents of sending their children to Chris Hani. "All are very poor," Jacobs said. "Many are not working. The cost for a child is 5 rands ($.45 US) per month."

Students wore dark skirts or pants and white shirts. Like other South African students, they had a school uniform. To get them initially, Jacobs composed songs, wrote poems and made up a play. She then took the children into the city for street performances: "White people throw money and I get the uniforms." She bought material, another woman cut out the patterns, and the pieces went home with students to be sewed together there. Jacobs believed uniforms important: "Children feel they are in school when they have a uniform."

Jacobs' dreams for her school included a larger staff and qualified teachers. She had submitted a proposal to the new Department of Education. Thus far, nothing had happened. "They keep promising," she said. "They are supposed to subsidize me, but they haven't."

She did arrange with the government for food for her students: bread, jam and milk. Her interest in her students extends to their families. She arranged group sessions of mothers to create beadwork rather than "sit outside and do nothing."

She stood outside the metal school building, a small figure, hand shading her eyes, to watch us leave. I waved and she did as well. Her parting words were "Jean Pease supported me, uplifted me."

Back at Cecily's house I sat on the deck in back and looked through printed materials I had picked up from Jacob's desk in the container. One told more of the history and origin of the school:

In 1991 parents and residents of the A.L.T.A. Hostels joined forces with Mrs. Maureen Jacobs...and founded the Nombaliso School.

•Most of the children have never been to a school, most parents are illiterate or semi-literate;

131

•Most of our children are from rural areas and do not have a birth certificate;

•Even with a birth certificate, the children would not be able to pass a school readiness test or be accepted into a mainstream school;

•Many students are older than 10 and unacceptable to public schools;

•Most parents are unemployed;

•Most children are Xhosa-speaking without language skills necessary to enter public schools.

In another pamphlet, I found a statement by Jacobs:

"Our special challenge is to help our children to develop the language and learning skills necessary to make certain that not even one child (and especially not another generation of children) is helplessly trapped in a life of illiteracy and poverty: without *education*; without *marketable work* and *life skills*, and without *hope*."

I read a bit more before putting the papers aside. I thought about the place I had been then shifted to the moment. Figs ripened on the tree next to the deck. Ferns and enormous elephant ear leaves covered the steep bank opposite. The invisible creek bubbled. Across the way tall willows and palm trees grew. Purple bougainveillia and deep pink and fragrant frangipani bloomed. Langa could have been a continent away rather than a short drive. What or who determined why I sat here and Maureen Jacobs in a ship container?

XI

❦ *Susan Conjwa*
Being in prison made me more strong, more determined

I didn't notice the traffic, or rather the lack of it, until Aldino waved at the empty street ahead. "There'll be lots of cars soon," he said, "coming from the mosque. The last prayers are taking place now. Then the Moslems will end thirty days of fasting with the feast of Ramadan."

The Indian/Asian community in Cape Town was near District Six, in a section that somehow had survived apartheid removals. But in the last few years Aldino said, residents had become militant and the area crime-ridden. "During Ramadan, they were very quiet, but they start again now."

Once again we drove across the bridge, that dividing line between white city and black ghetto, the bad old days reality and dream of the not-yet-begun future. We were on our way to Athlone-Rylands, to Jean Pease's offices. She had offered a room where I could speak with Susan Conjwa.

Aldino turned off the taped silken tones of Nat King Cole and talked, looking into his rear view mirror. "When apartheid was introduced," he said, "people spent the first twenty years laughing at it. After that, the government spent the next twenty years getting people to accept it. People had to be jailed and beaten up to realize they were serious. The end started in the mid-'70s when the school children stood up and said 'no more' and took to the streets. In the '80s the government became subtle. By the end of the '80s they didn't govern, they just tried to protect themselves."

Upstairs in the offices of Primary Open Learning Pathway (POLP), I laid out tape recorder and notebook in the room where Jean Pease and I had talked and read a sheet of newsprint tacked to the wall: Curriculum 2005, The National Educational Policy. As I understood it, by 2005 a school-wide program, "the basis of all education," would be in place. Fundamentals such as reading, writing, science and math would be taught relative to natural sciences, human and social sciences, arts and culture, language and technology.

I arranged my gear. POLP's funds didn't go for show. The conference tables in the big room were composition doors on sawhorses; the chairs, molded white plastic. I waited by the windows. I watched a knot of traditionally-clad East Indian women enter the cemetery across the street and branch out to take separate routes between the graves.

Conjwa arrived in a simple cotton dress in an African print. A scarf, knotted at the nape of her neck, covered her hair. On her feet, she wore those beach-type slip-ons anchored by straps between the toes. Her skin was very dark. She was short and round of body.

Born in 1923 in the Transkei, she had come to Cape Town to go to school, she said, because that was where her father worked. They lived in the city's township of Langa. Schools for blacks were then in churches and that was where she began her education. When a government high school opened, she continued there through Standard Nine. After leaving school, Conjwa worked as a domestic in Cape Town. After three years as a servant, she got a job at a hospital.

"While I was working there," she said, "I happened to hear about St. John's Ambulance (a volunteer national emergency service). Then I managed to take classes in first aid from St. John's Ambulance. My aim was to advance my education. But then I had to work more. My father also had brought my brother (to Cape Town) and we must now work together to send him to school."

But soon that became her task alone. She explained that after her brother left their Transkei home, her mother took over the care of the family's cattle and sheep and crops. When that proved too much for her, she asked her husband to return. He told his daughter, Susan, that after he went back home she must take responsibility for her younger brother who was in school.

"Langa school didn't have so high school fees then," Conjwa recalled. "I think at that time it was 12 rands ($1.33 US, probably ten times that exchange rate then) per year. I also saw to my brother's clothing and other school needs. He passed his matric (graduated). The children (rebelling students) then had become active. He joined them and was soon detained. But later, after he got out of prison, he married and educated his children. One is now a chartered accountant, one a teacher."

She also had married. Her husband, she said, had been a member of the Communist Party. "He is dead now. But he deserted me. I raised my six children by myself."

I had great trouble understanding Conjwa, even more so than Maureen Jacobs. It was embarrassing to ask her to repeat again and again. She had no teeth and some part of the problem was enunciation; quite likely most of it was because English was undoubtedly her third language.

I asked how she knew Jean Pease. "I met this one in detention," she replied. "In prison." They had been arrested in the eighties, she explained, for protesting during a state of emergency when no gatherings of any kind were allowed.

"There were a lot of things we were protesting," Conjwa said. "New apartheid restrictions. Arrests. Killings. House burnings. During the time of squatting, people picketing to protest no housing, and so on. We gave them moral support. Not with the ANC, no. I didn't know anything about the ANC because the ANC was banned. Then, those who protested belonged to the Communist Party that was working underground. My eyes opened in Langa, being with the school children. And I used to adore those women (Communist Party activists). And that's in fact, how I caught up. The white ladies were running a Nyanga welfare center. One of the women asked me to distribute (food) parcels to the community, to disabled people, to people who cannot work and the aged. I knew this old lady because I used to be in church with her daughter. The old mama was active until she died. And died not herself because if you had no ID number and so on, you have no identity. She did not have pension either. She said, 'I am not going to take the pass (book) because I want the pension. That pension can just go away.'"

"When I went elsewhere, I asked one of the white ladies at the Nyanga welfare to go and visit her. After that, they used to deliver her food parcels themself. Then the people from the administration came and those people in Nyanga had all their land confiscated from them. The people had worked hard to get that land. They didn't just pick up those lands, they bought them. Now they died without anything. This was the protest that put Jean Pease and me in prison. Jean left prison before I. We had quite a group of women. Sometimes from other cells we would hear them and we would all talk."

I wondered if prison had discouraged her from further protests.

"Being in prison made me more strong, more determined," Conjwa said with a laugh.

I asked when she had first begun protesting the apartheid laws. Since her school days, she said: "Not organized then, but organized later."

An early protest, perhaps the first, had been against the red tape involved in going from one place to another. Since she had been born in the Transkei and attended school in Cape Town, this restrictive red tape began with boarding the train. To leave the Transkei, Conjwa said, "you must have a permit from the local magistrate to say that you are visiting so and so. You must make sure you are visiting a relative. Like I was visiting my father. My first time to come, my mother brought me to Cape Town. My father had arranged a permit from Cape Town and sent it. Even the ticket was bought here in Cape Town and sent home. But now my father has gone and I must undergo all those things and it was nonsense. I hated that."

"After my brother left school, I went to work in Muizenberg (on False Bay south of Cape Town) and had to find a place to stay nearby because I wasn't sleeping in. Those squatting gave me a space. When I was staying there someone came to ask me to assist with people in another squatting camp, for coloreds, close to Muizenberg. So I used to go there and I also did char work every day."

"It was then we happened to meet ladies of the Communist Party, white ladies. Friends I had were involved, so I also got involved. And there was this man in the Communist Party who asked me to go assist (in educating) stranded children near Muizenberg, at that place called Free Ground. Those children used to come through the bushes to the only black school in that whole area. And the only ones able to go to school were with their fathers who were working on the docks at Simonstown and living at the squatters camp at Simonstown. So they must come to an age where they are able to go by themselves because it was quite a distance from the station to where they went. It is only now I read in the paper, those people that used to be there are given rights (to live in that squatter camp)."

She laughed and looked pleased. "They must like that very much because I put a school there and that school became a real school. So, my grandchildren schooled in that school and one of my granddaughter's sons is married to a girl who is teaching there. But we then moved to Guguletu. I had my school there in a church hall. We gave the school the name Elita. Elita means light. And it grew up. It is still there in Guguletu. It never faded. And also my other school in Free Ground, from the late '40s."

Conjwa sat back in her chair. She spoke so easily of those difficult times. Most of the time with a half smile on her unlined face. She was older, but I had six times the visible wear. That smooth, uncreased skin seemed remarkable, given all that she had endured.

Conjwa's arrest in the eighties followed demonstrations at Khayelitsha. She explained how that came about. "Khayelitsha is in two sections. There are squatters and there is now Khayelitsha township. The reason it is like that is the people that protested for sites were the homeland people. They'd lived in hovels at Langa and then it was overcrowded there. Then they started to show themselves, that they wanted to be seen to."

"They moved from Langa and Nyanga to an area nearby me. I was waked up nights by people suffering and opening my door. And it was a Catholic priest and some of the women I know (members of Black Sash) who started protesting against arrests of these people in the camp and deporting them (to the black homelands.) The protestors were brought to court. It was a real big scene. They wanted to jail them all, but the jail was not enough." Conjwa laughed. "Not enough space."

Those who were freed, she said, simply returned to protest at the same spots where they had been. "And of course we were doing monitoring of how people were treated. I think I was earmarked from that time."

Sounds of traffic came through the open window. Just as Aldino had predicted, the district's streets had come to life after the close of Ramadan services.

Since the change of government in South Africa in 1994, Conjwa had been involved with the refugees who began flooding into the country. "Now in my house I have refugees from Nigeria and Sudan. I am on the refugee committee for them. I was approached to join the committee because I'm keeping the Nigerians, but it was by coincidence I had refugees. I used to go to the Trauma Center and I got known by the Trauma Center community. During the unrest (leading to Mandela's release from prison in 1990) it was called Cowley House and it was where you went if you wanted to know about arrested people. It was run by a group of people who were concerned about the political problem and so on. The (Anglican) fathers were staying there at that time. There was a house in front where the Anglican nuns stayed. When everything turned over to normal, that place was turned into a Trauma Center for the victims of violence."

I asked how many refugees lived with her. "I've got four Sudanese and three Nigerians. The Nigerians when they came were six, but now they have sprouted themselves. Because they're working, they are able to pay the rent. There is unrest in Nigeria. There's unrest in countries all over Africa."

How had the refugees found her? "They were sent to me," Conjwa said. "I was asked by members of the Trauma Center to hold on to them until they got space. It is not easy for them to get space."

I asked what she thought about the new South Africa. "It is what we fought for," she replied. "It needs us again to put it straight. But my determination is that it is going to be OK. People were traumatized in South Africa. Others grew up with traumatized people. What can we expect from such a community? It will take time. We are not talking about something that happened only for ten years."

Earlier that week Conjwa had returned from the Eastern Cape where she had been surveying communities still marked by violence and trying to determine the causes. "In the places problematic in the Transkei there is all this fighting—you don't know who is fighting who. But there is a lot of shooting, a lot of killing. They say they are fighting the thieves, those who are stealing the livestock. But as long as there are still idle hands, the fighting won't stop. The European Union has given money for water in Transkei. How is this going to be implemented? There must be a lot of education to train people how to work. And who is going to be taken? To get the jobs, to get the training? Who is going to be left behind? My own way is there must be little training sessions, mini projects begun so they—I'm talking now about child, men, women—can be occupied with something."

"It's not only government that's got money. Churches have got money. But they've got hierarchy not knowing what to do. They can know what to do if they listen to the mothers. Christians have got to do something. Put it not on the shoulders of the government only. Families also must work. The other thing is, teachers are fighting for money, for survival. If we do things by the state, everything is political."

At the end of our conversation, Conjwa asked for a ride back to Cape Town. In the car, she said, "The country needs those who are aware. Between the top and bottom are the moderates. Only the moderates are able to look on both sides. They must coordinate their efforts. They've run to be in Parliament. Now they must coordinate themselves to what is Parliament." She termed the Truth and Reconciliation Commission "a good exercise." But afterwards that group has to look at what to do next, after the conciliation, after the apologies, once things are threshed out. "That is what the TRC is about, no longer pointing fingers but looking at now what do we do? We have to know each other. We do not yet know who we are. We've been only part of separated groups."

The taxi slowed as it passed through a business section. Conjwa pointed to tables set up along the curbsides where men sold packets of a popular South African brand of potato chip. These vendors were refugees, she said. They'd learned quickly how to tap the financial resources of the city. South Africans should take some lessons from them.

Conjwa asked to be let out at the Quaker Peace Center in Mowbray. It had been the peace center that had sponsored her delegation to the Eastern Cape. Once in Mowbray, she directed Aldino where to make the next turn.

"To me, " Conjwa said, "this is now a time of healing. For so long, we just got up every day and fought apartheid."

Aldino stopped where she told him, in front of a modest one-story building, tucked among what appeared to be small homes in a neatly kept, modest neighborhood. At the gate, she turned to wave before disappearing among the shrubs in the front garden.

On the drive back to Cecily's house in Newlands, Aldino clucked when passing a pocket of street vendors. Aggressive newcomers, he said, were taking money from the pockets of South Africans and there wasn't all that much to go around.

Conjwa had pressed another sensitive spot as well. "I beg to differ on what she said about apartheid," he continued, "about it being a daily fight. During the years of apartheid, many South Africans just got on with their lives. They worked, raised families and got them educated. They protested when there were protests and discussed apartheid, but it didn't consume them on a daily basis."

XII

☙ *Mary Burton*

Every Saturday and Sunday, we were marching or at public meetings

1

M ary Burton packed a container with ice and water to take to friends using the Burton tennis courts. I watched from the table in the room opposite the kitchen. The interior of her home in Rondebosch looked Mediterranean with its high ceilings and white, cool openness. While she stuffed bottles and packs, we exchanged comments on the weather, getting-acquainted small talk. It was Sunday and Cecily had dropped me off at her house.

Burton wore a just-above-the-knees tennis skirt and short-sleeved blouse, both white. She was a short woman with an attractive face and graying hair. Her features were regular and her expression pleasant. Not at all ordinary were the arresting blue eyes, a presence about her, a significance, and an accent best described as international.

Burton returned, trailed by a mellow yellow Lab. We sat across the table from each other in the dining room. The dog plopped down heavily and rolled onto its side on the cool tiles. Mary Burton was born in 1940 in Buenos Aires, Argentina. The family, she was one of three children, later moved to Brazil. After high school, she studied for a year in Lausanne, Switzerland. During a family skiing holiday in Austria, she met her future husband, Geoff Burton.

Both went on to university in London and continued to see each other until he returned to his home in Cape Town and she to Brazil, where she worked for an English-language newspaper.

During her visit to South Africa, at the invitation of his family, they decided to marry. After a wedding ceremony in Brazil, the couple returned in 1961 to live in Cape Town.

"I was so ignorant about South African affairs," Burton recalled, "I didn't realize that, while I was immigrating, a great number of white South Africans were emigrating in the Sharpeville and Langa aftermaths. Some left because they foresaw trouble and some because they objected to apartheid rule."

"In my first years in Cape Town—I tried very hard not to pass a quick judgment—I found myself drawn into charity work. In my immediate peer group were my husband's friends and their wives, people he had known all of his life. Every woman I met who was not working full time seemed to be involved in some charitable occupation or another. And I became particularly involved in driving a van laden with vats of soup into Crossroads, still then called the Cape Flats. It was before there was such tremendous density of population, so it was really driving into some sandy wastes. People either lived in very, very rough shelters or in sub-economic housing built by the state. We would ring a little bell and from every corner came a child or an adult with a container of some kind, and we would fill that with soup."

"I still think this is a wonderful thing to do," Burton continued, "but I began to question the reasons for the poverty and the fact that the poor people were always the black people. And the more I started asking questions, the more interested I became. Not only in the answers, but in the evasions."

"One of Geoff's friends was a lawyer who did all the legal work arising from the Black Sash Advice Office. His wife, through him, was invited to attend a Black Sash meeting. It was now, I suppose, about 1962. Maybe even '63, and the first wave of Black Sash members—Noel Robb, that generation—had been working hard for eight years and were beginning to look at new membership."

"We agreed she would go to this meeting of this organization with a funny name and see if it was any good and, if it sounded good, we would both join. And we never looked back. Both of us became increasingly involved and drew in another group of our contemporaries."

"So my friends and I started learning. We would go to meetings and we would listen to talks about the law and conditions. Then we began going with people like Noel to learn first hand about what apartheid did to people's lives. Because even then, it was very easy to live in white Rondebosch and not know what was happening."

"So when people now say they didn't know—though I know it's because they didn't want to—I also know how easy it was to slip into not knowing. Once we started to know, we could never go back. I always say that Black Sash gave me much more than I ever gave it in terms of helping me to come to terms with living here."

I was curious about whether she and her husband had considered leaving South Africa because of the government's policies?

"Geoff is in a family business and there was never much chance of going anywhere else," Burton replied. "I had, somehow, to make sense of living in a country which, as I was gradually coming to understand, was built on injustice."

"I remember so vividly," she continued, "going with Noel to the pass law courts where people were processed through like a sausage machine—a case very two minutes: found guilty and endorsed out; found guilty and endorsed out."

"Out" meant sent to one of the homelands?

"Yes, well, they weren't even homelands at that stage, they were native reserves. And I remember another thing Black Sash used to do at that time, go to ..."

The phone rang from the counter behind her. Burton spoke to someone of translating documents the French government had sent to the Truth and Reconciliation Commission: "I thought you might be willing to take that on." She spoke in a low-pitched voice, quietly, but with a persuasive authority.

Back at the table, Burton finished the sentence begun before the interruption: "Another thing we used to do at that time was to go to hearings of the Group Areas Board. The Group Areas Act had been used since 1950, but it was beginning to be implemented much more strenuously. The procedure was a public hearing where the public could discuss the proclamation of an area for whites or for coloreds or for whatever the classification was going to be."

"But you weren't allowed to oppose in principle; you were only allowed to say the boundary should be brought to this road and not that road, for whatever particular reason you wanted to make or claim. But Black Sash went to every hearing we could reach and protested in principle. Though we were invariably told to sit down before we got very far, we continued to do this as a way of indicating support for the people who were there."

"We were, inevitably, the only whites," she added.

She waited a time before continuing. "I often think, when I look back to those days, we made absolutely no difference at all to the decision. But now, when we talk about the forgiveness of so many people, I think it is because there were white people in this country who were prepared to stand up, to take the trouble, to show what they felt, to show what they believed. If it did nothing else, it helped to make relationships between the different groups of people. Racism isn't as rabid as it might easily be. Foreign observers tend not to understand that. And probably quite rightly, since the picture was painted as a struggle between white and black."

This good will, Burton said, was reinforced by the End Conscription Campaign. In 1985, the South African Defense Force numbered approximately 86,400 men and women: 17,400 army regulars, the rest conscripts who did two years of service, compulsory for all white males 18 years of age and up. After their service, they became part of the Citizen Force for the next twelve years, during which they must spend 720 days in uniform. They were then assigned to a kind of home guard and on call until age 55. There were many casualties as troops sent to the "Border," battled Namibian "freedom fighters." As in the days of the Viet Nam war, many young men chose to leave the country rather than fight for a cause they did not believe in.

"Year by year, apartheid bit deeper into every aspect of life," Burton recalled. "Another thing that particularly shook me—my mother remembers my writing to her in a state of fury—was the closing down of night schools. The greatest work of a number of Black Sash members was teaching in these schools. There was, as there continues to be, this longing for education on the part of people who knew they were getting an inferior education, or who had missed out altogether."

"Clearly, the government believed that what was taught in these schools was political, their teachers sent to these classes for political mobilization. Maybe some were. It's quite possible, I suppose, that small groups of young people, meeting to learn, also were taught political ideology, given ideas of freedom. I hope they were and not just learning to read 'The cat sat on the mat.' But I think of the women I knew, particularly the president of the Night School Association who dedicated years and years of her life to these schools. I really don't think she ever put a political idea into any one's head at all, except perhaps the idea that education was a right, an equal right for everybody."

"What was clearly important was that people should be educated, so there would be a chance for them to work, even under racial discrimination. Closing the schools seemed so contrary to good sense, quite apart from anything else."

Burton leaned forward in her chair, her voice and expression more intense: "The awful thing was, it just didn't seem possible to ever change anything. One would go every day and the Advice Office would be working every day and all it did, if anything, was ameliorate the situation a little bit, or give people some sympathy. It didn't ever change anything."

"Noel (Robb) was an inspiration because she just battled on and on, not the only one of course, but the closest one to us. The national president of the Black Sash, Jean Sinclair in Johannesburg, and later her daughter Sheena (Duncan), seemed very powerful, but very remote."

In Cape Town, membership of Black Sash fluctuated between five hundred and a thousand, with an active core of not more than a hundred, Burton said. That would be divided into those working on a regular basis in the Advice Office and those involved politically "in the legislation, in trying to change the system, in trying to make people think about what was going on."

Burton was among the latter, worked in the Advice Office only in emergencies, "when we had hundreds of people there."

"I gradually came to understand that the only way things would change was if voters were educated enough to understand what was happening and would vote for legislative change."

In the '60s that became, she said, the thrust of political activism among whites.

"We lobbied Parliament; we bearded cabinet ministers in their dens; we wrote paper after paper about the terrible hardships that African people, in particular, suffered. And the injustice of it. We kept thinking that if people only listened, somehow logic and good sense would prevail."

"And of course, we had all those mass stands. We used to debate the wordings of our posters. What can we cram onto a poster that will somehow change people? I still say, you have to believe people can change. Otherwise, we really were just bashing our heads against the wall."

During the '70s, a new opposition voice began to be heard. The ANC was underground or in exile and this voice was black and came from a banned man in the Eastern Cape village of King Williamstown. Steve Biko's Black Consciousness ideology spread like wildfire. His was a bold voice holding out new hope to victims of apartheid. Burton called it the articulate political view of black people at that time: white liberals were rejected; whites differed only in gradations. They would not change the country.

"Even if there were positive, friendly feelings toward whites as individuals, politically the gap was getting further and further," Burton recalled. "Someone said to me, 'I can't afford to come and spend social time with my white friend, because it makes me soft and I need to be hard.' Blacks distanced themselves in order to strengthen their own views, to remain untorn by divided loyalties."

"So working in the Black Sash became quite lonely because one was rejected by the government and those people as well. It sounded patronizing, even then, to say we were working for them. And it was not true that we were working *with* them. We tried and tried and tried to draw black women into membership, but it didn't work at all. Black Sash already had the stamp of a white organization."

Not until well after the student uprisings in 1976, Steve Biko's death in 1977, and the increasing oppression of the late '70s and the early '80s did an avenue for affiliation of blacks and whites appear: The United Democratic Front, an umbrella opposition organization, a loose alliance of hundreds of community, church, sports, professionals, workers, students, women and youth groups. Formed in 1983, the UDF became a powerful ally of the banned and exiled ANC.

A closer, cooperative relationship between blacks and whites had begun in the late '70s, Burton said. With Soweto, a new generation became aware of the ANC, a movement whose charter called for equality among all races. Burton said that touched a generation of blacks who had had little contact with people outside their race group other than employers or police.

"I suppose, inevitably, there was a reaching out to those who might be allies. Certainly the white student movement was very much drawn in. Having been rejected in the '70s, now there was a greater rapprochement between NUSAS and black student organizations."

"Even before the UDF was launched, we'd talked to people about new movements, new groupings. There were various initiatives to start a women's organization—and we were absolutely delighted about that after trying for so long to open Black Sash doors. I think we would have been happy, in the end, to close Black Sash and join up with a much broader grouping. But the '80s, as they wore on, became a period of enormous repression."

I was curious as to how she then believed change might come?

"All the thinking in the Black Sash, which was what I was learning and agreeing with, was of some kind of national convention," Burton replied. "We wanted people like Mandela to be let out of prison to participate and some way found in which leaders from all over the country could come together."

During the '80s, the frequency of large open meetings, public demonstrations, rallies, and marches increased greatly. Inevitably, police interfered, even if a permit to gather had been granted by a local authority.

"The police," recalled Burton, "would use tear gas to disperse the crowds, and went from there to bullets, first rubber bullets, pellets and birdshot and, increasingly, stronger and stronger ammunition."

After 1983, the UDF took on the role of organizer of public demonstrations and gatherings. Black Sash always was invited, she said, partly as a sign of solidarity, acknowledgment of non-racial commitment and "because some people said it, as a tribute to the long, hard road we had followed. And partly because the presence of white women, it was hoped, would reduce the levels of violence. And I think that was a reality because of people like Noel who had husbands who were pillars of the community and economic giants in Cape Town. Not so easy to detain her or arrest her as it was a black woman nobody knew."

"I remember at one of our national meetings, probably in '86, '87, Frank Chikane (general secretary, South African Council of Churches) was a guest speaker. He told us, 'You have space, political space, that many people in this country are denied. And you have to use it. It's your responsibility.'"

"To do that, we had to speak with firsthand knowlege of what was going on. And so, every Saturday and Sunday, we were marching or at public meetings where someone would get killed. The following weekend would be the funeral. That funeral would be dispersed with teargas and shotguns and somebody else would get killed and there would be another funeral the following weekend."

"Funerals became a way of being together, of singing the freedom songs, displaying the flags. And there were terrible scenes. The coffin would be lowered into the grave and at the last moment, an ANC flag would be spirited out of someone's pocket and laid over the coffin and the police would swoop. The funeral had been allowed to take place but with a maximum of two hundred attending; no flags, no singing, and so on."

Once again I was quite spontaneously washed by awe at the courage of South African women, particularly women who voluntarily stepped up to fight a battle that was not actually their cause at all. Their lives would be less comfortable, in fact, in a system where all people would be equal.

As for personal danger, Burton said, "I think realistically anyone who was in a crowd could have been the victim of a stray bullet. So, sometimes you were frightened and you ran with the crowd and you ran from the teargas, but no, I did not have a sense of 'I am a target.'"

She paused, then said, "I think one of the only times I remember being quite physically afraid was when I went with Di Bishop to protest against the behavior of police in Worcester. We went to see the policeman everyone was accusing of torture and terrible deeds done and we saw him in his office. I'm not usually a very fanciful person, but I was frightened just to be in his presence. Maybe it was because of things I'd heard. I just remember that sense of dread. But otherwise no, I wasn't afraid. But," Burton laughed, "I'm not brave like Noel. After one encounter with a policeman, I remember she told us, 'he was young and I was bossy.'"

In 1985, Burton had joined a march of hundreds to Pollsmoor Prison near Cape Town where, three years earlier, Nelson Mandela and four other ANC leaders had been moved.

Burton recalled, "We had many agonizing thoughts before deciding to go. This was the end of August and was the time of probably the worst repression. A state of emergency had been proclaimed here and in part of the Eastern Cape because of Matthew Goniwe and the three who were assassinated with him in the Eastern Cape in July."

Goniwe, she explained, was a charismatic young history teacher in Cradock and Cradock, police said, had become a center of resistance because of Goniwe. Security Police reputedly loathed him and his colleagues. Many threats had been made against them. Though they continued to speak out, they began telling someone where they were going, when they would leave, what time they expected to return.

One day, after a meeting in Port Elizabeth, they did not return. Some time later, their burnt-out car, four bodies inside, was found half way between Port Elizabeth and Cradock.

"Matthew Goniwe's funeral in Cradock," said Burton, "was an absolutely galvanizing moment—certainly for us in the Black Sash who were there. Many of us went up. Dozens of buses went from Cape Town to the funeral; dozens of buses from Johannesburg and everywhere. It was held in the sports stadium of this dusty little town. Not a blade of grass or a tree anywhere. A boiling, boiling sun. Black Sash members came from all our regions, after much agonizing over whether it was the right thing to do. People didn't know how he had died at that stage and the picture being painted of him was, here was a violent Communist."

"While we knew very little of the real truth about their deaths, we did know Matthew Goniwe. He spoke to us at our national conference in March of that year. He was close in our memories as a very fine man."

"There have been many, many investigations and the Truth Commission will eventually tell as much of the story as we've been able to prove. But people have sought amnesty for it and we know the four were murdered."

When the country began preparing for the 1994 democratic elections, Burton was appointed Provincial Electoral Officer for the Western Cape.

Burton smiled at memories of that time: "We were employed early February. We didn't have an office, we didn't have a telephone, we didn't have a piece of paper. We started working in my house, two of us, with a bridge table, two chairs and a telephone. Gradually we got an office, found the people, and staffed it, put up a team and eventually managed to hold an election. It went dreadfully with all sorts of mistakes which we sorted out except for one very, very, big hiccup."

"We had this huge, densely populated district which covered Khayelitsha and Mitchell's Plain, in other words, all first-time voters. Within the same district were colored and black, but mainly black. We had, in many cases, no roads, no halls. We had to try and find buildings we could use, all of them really unsuitable. Commissioners of the Independent Electoral Commission gave us these magnificent maps about how to set up a hall—a table here with seating, another table here and the polling booth there. We were lucky when we could squeeze two tables in."

"The system was very complex to prevent fraud. There were no voters' rolls, so people had to prove their identity. An identity book was the only thing that would allow them into a polling station. They had to dip their hands in a kind of ink which was very difficult to remove. But before they put their hand in the dye, an infrared light showed whether you already had some on your hand. If you did, you'd voted before and were immediately chucked out of the hall. That did happen a bit."

"After the dye," she continued, "you got your voting paper. These were poor people, often illiterate, but there were pictures with party emblems on the voting paper. Then into a secret booth to make your cross on it; put your vote in the box. Then you did the whole thing all over again because it was a national and provincial vote."

The masses of materials required were packed into boxes and sealed. These would be delivered by truck to polling stations guarded by monitors.

"We couldn't control all the delivery end of it," Burton said. "On the day of the election, people stood in these huge queues and the papers never arrived. And that could have been a recipe for violence."

"We were worried and the workers, who had gone through all this training, and who were tremendously excited about being voting officers, were furious with us."

"Parties bused some of their supporters in and out and that helped a bit. But mostly, people who had come to vote just sat. Nobody got angry. And reporters went to them and said, 'How are you finding this wait?'"

"And they said, 'Well, we are disappointed, but we are going to vote and we believe the papers will come.'"

"Eventually they did arrive, but late, late, in the day. Almost anybody you ask will remember what that day was like for them. Where they stood; where they waited; what they sang; who they talked to and so on."

"We were granted an additional day, so when the paper did all arrive, people could come back the next day. But because we had lost control of the delivery process—though only in that one district out of thirty-nine—we also lost control of the collection. The same system used to distribute all the voting materials should have swung into operation to bring everything back."

"We should have been able to get from voting station X the exact number of ballot papers we'd given them. The trucks were going out at 2, 3, 4 o'clock in the morning. They shoved everything together, from all these polling stations, instead of keeping it separate."

"Everything was in a muddle and it could have been a real disaster. We had an emergency meeting. All the organizers and the strategic planners agreed: 'The only thing to do is to put all the ballots together and count them together rather than separately, according to each polling station.'"

Though that appeared the only solution, voting officers were extremely upset, Burton said.

"They said, 'Once again, you are telling us that we black people don't matter. We want our votes to be counted exactly the same as the white peoples' votes.'"

"I said to officials trying to push this decision, 'I think we can't make this decision by ourselves. Even though I believe it is the right decision, if we haven't got support for it, we won't be able to manage.'"

"I went to the township and called the voting officers together,"

Burton recalled. "They were angry; many were in tears. But we talked it through and eventually they decided the only thing to do was to count the votes together. They understood it had not been deliberate. It was inefficient but not criminal. We had sealed the trucks and signed over the seals and I could assure them, 'All your peoples' votes are there. But you need to be satisfied about that.'"

"At dawn the next morning we invited everyone, all the voting officers, all the international monitors, all the church people, to an enormous great hangar where the trucks had parked on land owned by the government, which was absolutely secure, had 'round the clock protection."

"We used a hailer to address them all; then everyone sat in groups on the sand and talked it through." Observers were open-mouthed, she said. They had never witnessed decision-making like that.

"Eventually everyone said, 'Yes, we're happy. But we all want to inspect the trucks.'"

"And representatives of the Muslim party and the clergy in their robes—all the officials, all the political parties, everyone—clambered in and out to inspect the seals, inspect the boxes which had been thrown in with chairs, pencils and all the other paraphenalia of any election. Then we all went off and counted."

Elections over, in late 1994 Burton returned to work with Black Sash. By then the organization had changed. Executives had restructured the organization, closing membership participation and directing resources into Advice Offices with full-time salaried staffs.

Burton recalled, "This had required an enormous amount of time and energy discussing how we should do it and whether we should do it and so on. I went back into quite full-time organization work within Black Sash and learned a lot about management policies and practices which I knew absolutely nothing about before."

She was named one of twelve trustees on the board of Black Sash.

In 1995 President Mandela appointed Burton to the Truth and Reconciliation Commission.

2

As of 1995, fifteen truth commissions existed worldwide. The first appeared in the mid-1970s. These commissions operated elsewhere in Africa, Eastern Europe, and South America. Not all work in the same way. For example, unlike South Africa's Truth and Reconciliation Commission, some granted blanket amnesties to groups. South Africa specified individual disclosures of apartheid-era crimes and strictly voluntary participation.

The TRC began its work in late 1995 with seventeen commissioners, the maximum number called for, appointed by President Mandela. One resigned at the end of 1997 to take another post and was not replaced. The TRC, according to its mandate, would sit for eighteen months.

The Commission is made up of three committees: Human Rights Violations; Reparations and Rehabilitation; and Amnesty.

The Human Rights Committee, to which Mary Burton belonged, hears from victims.

"For two years," she said, "I've listened to terrible, terrible stories" — of sons taken from their homes late at night, of husbands who disappeared forever, of betrayal, of beatings, stabbings, shootings, electric shocks, deaths by asphyxiation, torture, bodies burned, homes ransacked.

Approximately 20,000 victims voluntarily filled out statements to tell their stories. Testimony began mid-1996, six months before amnesty hearings began. About five percent of her committee's hearings were picked for reporting on television, radio and in newspapers. These represented a cross section of cases. It was important, Burton said, that other victims felt that, in some way, their story was reflected among those told publicly.

The Committee on Reparation and Rehabilitation would decide how victims should be compensated. The Committee on Amnesty, chaired by a judge, considered politically motivated acts and gross violations of human rights committed between March 1, 1960 and December 5, 1993.

Approximately 8,000 had applied for amnesty. This number was believed to reflect only the individuals who believed they might be found out, far less than the actual total of those personally involved in such crimes. Being granted amnesty, after a full and honest confession, brought protection from later civil or criminal action and was only given for acts admitted to, the details of which would be published.

The decision to grant amnesty to those responsible for past gross human rights violation had been one of the last stumbling blocks in pre-election negotiation.

Burton said, "There had always been a very strong feeling that amnesty had to be given for the sake of peace and the sake of the success of the negotiations. But it should not be just a wiping the slate clean, which is what the National Party wanted and they used that expression very often. It needed to be amnesty, but with acknowledgement of what had happened."

With basic tenets finally agreed upon, the examination of truth commissions in other countries began. Among those doing the research were members of Black Sash. "Not officially as Black Sash," Burton said, "but as people interested in what was going to happen. We began to read and think and talk about this, then to write about it. We were one of a number of organizations expressing opinions, engaging in debate, because no one knew exactly how it should work."

An organization called Justice in Transition was put together by

Dr. Alex Boraine, former Progressive Party Member of Parliament and Moderator of the Methodist Church in South Africa. Its purpose was to coordinate thinking of how such a commission would be set up.

Burton continued, "They had a lot of discussion, particularly with the Chilean truth commission, but they looked at other models as well. As individuals, we in Black Sash participated in that."

"The new government of the ANC had already established the Human Rights Commission and we had been critical of the way it had been set up. People were allowed to make nominations and candidates were interviewed in public, but the process of selection seemed to us very unclear. We campaigned for a more transparent way of electing or appointing public commissions. One of the things we said was, whatever commission is set up, there must be a proper way in which the whole country can have an opportunity to see who will be a part of it. The president did listen to that."

A multi-party committee was appointed by President Mandela. The public was asked to make nominations to that committee. Then its members made up a short list of nominees they thought suitable. Those on it were interviewed by the committee and these sessions televised.

"I had declined nomination from Black Sash," Burton said, "because I didn't think I was tough enough to do this job. And then the ANC Women's League asked if they could nominate me. I explained I'd refused nomination because I didn't think I had the capacity to pursue people hard enough. Then at some social occasion I met Albie Sachs (member of the Constitutional Committee of the ANC) and he gave me a lecture: I didn't have a right to refuse nomination. People of different skills would be required."

"My husband and I talked about this. He agreed with Albie and said I'd ought to allow my name to go forward. Even then I didn't think I would be appointed, but here I am."

Burton's commission duties began in December and at the time we spoke, in February 1998, the Human Rights and Amnesty committees had completed two years of hearings.

I asked about procedures of applying for reparation and how individuals qualified.

She explained that when her committee determined an individual had suffered a gross violation of human rights, that name was passed to the reparations committee. Their first step was to determine if immediate treatment was required. If so, medical care or psychological counseling for the victim was authorized.

Burton said members of her committee on Human Rights had hoped that all victims would receive some payment right away. "That hasn't happened," she explained, "in part because our own process hasn't moved rapidly enough, partly because things have to go through different departments."

The proposal at that time was that each victim be paid a certain sum: "the same sum, no matter whether they lost a husband or a child or they themselves were tortured or even experienced a lesser degree of suffering, because it isn't possible to measure suffering."

Whatever amount is decided upon, the commission recommended that payments should be made annually for six years rather than in one lump sum. Partly, Burton said, because the certainty of income would be helpful and partly because it would be less of a drain on the state.

The amount and method of payment would be decided by Parliament. Debate had not yet begun. Burton thought the commission's suggestion, between 17,000 and 20,000 rands ($1,888 to $2,222 US) annually, might be more than Parliament would approve.

The original term for the the TRC would have been up in mid-1997. Burton said it became obvious very early that eighteen months would not allow enough time. Application was made to the president for the previously agreed upon six-month extension and this was given. Then it became evident the Amnesty Committee would not wind up its work when its term expired the end of 1997. In August of that year, when Archbishop Desmond Tutu, chairperson of the TRC, was in the U.S. for cancer treatment, commission members, led then by deputy chair Alex Boraine, set a new time limit. Work of all but amnesty would end in December 1997. The latter would request a minimum six-month extension to complete its tasks.

When the Archbishop returned, he rejected that and called the entire TRC together: The amnesty process, he told them, reveals the worst crimes. The hearings are open and public and the revelations hurtful and horrendous.

"He said," recalled Burton, " 'we cannot let the country go alone through that terrible agony of hearing what was done. Our part of the work is supposed to help toward reconciliation. If we aren't here to do that, it's not responsible of us.' "

"So he persuaded us to reverse that decision and to agree that we would all go on until June this year (1998). Absolute deadline. And that's just as well," she added, "because we're nowhere finished our work."

Her committee planned to take the month of July to complete its report and to present that to the president by October 31.

"At our meeting last week," Burton said, "it became very clear that the Amnesty Committee won't be finished this year, let alone by June. We don't even know how long it will take. The number of people who applied for amnesty (approximately 8,000) is much, much greater than we anticipated. And they have a consitutional right to be heard. A great deal hangs on the balance for them."

"While the Amnesty Commitee can't go out of existence, neither can we go on forever waiting for them, now that our part of the work will be finished. We've now gone back to the decision taken last year: the Amnesty Committee will go on and we will not. It's been a hard decision and the Archbishop is very sad about this. But it's not possible — too expensive, apart from everything else."

I asked how many appealed to appear before her committee?

She said, "21,297 statements were taken, far more than anyone imagined. And one of our problems now is that about 5,000 applications came into our Durban office the last week that we accepted statements. The only explanation that makes sense is that the IFP (Inkatha Freedom Party) finally realized that if they didn't encourage their people, the majority Zulu who live in that province, to participate, they would be denied reparations."

"So that has placed a huge burden on us. My race at the moment," Burton said, "is to finish my work by next week so as to help in Durban, or have the statements brought here, whichever works out best."

I asked if she could determine whether those testifying had been truthful?

She thought a minute and said, "My understanding of what we have been told in the Human Rights Violations Committee is that the stories are probably all true. Maybe people forget details, dates, or their memory is that 'I was held in a black cell with no lights and with no food or water for weeks.' In fact, they would have died if that had been the case. It was probably days, but I'm sure it felt like weeks."

"So I think it's that kind of thing that is not absolutely accurate."

I had read about the Commission's sophisticated computer system. Software would link up sound-alike crimes. If those confessing didn't make full disclosures, testimony by other victims could incriminate further. Had disclosures of crimes been complete and honest?

Burton believed not. "The perpetrator is much more difficult to judge. We find ourselves quite far from the Amnesty Committee because the previous government, in drawing up the legislation, fought very, very hard and succeeded in getting the Amnesty Committee to be fairly autonomous. Though it's a committee of the Commission, the Commission has no power over its decisions. They, the members of the Amnesty Committee, decide who has been given amnesty then tell us, often at the same time as they announce to the public. That is why this recent brouhaha over the thirty-seven members of the ANC leadership given blanket amnesty."

"If we'd had a chance to discuss this with the committee, it might not have happened. But that's the legislation. And maybe it does give people a greater trust in the committee."

Burton said she personally felt quite distant from the Amnesty Committee and seldom attended its meetings. Partly because she did not have time, also because committees seldom meet in the same cities at the same time. TRC headquarters are in Cape Town with additional offices in Johannesburg, Durban and East London.

She understood from the Commission's investigative unit that Amnesty Committee members were often frustrated with the testimony given. Particularly with Security Police "who clearly discuss with each other what they will say. So you can't break their story even though you don't believe it. In many cases their confessions would be the only way of getting the truth because things happened in secret."

"That is hard for the victims." Burton continued. "Since they get so little and, since the provision of amnesty will prevent them in future from bringing civil claims against those people, they feel they have been denied justice. And if they don't even get the truth instead, it is very hard for them to bear."

"That is one of the reasons why the work on the Commission is so draining. Because one is dealing with issues like that. And we want it to be just and satisfactory to everybody and I think in the end it will be, but there are so many things in it that are not perfect."

Burton talked again of the work that remains.

"What we have done now, arising out of last week's decision (to adjourn in mid-year), is ask the Amnesty Committee — and I don't know yet if they are willing or if it is possible to do it — to give urgent attention to the very big cases which will make a political difference to our report."

"For example, they have not yet given any attention to the question of atrocities committed in the ANC's camps in exile. We know there are applications and we have certainly been given stories about what happened to people. But there has been no public sign of that being heard. They will be dealt with, but we want them to be dealt with before we go out of existence so that we can provide a balanced report."

Burton said her hope that charges made against the ANC would be dealt with by the Amnesty Committee before her committee disbands may not be realized. The Amnesty Committee could tell the Commission that first it must complete its first priority: by law that is dealing with individuals currently imprisoned.

The final report of the Amnesty Committee, Burton said, is likely to be a list of findings, "not any kind of analytical document. Which is why it is important for us to have a balanced content to put into our final report."

I passed on Susan Conjwa's comments — that once the hearings were over, the finger-pointing done, the TRC should look at what next. Did Burton see a future role for the TRC?

"No," she replied without hesitation. "Our task is to make recommendations about how reconciliation can be furthered in the country, but not to *do* anything. We will have no implementing capacity. We have already been in discussion with churches and other structures. And I think probably some of us would like to see something laid down that will commit not only this present government, but future governments, to making reconciliation something that is part of a state responsibility."

"We've had several useful seminars and think tanks with others, looking at what reconciliation means and how it can be achieved, but no further than that. And we'll probably need to do more of that when we have the time."

I told Burton that I understood she donated part of her Commission salary to Black Sash.

She said, "Commissioners are paid an enormous salary which is extremely uncomfortable for me. I know some commissioners came from well-paying positions and I think it's only fair they shouldn't lose by joining the Commission. But I don't think it's appropriate that the government should pay such salaries."

Pay policy of the IEC (Independent Electoral Commission), to which she belonged earlier, had been no loss, no gain. If the individual came from a highly paid job, he or she received the same salary; a lesser paid job worked the same way.

Commissioners initially received an after-tax salary of approximately 12,000 rands ($1,333 US) monthly. Since taxes were about 43 percent, take home was about half the total. Within six months, that salary was raised by another 4000 rands ($444 US) per month.

"I thought that was terrible," Burton said in a cross voice. "We'd all taken the job on the understanding of what the pay was and understood it was a maximum of two years. I tried to refuse that. They didn't know how to do it."

What she did was to give a regular amount of her salary to Black Sash and also pay the equivalent amount, after taxes, of her increase to the Black Sash State President's Fund for Reparations, from which part of the TRC-recommended reparations will be paid.

I said I also understood that she had refused an official vehicle.

Burton laughed: "I often say that is the only thing for which I'm going to be remembered. At the end of my life, they'll put on my tombstone, 'She didn't take a government car.' "

I asked if she hoped to serve in any kind of official capacity in the future?

Burton shook her head. No official role, she hoped. And, she added, she never wanted to be on another commission. There were objectives she'd like to further, though at that point she was not exactly sure how.

"I'm very worried about crime and violence," she said, "And how you bring about a better life for people."

"I think we are now facing realities that the government should have faced twenty, thirty, forty, fifty years ago. We need education desparately; we need jobs desparately. There's an enormous amount of work to be done. And I won't see its benefits, probably, in my lifetime. But I'm very excited by the events in this country and I wouldn't be anywhere else in the world."

TRC history (much of it taken from *A Country Unmasked: Inside South Africa's Truth and Reconciliation Commission:* Alex Boraine, Oxford University Press 2000) includes the following:

> •1995: Late in the year, police applied for blanket amnesty for 3,500 of its forces. Black Sash opposed a companion bill which would have made the details of these

crimes secret. According to its statement, 'The commission's purpose is to disclose the truth. To achieve that purpose we have compromised on accepted international norms regarding the prosecution of perpetrators of torture, assassinations and the like. We cannot compromise on the truth being heard.' Blanket amnesty was denied.

• April 16, 1996: Nohle Mohapi is first to testify at the first hearing of the TRC in the City Hall at East London. Her husband, Mapetla, had died in detention in 1976. His captors claimed he had hung himself by his jeans in his cell.

• August 1996: The ANC submitted a 90-page document to the TRC summarizing apartheid-era crimes. The National Party's 35-page document to the commission reportedly was a justification of government violence during apartheid.

• January 1997: Details of the deaths of the Cradock Four, Matthew Goniwe and three companions, were revealed by the commission. The four were pulled from their car: one was shot trying to escape; the others were beaten with an iron implement, then stabbed to make it appear their deaths were vigilante killings. Their bodies were burned.

• February 1999: The TRC refused amnesty to four former Port Elizabeth police officers who claimed that Steve Biko's death in 1977 had been accidental. None admitted to any crime, saying they had acted to defend themselves, that he had become agitated, refused to stand and fought back during questioning. Reports at the time of Biko's death were that he had been beaten with a hose and his head rammed into the cement wall of the interrogation room; that after his collapse he had been thrown, naked and shackled, into the back of a police van and driven more than 500 miles to Pretoria for medical care. He died in a police cell before he was taken to the hospital.

The lengthy ruling by the TRC cited several reasons for denial of amnesty including that the officers had lied about what happened and that their account of the death of Steve Biko was "so improbable and contradictory that it has to be rejected as false."

XIII

❀ *Virginia Engel*

Secretly I became the link between the ANC and the unions

That morning's traveling music turned out to be *The Second Time Around*. Invariably when I transcribed notes from an interview, somewhere, on some page, would be a scribbled title, *Just the Way You Look Tonight; New York, New York; Sweet Lorraine*.

Listening to the music Aldino played reminded me of something Cecily said. After a year of travel around the world, coming home was going back in time twenty years. South Africa was exactly that way to me. That feeling of landing in another, simpler era had been especially true in the 1970s. No TV to talk about or look at; uniformed school kids with regulation haircuts who stood at the back of the line at the bus stop; advance bookings for the movie and tall urns with flowers either side of the stage below the screen.

But the nostalgia was fleeting. On the drive into Cape Town, the main thing on my mind was a non-functioning tape recorder. I had checked it out just before leaving the house, and when I pushed "record" nothing happened. Aldino offered to take a look at it.

He stopped at the Parliament gates and told the guard we were to see the President, which was not exactly true but we were waved through. Aldino parked on the opposite side of the square, in front of the pillared presidential office building. He tried a few things with the recorder that didn't help and said he would take it back to the shop. One of the men who worked for him was good with electronics.

That meant this interview would be notes only.

Just inside the entrance, I signed in with a guard who called to verify the appointment and walked me through a metal detector. An aide led the way across oriental carpets through an elegant formal entry hall into a dining area with a polished table, long enough for eighteen chairs. The rooms were spacious, rich with dark woods. Elaborate chandeliers hung from high ceilings.

We turned into a hall down one wing and passed an open door. The man ahead motioned into it: "Virginia is busy with the president."

A woman at a desk glanced at us briefly, smiled, then turned back to the individual hidden by the door. It occurred to me that, if I dared, I could step across the hall and peer around the corner to see Nelson Mandela. To my lasting regret I did not.

The day before a steady parade of helicopters had droned over Cecily's house, delivering the president, cabinet ministers and other officials to Cape Town for the February 5 opening of the 1998 parliamentary session.

As the hall continued, ceilings lowered and rooms off from it became less grand. We entered one of these. A young, smartly-dressed black woman at one of the two desks listened to rock/rap radio. She and the other staffer, a man with lighter skin and East Indian features, fielded a steady succession of phone calls: "President's office. Who should I say is calling?" They spoke to each other and to callers in a mix of Afrikaans and English: "Goeie more, meneer . . . I'm well, thank you."

A tray on the low table in front of my chair held a jar of Nescafé Instant, a carton of long-life milk and a bowl of sugar. After one call, the man said, "The President is still with Virginia. As soon as he leaves, she'll call."

A young, tall, substantially-built, white woman came to use the fax machine at the end of the room. Waiting for the papers to feed through, she turned to the others.

"You can't just give away tickets to anyone for the opening of Parliament, you know," she said in heavily accented Afrikaans. "That is a security risk."

Neither of the two looked at her or paid the slightest bit of attention. "I'm not just being sharp," she added. She looked at them, waiting for an answer. The two continued what they were doing.

The intercom crackled and the young black woman asked for a
repeat. "The President is still with her," she said to me. "He was supposed to be gone at 12:30. Five minutes more." The white woman
left. I looked at my watch. Scheduling back-to-back interviews obviously had been a bad idea, but I had had no choice. Both women had
packed calendars. I had taken what I could get.

The man at the desk asked his colleague if she had a copy of the
letter to the President of the Congo confirming his appointment on
the eleventh. She shuffled through a stack of papers and shook her
head. He called another office to ask if it had any documentation.
No. The next phone call concerned arrangements for a meeting of
President Mandela and the ruler of Denmark.

"Is government in the United States like ours?" the man asked
during a break in the action. I said something noncommittal like "I
imagine they're all the same," then thought about it. More layered in
the U.S., more rules and formality, more organized perhaps, less
accessible certainly. Did it work better? Maybe not.

The appointment, scheduled for the lunch hour, began almost an
hour late. Virginia Engel, Nelson Mandela's private secretary, had a
fine office. National flags on standards flanked her large desk. Light
came through tall windows, highlighting the gleaming surfaces of elegant antique furniture. Engel left her desk, walked across the carpet
and sat on a couch facing a pair of chairs with curved, wooden arms and
legs. I took one of them. Behind the couch was a fireplace. Engel was
young middle-aged, tall, slender and good-looking with fine and classic features, high cheekbones and skin the color of coffee heavily dilut-
ed with milk. She spoke quietly and exuded calm assurance.

She thought for some time about the question of her involvements during the apartheid era.

"You have the capacity to store experiences, remove them from your present consciousness," she said finally. "So much one wants to put behind. Some time ago an old friend phoned. 'Do you remember the day we fetched Chief Buthelezi (Zulu leader) from the airport?' 'No,' I told her, I didn't remember. 'We were students then,' my friend said, 'campaigning for free universities instead of bush colleges for coloreds.'"

Two white men in dark suits came through a door opposite the one off the hall. Engel got up to talk with them by her desk. They spoke mostly in Afrikaans. Just before they left, they talked together briefly in English. About a name on a gravestone. Engel returned, still holding a couple of clippings that had figured in the conversation. A school friend had sent an obituary of her father—"a good comrade who committed suicide last year. The struggle was his life. It sustained him and when it was over, he had nothing. No job, no interest."

The conclusion to the story was that the schoolmate, in sorting her father's possessions, came upon an early photo of Nelson Mandela, standing in front of a street stall. Now the woman hoped to exchange the old photo for a headstone for her father's grave. The president's office had agreed and apparently also would contribute an inscription.

Engel was born in 1950 in the Western Cape magisterial district of Good Wood. Very soon afterward, the area was proclaimed white and residents removed. Her family resettled in Landsdowne, a Cape Town township, and that is where she attended school.

"Our principal at primary was involved in the Non-European Unity Movement (a colored, anti-apartheid organization)," she said. "I knew there was something very strange connected with this because adults in our community were scared of the teachers, knowing they were politically active."

Engel said her first consciousness of apartheid came in those early years when she watched marchers from the black township of Guguletu. "That march by the Cape Town community was in support of those who died in the Sharpeville massacre of 1960. I remember we were sent home early from school and told to stay indoors." But Engel joined the crowds on the street, got caught up in the excitement.

"That was my first realization that something was terribly wrong." She said that until then she had been unaware of differences in skin color: "In South Africa's compartmentalization of people, as a colored, we lived separately from the black and white communities."

From that day on she paid attention to race.

"I witnessed the interaction of people," she recalled. "Saw police stopping buses and raiding people on them for passes. I couldn't understand what a pass was. I watched people fleeing, trying to get away from the police. I saw an African woman with a baby tied to her back, thrown into the back of a police van. The baby's plastic bottle was flung to the ground. That bottle lying in the gutter was a disturbing sight, one that I never forgot."

"We then had school in churches and I went from primary to Livingston High School. Basically, what I learned there was respect for human dignity and a creed that was essentially the program of the Unity movement."

When a teacher at the school was arrested and sent to Robben Island, students rebelled. "We stayed out of school two days to protest," she said. "It was my first experience of a boycott."

Meanwhile, Engel had moved from her family's home at Landsdowne to her grandparents' home in Claremont which was closer to her school. At Livingston, the colored high school, children of professionals or those whose parents were involved with the Unity Movement were invited to join political discussion groups. Engel was not among them.

"I was never certain if this was for security reasons or a class thing," she said. "I had a clear working class background. My father was a laborer. There was no politics in our house. However, two of my uncles who were teachers had been arrested. Though they were not politically active, they owned a printing machine and did printing for the movement."

"I could never understand the secretiveness. Though I knew politics was risky, it wasn't until the early 1970s that I first saw police beating schoolchildren. I wanted to become politically involved, but I didn't know anything then about the ANC."

Two men in work clothes and another in a suit appeared at the hallway entry. They carried a new door to replace the existing one and talked with Engel about this. When they began installing the door, we moved to chairs in the corner of a large adjoining room.

What had been her plan after finishing high school?

"I was going to become a teacher," she said, "The question was, would I go to Teachers Training College or the University of the Western Cape? Since graduates of my high school boycotted UWC because of its designation as a colored university, I ended at the teacher's college."

Her cell phone rang. She listened and responded calmly, quietly and decisively: Yes. She would call the minister and explain the problem to him. "I will take care of that for you," she said.

Engel said she knew only Unity Movement politics until college. There she was introduced to NUSAS (National Union of South African Students), an anti-apartheid, politically active organization in white colleges. One of the speakers at a NUSAS conference had been Steve Biko. Listening to him, she knew she had found an anti-apartheid philosophy that she could support wholeheartedly. Biko told the audience there was no place in NUSAS for black students.

Engel continued, "I saw myself very much as part of the black community. I trace this back to traveling with white students on the train back to college. I never felt free with them somehow. I met good people in NUSAS, but only token blacks and I just didn't feel at home."

"I realized there'd been a breakaway of black students from NUSAS, but I had very little understanding of why. I began to ask questions. This was in the early days of SASO, Steve Biko's South African Students Organization, and it appeared to be an alternative anti-apartheid movement to NUSAS. I chose SASO."

Engel studied two years at Teachers Training College then went on to the University of the Western Cape to earn her teaching diploma.

By then she had become deeply involved with Black Consciousness politics through SASO. After returning from a 1973 SASO meeting in King Williamstown, her father met her at the door of their house. The security police had been there. She must report to their headquarters.

"We had brought back with us in a bakkie (pick-up truck) the first SASO booklets printed," Engel recalled. "The back end was full of these books and we sat on canvasses to hide them. I remember we had to hang on to the pipes overhead to keep from sliding around. The man with me, the man I later married, had the skin rubbed off all his knuckles from the canvas covering, but we brought them safely to Cape Town."

She had been living at home while at UWC and had hidden the pamphlets in her father's garage. "He was furious when he found them, I believe he was scared for me, and he burned them all. I went to Caledon Square Police Station. When I was taken into this big room, I saw others from UWC who had been pulled in. The Security Police said they knew I was treasurer of SASO."

" 'Why,' they asked, 'are you associating with these kaffirs (niggers)? You come from a decent family.' They didn't treat me roughly. They really smacked some of the others, but handled me differently. I think it was just a warning. I think because I was a woman and colored rather than black. This did not deter me. Definitely not."

"At the end of 1973, I was required to teach in a township school in a colored area. I went to Hanover Park Secondary School, but was kicked out after a term because I was a political activist. I know I had an influence on some of my students because I heard from them later. Some landed in the MK. One I adopted as my own child."

Engel sighed. Her voice dropped a tone. "So much happened."

"At the end of 1974, I was told I could not teach nor could I enter any school property. The principal had been informing on the teachers at that school. Ten of us lost our posts because of that informer. I was devastated. My parents were so proud that I'd become a qualified teacher and teaching was the only thing I could do, the only thing I knew. I then wasn't earning money. I did keep up my contacts. But I was not productive. A big chunk of my life had been taken away."

"What sustained me was my strong belief in Christianity. I believed I had moral justification for political involvement. To be a true Christian, I had to be politically involved."

Barred from teaching anywhere in the country, Engel applied for other kinds of jobs, accepting temporary posts to earn enough money to live. One post she tried for was as youth organizer for the Institute of Race Relations. While she did not get it, it led to another. Soon after, the person at Race Relations who interviewed her moved to the Food and Canning Workers Union and hired Engel.

"My motive was to have a job that would make a difference," she said, "and this seemed to be a meaningful job since the object was to improve wages. My father was a laborer and I knew workers couldn't live on working men's wages. I knew nothing about trade unions, but gradually I learned and through that work, I moved to a different level of political consciousness."

To understand more about trade unions, Engel began by reading: newsletters of other unions, other documents, anything she could find that was at all relevant to the workers' struggle. Among the papers, she discovered a letter written by Nelson Mandela to the queen of England. He had requested her intervention in South Africa in behalf of human rights.

Engel also continued her involvement with Steve Biko's Black Consciousness movement which by then had become a political party, the Black Peoples Convention.

"When Steve and Peter (Peter Jones, Biko's second in command) came to Cape Town," she said, "they contacted the three of us, we were all women, who had been selected to attend a BPC meeting in King Williamstown. We had planned to fly and had made arrangements to be picked up at the East London airport. Steve and Peter wanted us to travel with them by car to King Williamstown to save money. I remember so well our heated discussion. But I was married then and had a child. I considered it too big a risk: Both men had been banned, were under house arrest and traveling illegally. So we flew up."

One of the speakers at that meeting had been Dr. Mamphela Ramphele, then a BPC activist, now chancellor of the University of Cape Town. At some point during that 1977 meeting in East London, Ramphele announced that Biko and Jones had been arrested by police on the way to King Williamstown from Cape Town. Both men had been detained and the group must carry on in their absence.

Biko never came out of prison. He died there in the days following.

Speaking of Biko reminded Engel of a talk she had had recently with his son. "There was in those days a very strong chauvinist element, not only in SASO but in mainstream black politics. I told Steve's son, 'One thing I am not certain of, is your father's views on women.' We often argued about the position of women in society. I remember arguing about this after one of our meetings. We always had meals with these meetings and we were standing near a table with dishes all over it. Steve had books under his arm. 'Virginia,' he said, 'could you just move these plates and things so there's room to put these down?' I reached for his books and said, 'I'll put these away and help you pick up the plates.' He laughed. 'You Cape Town women are all alike,' he said, but he put the books on the chair and we cleared the table together."

In the months following Biko's death and the banning of the BPC, Engel became active in the multi-racial United Women's Organization. "We formed it," she said. "The women's organization was critical. It was conceived by the ANC as an extension of the Federation of African Women and became a community-based organization. I organized the Cape Town and Western Cape branches and workers at the same time."

"I became involved in a cell, basically a small group of people who helped me understand the struggle further. During the BPC days, some members were anti-white. In the women's group we had every hue. That shocked me. Then I met Beyers Naude (an Afrikaner minister, founder of the anti-apartheid Christian Institute). I have great admiration for him. This made me realize all white people are not bad. I saw good and bad ones, irrespective of color. This was, for me, a shift from BPC politics to the ANC which was non-racial."

"Trevor Manuel, now Minister of Trade, Industry and Tourism, was key. You had to be invited to join the ANC. He invited me."

"I was with the women's group and the unions then. My public work was with the unions. Secretly I became the link between the ANC and the unions. But my union work had to be completely separate from my political activities. Since the union could not afford to be banned, I only associated with those in my cell."

In 1983, Engel left the Food and Canning Workers Union to organize the Textile and Clothing Workers Union. Unions were then in the Federation of South African Trade Unions which was the forerunner of COSATU (Congress of South African Trade Unions). She worked as a union organizer until 1986.

"By then, harassment was taking a toll of me," Engel said. "My husband is a priest in the Moravian Church (a Protestant religious sect, founded in Saxony in 1722 by emigrants from Moravia) and in 1986 he was posted to a remote spot, to Wupperthal. I then had to decide whether I would leave (political and union work) and become a family person."

"It was a difficult time. Many had already been detained. We knew in '86 they would come down heavily on us. And I was detained. At the time, one large firm whose employees I worked with, was in the middle of wage negotiations. This was a multi-national company and because a strike was threatened, the firm's executives intervened in my behalf: Police should release me. I was not that dangerous."

"I was only three days in detention, but after that I decided I would leave and go with my husband to Wupperthal. A decisive factor was the tension between those who were ANC people and those who weren't. It could have meant long detention if it was known I was giving the ANC union information."

"I remained in Wupperthal for seven years. It took me a long time to get used to not being active in politics. But I did a lot of women's work, organized a creche and a program for the aged. People on the run also stayed with us. I'd applied to go back to teaching and received permission to return in a temporary capacity. A year and a half prior to the election I got involved again, started organizing for the ANC and began teaching at Mitchell's Plain."

The interview ended when Engel answered her cell phone. The President needed her.

In the seventies the major black voice had been Steve Biko's. He lived nearby in King Williamstown. Fraser and I talked with him there just weeks before his death. Though he and his Black Consciousness movement were banned, this had been the only revolutionary activity I knew much about. Nelson Mandela had been in prison for many years and members of the ANC operated underground and out of the country.

One of the Elderhostel lectures had been on Mandela. He was born in 1918 into a royal Xhosa family who lived in a small village in the Transkei region of the Eastern Cape. Only a few black children from rural areas had access to mission schools. Mandela was lucky enough to be among them. In 1937 he entered Fort Hare, some eighty miles from East London. It was South Africa's sole college for blacks and run by Scottish missionaries. After a year and a half he left to take a job as a watchman in a mine near Johannesburg and later as a clerk in the city. There he acquired a reputation as an excellent amateur boxer, a good dancer and a snappy dresser who enjoyed the city's "high life." During this time, he took correspondence courses through the University of South Africa and earned a bachelor's degree.

In 1944, after a stint as an articled clerk with a liberal Jewish law firm, he entered Witwatersand, becoming the university's only black law student. While there, he helped organize the African National Congress Youth League. Mandela emerged as a national presence during a 1952 defiance campaign which stepped up the anti-apartheid action. He was among 150 charged with conspiracy to overthrow the state. Trials lasted from 1956 until 1961. During that time he divorced his first wife, Evelyn, and married Winnie.

The case was dismissed in 1961, a year after the banning of the ANC which had been founded in 1912. The banning did not deter Mandela. He worked underground, mainly organizing guerilla fighters, until 1964 when he was again arrested. He was tried for sabotage and convicted. From then until his release in 1990, he remained on Robben Island, a mound in the Atlantic, visible from Cape Town, and a prison since the 1500s.

XIV
❧ *Elsa Joubert*
Everyone said, 'you've torn the veils from our eyes'

Before I met the Afrikan's author, Elsa Joubert, I read her most notable book. What follows is the synopsis of *The Long Journey of Poppie Nongena:*

Poppie is a Xhosa woman who tells Elsa Joubert the story of her immediate and extended family and her own life in South Africa over forty years.

Poppie hears of the Boer War from her mother who in turn was told of this and other events of the early twentieth century from her mother.

Poppie's contented childhood in the Cape province ends when she marries a migrant worker and moves with him and their young children to a crowded township outside of Cape Town. No sooner has Poppie settled there than the authorities pressure her to move to the Ciskei, her husband's homeland. But he, as a migrant worker, may stay in the Cape.

On a brief honeymoon visit to his people, Poppie sees enough of the very different tribal way of life of the Xhosas to know her own forebears left this way of life behind them three generations earlier. To them, and to her, the Ciskei is the past—urban blacks dismiss it as 'Kaffirland.'

For ten years, Poppie fights the pass laws, winning limited extensions to the permit which allows her to stay and work in Cape Town in a struggle to hold her family together and educate her children, even if this means 'sleeping in' jobs and seeing her family fleetingly. Just the process of getting to the authorities—the time, distance, and expense involved—was monumental. When the extensions stop, Poppie and her children are 'resettled' in Mdantsane, a raw, new township outside of East London.

Set against this continuing struggle with white bureaucracy are the equally inescapable demands of the tribal way of life. Poppie must come to terms with these as well. She experiences the unrest that began at Sharpeville and comes to Soweto in the early sixties. In Cape Town once more, its aftermath envelops Poppie and her children.

The interview with Virginia Engel had continued until well after 3, which was the time of my appointment with Elsa Joubert. Being late disturbs me beyond all reason. Walking out through the corridor in the presidential office building I had panicked. Sometimes Aldino wasn't there and I had to wait. What if? I stopped on the porch to look around and felt great relief to see his blue sedan near the gate.

His daughter sat beside him. Sheena was a shy, pretty child, in her first year of primary school. After delivering me, he would pick up JC and CJ, his three-year-old twin sons, from day care and take all of the children home. He passed the tape recorder back over the seat: "It works fine now," he said.

Getting lost on the way to meet Joubert made us still later. Oranjezicht, where she lived, was an Afrikans neighborhood in the hills above Cape Town. She later told me she had lived on this street, Belvedere, for thirty-five years. Not too long before, she and her husband had moved from a larger home a few doors up to a smaller, single-level house. I pushed the button on an intercom next to the heavy, locked gate and, after a few miscues got buzzed in.

A path bordered by gardens led to steep steps and a broad verandah. Joubert, preceded by a chubby yellow lab, stood in the doorway. The home was traditional Cape Dutch, both outside and in, with curved gables and white plastered exterior walls. As I followed Joubert into the house, I caught a glimpse of heavy European furniture on quarry tile floors in rooms either side of the entrance hall.

We sat down at a large table in the dining room. I apologized for being late. After Joubert banished the friendly lab, she grilled me and ended with who else was being interviewed. Her voice was forceful, unhesitating and slightly raspy. Joubert had hennaed hair, gray eyes and a bit of a chip on her shoulder which eventually I either got used to or she got over. She wore a silky blouse of many colors in a flashy pattern above a quieter red skirt. She spoke as if she had been interviewed countless times and it was a great relief to have the recorder back. I could concentrate on her and the direction of the conversation while I made notes to myself rather than feverishly working to get her words down.

Elsa Joubert was born in 1922 in the Western Cape town of Paarl. She said that her father, the head of Teachers Training College for primary teachers, was very well-known in the field of education. Her mother was a De Villiers, a family of professionals, ministers and missionaries. The family was Afrikaans-speaking and of French Huguenot descent. Joubert's French Huguenot forebears came to South Africa in 1688. After twelve generations in the country, her family did not consider itself colonists: "We are not here on a temporary basis," Joubert said firmly. Her point was that her heritage differed significantly from English-speakers descended from the English immigrants, most of whom dated their residency in the country from the early 19th century. This sort of comment combined with her rather haughty manner came through to me as self-righteous superiority.

"All of my people were in service to the community and good role models," she continued. "That taught me that the importance of life is what you give to people, not what life gives to you. My husband came from the (Orange) Free State and a family with both sides in education or ministry, same as mine. We learned later that our fathers had been contemporaries at Stellenbosch University (an Afrikans institution).

After schools in Paarl, I also went to Stellenbosch. It is traditional. In 1910, my mother became one of the first women to study there. My daughters and son went to Stellenbosch, also my grandson."

After earning a BA as well as a teaching degree, for a year Joubert taught Afrikaans, Dutch and history in the small, Eastern Cape town of Cradock. Upon deciding she "wanted to be closer to the written word," she returned to the University of Cape Town for a master's degree. That was where she met her future husband, Klaas Steytler. Both went on to work as journalists, he in Johannesburg, she in Cape Town.

In 1948 she took off to see the world. Following her interest in the continent of Africa, she traveled to Kenya and Uganda first and later followed the Nile to Cairo. Sending articles back home about her adventures helped to cover her expenses. Joubert recalled speculating that with so much political turmoil in South Africa, there would be little interest in what she wrote from outside the country. But someone recognized book material. This trip turned into her first book, completed and published eight years later. Then, as now, she wrote under her maiden name. A succession of travel books followed, both before and after her marriage to Steytler in 1950.

The couple made their home in Cape Town where she raised their three children, freelanced, took off to travel and wrote about her experiences. One book, about journeying by bus and train through Madagascar, she called an inner journey as well: "when I had to come to grips with absolute primitive company and came to new insights about the question of who is your neighbor."

She explained that in this way: "There was a pregnant woman sitting next to me on the bus, naked with this big tummy. I felt her baby kicking me and, for a moment, I thought I was pregnant with my child. I knew that kick so well. Suddenly I felt, this was also a baby. A baby like my baby. And this is my sister with her baby. I felt a unity with life, with mankind, with everything that lives. I couldn't have felt it if I hadn't gone through that—the utter fear, the utter distaste, that utter alienation at the beginning of the trip. I couldn't bear to go crouch in the veld with the other women to relieve myself. It was to me hard. I didn't even want to eat anymore because if I didn't eat, I would not need to relieve myself. I couldn't face the squalor and all that. This experience really put everything on a different level."

Many years after its publication in 1964, a travel book about Mozambique brought an unexpected bonus. "The other day," Joubert said, "the office of President Mandela rang and said, 'Mr. Mandela wants you and your husband to dinner.' We didn't know what on earth. Probably a lot of journalists. Or maybe writers. But no, we were the only guests." It turned out that President Mandela had read her Mozambique book during his imprisonment on Robben Island. "Not only had he read it," she said, "he quoted scenes I had forgotten. He said it had been a great influence. The first time a white South African had envisaged black Africans having lives. He spoke more about that book than *Poppie*, though he'd liked *Poppie* very much."

The history of *Poppie*, her most famous book, had begun with her research for a book on South Africa. Surprisingly, she had written only about other regions of the Southern Hemisphere. But in the mid-'70s, her publisher told her the time was right for a book about her own country. She began her research: visiting the homelands, Transkei, Venda, Ciskei, the black townships, schools, courts, black churches and homes—"every place I could go for a book on know-your-own-country. So few people knew. Then a very fortuitous thing happened. Poppie came to me. I met her on my front stoop, the day after Christmas '76. We were about to leave on holiday. I opened the front door and she said, 'I must talk to you. I must talk to somebody.' I said, 'Come in,' and I left all my packing. Two days before my eldest daughter had got married. My son had an elbow op (operation). We were really busy, but I put everything aside. I said, 'Come. I'll make a pot of tea then you can tell me.'"

"I think she was just sent to me. Actually, Poppie had worked for me for awhile. She was Xhosa and we always spoke Afrikaans. I'd noticed then, when she spoke about her aunts, she would say, 'Auntie Lena,' or 'Auntie Hannie,' or 'Auntie Nelly' which are all Afrikans names, so I said, 'Where does this come from?' And then I got into her story. She grew up in Upington, an Afrikans community, actually what they call a mixed community, colored, white and non-white. She started telling me about the Christmas uprisings of '76 where those they call the city-borners, Africans living in the city for one or more generations, clashed violently with what they called the people from the land—homelands—the hostel dwellers. She'd had to flee with their children. In the bush the whole night. And then to me. I comforted her and said, 'We must talk some more. After the holiday.' She was also going to her people for a few weeks holiday. I said, 'When you come back, we must make a plan.' I talked to my family about this and they all supported me and I started having sessions with her, taking her back to her childhood, to her early youth."

As the book jacket said, and as it was to me when I read it, Poppie's story as Joubert wrote it was touchingly personal as well as universal to black families in South Africa.

"You know how it is with somebody: they give you a lot of facts, just at random," *Poppie's* author continued. "But you've got to make a story. You've got to dramatize it, blow life on these facts. I think it was meant to be. Dear God prepared me and sent her to me. If she'd gone to the woman next door, that woman would have been able to do nothing. Not being a writer, she wouldn't even have thought of writing down a story. The woman on the other side was English-speaking who would have had no idea. I'd been preparing for this travel book and I knew every situation she'd describe. When she told me about initiation rites in the homelands, I'd been there. If she told me about eviction, I'd been there. If she told me about the courts, I'd been. I'd been in the schools, to the funerals. The penny dropped into every slot."

"I worked very hard. And I checked every statement she gave me. If she told me they were moved from one neighborhood to another in Lambert's Bay, forced to move, I didn't take her word, I went to the library and got the municipal report of that year from Lambert's Bay and checked if it was like that."

"After the book appeared, not any fact was ever questioned, not one single fact. If I'd slipped up on one fact, my credibility would have been gone. In my travel books, I'd also been very meticulous. I had that reputation and they believed what I wrote and that's what caused the big furor about *Poppie*. I almost could not explain. The response was just overwhelming. Every day I'd get more letters in the post. Every day I had phone calls. Everyone said, 'You've torn the veils from our eyes.' I remember one man, one morning very early, I was still lying in bed. I don't know where he got my phone number. He called from the heart of the Free State, it's supposed to be a very conservative part. He said he'd read the book all through the night. The next morning he'd had to bring his children to school in the town. And he passed the township he passed every day. Always he regarded it as a squalid collection of huts, covered by smoke and debris. 'I drove past that morning,' he said, 'and thought there are Poppies and their husbands and their children living in there—with stories and relationships like I have myself.' He was in tears on the phone. And a professor from Pretoria called me. He said he went out to the street the next morning after finishing the book and it was as if the population of the country had doubled."

After I had read the book and noted the 1978 publication date I had been amazed that, in a time of increased censoring of anyone and anything remotely critical to government, *Poppie* had escaped.

"They couldn't ban the book, because everybody knew it was the truth," Joubert explained. "People then suddenly realized their own housekeeper had to have a pass. Another reason they couldn't ban it was I was in their establishment. There would have been an uproar if they had. I won't say esteemed, but I was a member of...." Joubert often paused, as she did then, searching, and nearly always successfully, for an English word. "I was not an outsider, a liberal immigrant coming to criticize them. That would have riled me, too. These outside people coming in to tell us, with half knowledge. But this was one of their own people and my parents and my husband's parents had good professional standing. My father was called the father of primary education in South Africa. I'm not saying this to boast, just to try and explain this. I'd been born and bred in the inner circle of the people of the Afrikans' world. They could not *not* accept it. They accepted it."

"There was a journalist here the other day and she also couldn't understand why it wasn't banned. I told her the following. Perhaps it would interest you. I said to her, for the first time a huge literary prize was going to be awarded. In those days, 10,000 rands ($1,111 US) was a lot of money. Nothing today, but in those days a lot. There were five contestants and *Poppie* was one. And we all went flying up to Johannesburg for a formal do at the house of a millionaire where the winner would be announced. Now you won't believe this, but while I was packing, the phone rang. Who was on the phone? Mrs. Elize Botha, wife of PW (Prime Minister Botha 1978-1983, State President 1983-1989). She said, 'Elsa, I'm holding thumbs for you, that you'll get the prize.' We'd been contemporaries at Stellenbosch. We knew each by sight and to say hello, but no more than that and she said, 'I'm holding thumbs for you.'" Joubert's tone of voice and face mirrored the pleasure and awe that had accompanied that phone call many years earlier.

Poppie, Joubert said, took the country by storm. It went on to become a successful play. Initially it was adapted as a "library play," which is a dramatization of a book by the library system, taken to various towns within a district as a cultural project. Joubert recalled, pride in her voice: "The woman that dramatized it phoned me and said, 'You won't believe it, but farmers are bringing their families and driving night after night to see it again. Driving to the next town.'"

Why did Joubert believe the story had such widespread appeal? She replied without hesitation: "Because people had been feeling unhappy all along about the whole situation. About the passes, about discrepancies. This may sound strange to you but, basically, the Afrikans people are a good, religious people. They just went funnily wrong with this apartheid scheme. They're not cruel people, not the evil people you see every night on TV, like the policemen testifying at the Truth and Reconciliation Committee (*sic*). I think that's terrible the way that's going on. In every society you will find a few brutes. Basically, Afrikaners are kind to their people. But the publicity is always given to the one farmer who isn't. They felt the need of that book. They wanted to be told the truth."

I said I had thought it possible the National Party government might modify its apartheid policies as a result of her book. "People ask me about that," Joubert said. "We had a very good friend. He was a doctor, a colored. He was cruelly murdered by gangsters. It was a homosexual murder and it really shook us up. Two youngsters, a few years in prison. They're out now, but Richard is gone forever. And it wasn't over the homosexual, it was just..." She shrugged, "I don't know what happened. In any case, he always said to me, 'Elsa, a writer can change the climate in which change can take place. But the writer cannot change laws.' That is my answer."

Joubert's principal complaint about the new majority government in South Africa was its consitutional sanctioning of eleven official languages: nine tribal languages plus English and Afrikaans. She believed that by doing that, the ANC broke its promise to Afrikaners to preserve their language. From now on, she said, English and tribal languages would be promoted, though she does not see how schools possibly can accommodate African children whose parents demand they learn in their home language.

Afrikaans, "the language of South Africa," she is certain is doomed to die. Joubert was bitter about this and visibly angered.

"People think very simplistically about South African politics," she continued, "but it wasn't so simple. '85, '86, when those terrible states of emergency were proclaimed, et cetera, one must always see in the perspective of what was happening in the world. The Cubans were on the border in Angola. Our sons were being sent to fight them. The Russian danger was an actual fact. Young people don't know today, but the Cold War was a fact. We lived our whole married life under the cloud of the Cold War and the atom bomb. The Chinese were in Tanzania; the Russians were financing rebels in the Congo. When PW (Botha) said, 'We've got a total onslaught,' it wasn't just rhetoric. You Americans know the fear of the Russians. And here we were—the Cubans just here, at our borders. When could they, with one slash, tear asunder everything of apartheid? The moment the Russians collapsed and the wall collapsed, the Russian threat collapsed. That minute, apartheid could and did come apart. People forget that it was an actual thing, this threat. And all these terrorists, now we call them freedom fighters, were all being supplied with weapons from Russia. Really sophisticated weapons we were up against."

"The perception persists here that America got us into the Angolan War. That story must still be told. Americans wanted to stop the Cubans in Africa and the South Africans were almost at the point of entering Luanda (Angola) when the Americans just withdrew, just left them in the lurch. They'd pushed us. Held the carrot in front of us. Cajoled us to come further up—up—up into Angola. When they got us to the point they wanted us, and we'd defeated the Cubans, the Americans just withdrew, said Africa is not their business any longer. Now honestly, there the Americans have a lot to account for. The Angolan War is one of the reasons it took so long for apartheid to go under."

I felt abysmally ignorant of America's past role in southern Africa, our vested interest in any of this. But it was also impossible to believe that America was responsible for apartheid which the Afrikaner had constructed beginning in 1947.

"I'm putting it very simplistically," Joubert said, "but it isn't simple. If the Russian threat had continued, this Cold War continued, Russia would have kept sending Cubans and soldiers and more soldiers to South Africa. It would have been a naked war. We don't know if America would have had the guts to come and keep this war from us. We don't think so, because of the betrayal in Angola. The Russian collapse was propitious."

Joubert smiled suddenly, relaxed in her chair from straight back and forward posture. "But listen, I'm talking as a complete amateur. I'm not a politician, I'm a writer. But that was the way people felt."

She said young South Africans in Parliament today had a picture of past absolute oppression and cruelty but lacked the background to put that history into perspective. For instance, in the late 1940s, she and her future husband had been the first Afrikaans journalists into Berlin after all supply routes to the city had been cut. They flew in on a South African Air Force plane taking coal to the beleaguered citizens. There they saw the face of Communism. "These youngsters today, they just condemn. They haven't got the big picture. If there hadn't been all these threats from outside, the government would have dealt with the apartheid system. There were all these outside demands. It could not focus on its internal system."

Joubert told of a recent visitor. In *Poppie* she had written about a boy who fled after shooting and injuring a police officer. Sometime later, his parents got a cable: He had left the country. "And he now came to visit me, a big strong man. He had had a whale of a time in Russia. He'd spent all these years there. He speaks Russian and he had a very good singing voice and ended up touring around Russia. When everybody could come back here, he came back. And he was now very, very, distressed. He had nothing to do: He wasn't a hero anymore, wasn't being lionized by the Russians. He had to find a job and the ANC couldn't give them all jobs. He was very disillusioned."

The ANC provided a good prompt. Had she been surprised when Nelson Mandela's release was announced? "No," she replied. "We were wonderfully happy. We'd been expecting it. Even from PW's (Botha) time there was always speculation: 'When is Mandela coming out?' 'PW is having talks with Mandela again.' " Changes had been coming gradually, she added, beginning in the middle eighties.

"The state of the country today? I don't want to talk about politics. I think Mandela led us up the garden path regarding our language. Afrikaans is my language. I was born and bred in it. It's my being. I cannot exist without it. After everything had been granted, the ANC supposedly felt they needed a way to denigrate Afrikaans. But Mandela had publicly said no language would lose its status. So in what way did he denigrate Afrikaans? He uplifted nine African languages so that, with English and Afrikaans, we have eleven official languages. Nobody on earth can speak eleven languages. So, in effect, English is going to be the official language. Afrikaans, previously one of two official languages, has been equalized with the nine African languages that have been lifted up. Do you see what I mean?"

Did she mean there would not be schools teaching in Afrikaans?

"Of course there will be," she said impatiently. "But the constitution says every child has the right to education in his own language or the language of his choice. Now there is a predominantly Afrikaans' school in a predominately Afrikans neighborhood. Ten black children come—and it's not the point these black children are coming, but these black children can't speak Afrikaans so they demand to be taught in either Xhosa—or in English or Zulu or whatever. Can you see the point? But what's even worse, (Sibusiso) Bengu (ANC minister of education) has said every student has the right to a tertiary education, so any student can go to Stellenbosch, our Afrikans university, and demand to be taught in his own language or in English. In this, the Princeton or Harvard of South Africa."

"Tuesday," Joubert continued, "I'm flying to Bloemfontein to do the opening address for the new semester at the traditionally Afrikaans university there. And they warned me, fifty percent of the students already are black, or from Lesotho, Sotho-speaking, and the stress is on multi-cultural education. I must remember that in my speech. They say every lecture has to be duplicated in Afrikaans and English because every student has the right to be taught in the language he has a mastery of. Can you see in what a subtle way Afrikaans is being swept aside? That's my greatest grievance."

"My youngest daughter, she's head of the department of rare books at an Afrikans university in Johannesburg. Wits (Witswatersrand University) was predominantly English of course, so the Rand Afrikans University was established about 1960 for Afrikans students on the Rand. Even that university is already 50 percent English. That's the truth, and that never gets written about."

"My children went to Jan van Riebeeck School. Today you see, very happily, very easily, no strain whatsoever, black, white and colored students in school uniforms, chatting away. There's no problem because they are mostly Afrikaans-speaking black and colored children. No problem as long as English-speaking black and colored go to English schools because there are plenty. As far as regards their own university, I suppose you've read that the University of the Western Cape is closed down because the students haven't paid their fees."

"We want the black and the white and the colored peoples to have every opportunity, but we are not happy with the situation with Afrikaans. You can go into every smart shop, every doctor's office. They will say good morning in fluent Afrikaans. The point is, most people speak Afrikaans."

On the way back to Newland, Aldino toured through the old District Six area. It lay in the shadow of Table Mountain, rolling upwards and taking with it fine views of the sea, the harbor and the city. Even in full light, it was a strange, ghostly place, barren and empty and criss-crossed by deserted streets with weeds pushing up through cracks in the pavement.

Aldino slowed down and pointed to one of the weedy lots: "We lived right here. Our house was on this corner." Still inching along, he turned right. "People used to walk up and down here. Houses here," he pointed side to side, "there, others. Caledon was a main road through District Six."

The area had been cleared of its residents after the Nationalist government declared it a white area in 1966. No houses had been built since. Cecily had told me the razing of District Six had been so controversial that no self-respecting Cape Townian would dream of building a house there. The only buildings added had been a technical college and large fire station.

Weeds and blowing dirt had replaced what old photos recorded as packed-in shanties, shops and colorful small houses, traffic-choked narrow streets, and crowded sidewalks.

"There's the old Methodist Church," Aldino said, pointing to a brick structure. "A mosque and Anglican church also survived relocation." They sat apart, isolated from one another and from their exiled congregations. I asked if he thought the district would be rebuilt now the apartheid government was gone? He shrugged. "No matter what happens, we can never revive District Six."

We moved on to an obviously lived-in area. Walmer Estate, Aldino said. It bordered District Six. Coloreds with more money bought houses there. In recent years, the area had become Muslim-dominated. He turned onto Coronation Street where, he said, Indian traders lived. He then climbed the hill to the topmost street, Premier Road, across the side of Table Mountain. Portuguese and Jews lived there alongside coloreds. Stolid, plaster-walled, middle-class houses that looked as if they had been built in the 1920's and 1930's lined the street. The view of the harbor and sea and city were priceless. Business people mostly, Aldino said. Tour over, he wove through streets without markings or reference buildings and then onto the highway.

"At one time," he said, "all streets led to District Six."

Back home that night, Cecily and I drank wine on the deck and talked about what we had done since breakfast, like a comfortably married couple after a day of work. When it was my turn, I told her about the President's secretary and Elsa Joubert. I said that Joubert worried that Afrikaans would fade away.

Cecily sounded annoyed: "Oh, that language thing. They forced Afrikaans on us. Now they have to fight for it and they don't like it."

Regarding Joubert's description of herself and the Afrikaner as native South Africans, "She would consider me and everybody else who speaks English as a colonial," Cecily said, still steamed. "My family has been here for just about as many generations as hers. In our family we chose to speak English. My father's language rather than my mother's."

XV
🌿 *Janice Honeyman*
Theater so often reflects what's going on in the society

Hiddigh, original site of the University of Cape Town and now its drama and arts campus, was tucked into a tree-shaded section of the downtown area with Table Mountain as a backdrop. Cecily dropped me at a corner and I walked past a mix of old and undistinguished buildings separated by parking lots, walkways and patches of lawn.

I had come to talk with Janice Honeyman. She was among the founders of the second multi-racial theater in the country and currently director of the Johannesburg Civic Theatre. She was in town to direct UCT drama students in a production of *Othello*. I found her on the top floor of the Little Theatre, a gym-like space with open rafters and echoing voices of rehearsing actors. Gabriel came to the door, introduced himself as Honeyman's assistant and took me to a chair on the near wall. Ten or fifteen students sprawled on chairs opposite. They looked like students anywhere in their tie-died shirts, pony tails, floppy sandals, no shoes and scruffy beards. One had on a "Ban Animal Tests" shirt.

In the center of the big room two actors, holding scripts, stood on a school desk with a wood top. After dialogue between them, they peered toward a distant horizon, hands shielding their eyes. A third character approached and called "News, lads. The wars are done."

Honeyman, in slacks and an oversized sweater, stood just beyond where the actors worked. She was tall with wavy, shoulder-length blonde hair. Her features were classic with movie-star good looks.

She was animated and usually on the move, radiating energy and enthusiasm, both physically and vocally.

Honeyman stopped the scene and engaged the three actors in a discussion of the preceding events, the personalities of their characters and the existing weather. The actors ran through it again and after a couple of stops and restarts, went from the beginning straight through until Honeyman declared, "Fantastic."

"Good, guys," she said. "It's beginning to take shape. Now, once again." Behind me, three students came in struggling with a tub filled with props and hauled it across the back of the room to the opposite wall. In the middle of the room, Gabriel took over as director.

Honeyman and I picked up sandwiches at a cafe across the street. On the walk back to the campus she said she was second-generation South African of Scottish and English ancestry, born in Cape Town in 1949.

We found a shady place with some grass and sat there to eat our lunches. She told me she got into theater quite by chance. Her long-held dream of becoming a veterinarian had vanished when she failed to qualify in math and science at the University of Cape Town. By luck, she ended up in an English literature course. Characters she met in books so interested her, she said, that she pursued them further in the university's drama classes.

"I was quite a shy person and used to disappear into my own world," Honeyman said. "For me, every situation in life seemed difficult. But this particular drama teacher, in some way, enabled us to lose our inhibitions. This was a new thing, a release, a self expression that I found great."

After university and two and a half years into a professional acting career, in 1971, she broke a leg ice skating. With time left in her contract with PACT (Performing Arts Council of the Transvaal), "Manny, who was then head of PACT, said 'You're not going to just sit around,' so I started directing." She had some experience in that area. At UCT she had staged three children's plays that she had written.

"Two years later," Honeyman continued, "we all broke away

from PACT because it wasn't multi-racial. Black people were not allowed to act on stage and the staff had separate amenities, all the rest of it." She said most everyone in the arts was against the country's apartheid policies.

"There were a few in PACT who were separatists and we had enormous fights. I remember one argument in the director's office very clearly. Some actors in our company had objected to black stage staff showering in the showers they used as well. And that event, in fact, was the one that turned me. I thought, 'I don't want to be here anymore. I don't want to be with people who think like this.'"

"So just after the director, Manny, broke away, I thought, 'Well, I'm going too.'"

"There was also a director who had come to PACT and done one or two productions for them. A lot of us had become fascinated by his directing methods and his ways of thinking. So when he and the former head started this group called The Company, some of us left PACT to go with them. The Company was a band of eight or ten actors who lived off their box office receipts: no salaries, tiny rooms to live in, an excess of hard work."

"Shortly after that," Honeyman continued, "The old Indian fruit market in Johannesburg, which had been closed for years, became available. Everybody in the community put in tenders for what they would like to do with it. Barney and Manny, the breakaway directors with The Company, put in a tender, saying they would like to turn it into a theater. And they won."

"We had to paint it ourselves, turn it into a theater by ourselves. And it was just an incredible experience. Apart from the Space which was in Cape Town, that was, I think, the first completely multi-racial theater. And the Space was an ideal for all of us, what we wanted to be as well. The Market is just huge, much bigger than the Space, with one, two, three theaters in it."

"We negotiated a good deal with the council. They didn't make us pay rent. The initial remodeling was done with the help of the council, but after that with private money. A huge amount of fund raising was done and it kept going by box office and private money."

"Kinds of plays? All sorts. It started with *The Assassination and Persecution of John Paul Marais*... It's a long title with many, many more words, but it's a play about Marais and the Marquis de Sade set in a lunatic asylum, highly alternative theater for South Africa at that time. And we did Chekhov's *Seagull.* Interestingly enough, at that point it was predominantly white theater and predominantly white audiences."

"And then for personal reasons," Honeyman said, "I went off and lived in London, '77 until '79." She straightened her legs, leaned against the trunk of the tree. "I'll never forget the night I came back. The first thing I did, that very night, I went to the Market Theater. Athol Fugard's *Sizwe Banzi Is Dead* was on the main stage and the audience was, I would say, 60 percent black and 40 percent white. It was fantastic."

"That was what the Market absolutely worked for—untiringly— theater for everybody."

"While I was there I directed various Broadway and West End hits, but they were things like *Torch Song Trilogy* which dealt with an alternative kind of morality; plays like *Driving Miss Daisy*, which has black leads and white leads and deals with harmonious living together. These were different to what a lot of the rest of the Market was doing which was protest theater and various black directors had come in."

"So there was protest theater which was absolutely necessary at the time because there was so much to protest about. Yet, for myself, I had the belief that the techniques of theater were still important, the well-made play and all the rest of it. So I tried to find plays that spoke of the political situation without being blatantly political. A fine line. I don't know that this was entirely accepted by the black people, because they needed more of the protest stuff. I think now the 'Driving Miss Daisies' would be more acceptable. But the Market did everything, across the board sort of work."

Honeyman remained at the Market for several years and became resident director.

I asked about the theater season in South Africa. "All year 'round," she replied. "That's the weird thing about South Africa. We don't have a season so we find ourselves with a smaller audience than anyone else, doing more work that anyone else. In the theater I'm running in Johannesburg at the moment, we do between fifty and sixty productions a year in our five venues. Which is a hell of a lot."

"People have talked about maybe we should have seasons: We might get bigger audiences that way. I'm not sure. Theater is such a drug we're addicted to doing that one can't imagine working only for the winter, or only for the summer."

"At the moment, I probably do between three and four plays a year. I used to do more, but the job I'm doing now, Executive Director of the (Johannesburg) Civic Theatre, there's a lot of administration. I'm the artistic director as well so there's a lot of organization of other people."

I asked what the job of the Executive Director involved.

"To get a nice mix of theater, broad-based; and more than anything, audiences. Johannesburg has an ever-dwindling audience," Honeyman said with a sigh. "It's the crime, the situation of Johannesburg with the townships so far away. I'm struggling at the moment with quite a difficult predicament, in that a huge number of white people have emigrated. The people who can afford to leave the country, or even what they call 'semi-grate,' which is moving to Cape Town, are the house-owners, the middle-class, the people who have the money to come to the theater. They were the theater-goers. And they seem to be getting out of Johannesburg as quickly as they can."

"In the meantime, the Civic Theatre, where I'm working now, was closed for five years. Before it closed it was a white palace, opera and ballet and an exclusively white audience, exclusively white performance. One of the things I've had to do in the four years since I've been there—it's only been reopened for five years—is try to turn that upside down and say it is a theater for everybody. That's being accepted more and more, but it's going to take a long time."

"For the place to keep its credibility, one's got to do the stuff black people believe in. It's also turning them into a regular theater-going public and that's not easy. From '76, when I believe their lives were turned so upside down by the unrest and the violence, theater was the last kind of luxury on their list. From 1976 to 1996 is a long time. There's a lot of building to do."

"How? Choosing plays I believe the black people, the middle class, will want to see. We also have a very active education and development department, where we give new young playwrights a chance, where we do readings and tryouts and give community groups the opportunity to work in the theater. I think the real aim of it is to work to the point when you don't need a development department anymore. That's going to take time. It's easy a five year job."

I asked what kind of theater appealed to multi-racial audiencences? "Not the plays one might necessarily expect," Honeyman replied. "I've just done a pantomime at the Civic. There's not a great tradition of pantomime in this country."

"Pantomime is a British tradition that has drawn from the music hall, the ballet, stand-up comics, even from much earlier Italian comedy. They're always based on fairy stories, but they always have topical references and a comment to make on society today. In England they have a beginning and an end and, in the middle, a whole series of individual acts."

"I don't do pantomime like that and I've written seven so I've honed the art. I try to get good comedians in, but then they play roles. I have a story with a beginning, middle and end that gets enacted all the way through. I started with *Snow White and the Seven Dwarfs* and apart from having a few blacks in the cast, and lots of modern music, it was pretty traditional, straight."

"Over the years, I've localized and South Africanized them more and more. Last year we did something called *Robin's Cruise-ou* with a completely multi-racial cast. 'Cruise-ou' is a pun for a sailor and I set it in the Cape and the island was off the coast of Africa. Robin didn't meet Man Friday as a noble savage; he'd been here to a finishing school but decided against this culture and went back to Africa to find his own."

She said reviews were good and audiences racially mixed. The capacity of the theater is a thousand and while it "didn't play to chock-ablock, it played to good houses." The run was six weeks, eight shows a week.

"I'm getting a little bit older now, so it's more difficult energy-wise," Honeyman said, "but I've always had an enormous amount of work energy. I must be honest. I don't enjoy the administrative side of the Civic as much. In fact, this month, after two years of trying, I've finally got an administrative director. Artistic director is far more my line."

I asked how she came to be in Cape Town.

"In a funny way, I shouldn't be," she replied. "We'd hired the Civic out to a dance company that's done a new, vamped up version of *Ipi Tombi*. No, we didn't produce it. As a matter of fact, we definitely didn't produce it. What happened was, with only two weeks notice, they cancelled the booking because they'd got a better one in Australia."

"Then the University of Cape Town offered me this because they thought it would be good for students to work with a professional director. I, of course, am Shakespeare-obsessed, so I said yes immediately."

"But I've patched things a bit. A show is moving into the Civic for ten days and I'm down here, doing this with the students, which I'm loving."

Honeyman had put together a pared-down version of *Othello*, condensing it so that the story comes over clearly, where the main aspects of the characters' personalities are apparent. This would take place in the present with modern day clothing and references that would include contemporary events such as the Gulf War. Rehearsals had begun three days earlier. *Othello* would open three weeks from the coming weekend.

The company of seventeen was composed of first to third year university drama students.

"I auditioned them," she said, "but in a way there are only so many kids and they all need to be used. It's part of their training and part of the exercise of learning stage craft and theater craft."

A recent newspaper report had noted the soaring prices of theater tickets in South Africa. She agreed that was true, but there were ways around it—block bookings, 11 rands ($1.20 US) tickets on Mondays, and senior and student discounts.

"At the moment," she said, "we are only self-supporting in that we set ourselves a goal of about 4 million rands ($444,444 US) income a year. The entire production budget is twice that. The running of the building and the paying back of the renovations and all that subsidy is actually 29 million rands ($3,222,222 US) that comes from the city of Johannesburg."

So she doesn't have to worry about overhead?

Honeyman shook her head vigorously. "We do worry about it, constantly, particularly because it's not secure. It's a subsidy that's at anybody's whim and a non-arts lover could stop it like that. So we do live a bit on tenterhooks."

The Civic does not have the funds for a permanent company. Honeyman wishes that were different.

"It's a pity we can't employ actors full time," she said. "I would love to have a permanent company and I think the people that do deserve money in the arts are the artists. I suppose, in another way, with the number of theaters we have and the number of productions we do, we give more people opportunities to work, just not as consistently."

I asked if any Civic Theatre productions had played overseas.

"The revival of the Zulu *Macbeth* we did played at the Lincoln Center in New York and then at the Globe in London. And I hope we'll do more exporting of stuff as we become more established. Four to five years in the life of theater is very young. Because of that five-year closure of the Civic and because of that complete switch-around, changing the whole dynamic of the theater, we've still got a long way to go."

PACT, she said, works vigorously to attract multi-racial audiences. "But all too late. It would have been great if, when the Market started, all the performing arts councils had switched to that way of thinking instead of arrogantly saying, 'We're doing fine' and 'Art for arts sake.' They're trying to put it right now, but I worry it might be too late."

I asked about professional goals for herself.

"I'd like to just be a director again. My first goals, to become a theater director, I did; to work for the Royal Shakespeare Company, I did. I still want to work for Peter Brook (British-born, internationally renowned director). He did some magnificent work in North Africa, using actors from all over the world, I just think he is a magnificent theater person. He's honest and innovative and his work is inspiring."

How does she interpret the current government's position to the arts?

"I think there are areas of our government in support, but I don't think it is a priority, which is sad for me. They've got to get the country right, but it would be nice if they'd slip us a little on the side so we can help by feeding people's minds."

We got up, brushed off, found a container for the papers, and walked slowly back to the Little Theatre building. I wondered about the future of theater in South Africa?

"I'm very optimistic about it," Honeyman said. "Theater so often reflects what's going on in the society. For me, what's encouraging about society now is that everybody's chances are so much broader; There are so many more possibilities. I believe what has happened in South Africa, whatever anybody says about the crime and the violence, is a miracle."

"It's astounding that we were civilized enough, or I think big-hearted enough, to merge. I'm actually saying that in a political way, from the black perspective. I do believe that everyone has to be punished for what they've done and I do believe the whites are still going to be punished in some way or another. I think they are being punished at the moment. But I think the transition has been miraculous and fantastic. We are all now going forward together and merging as a nation and we are finding a way through."

"And if theater reflects that, theater will find a way through as well. It might take twenty years, but we'll have an entirely South African-based culture with all the elements of all the cultures here and that's what I would love to work towards. The tapestry is so rich and if we can keep that, instead of doing what happened in the old South Africa where we were in all our little groups, if we could just pull all the threads together to make one picture, I think this would be an amazing culture."

XVI
Trudy de Ridder
I did intensive research on children in prison

Aldino turned onto the highway approach at the end of the main street through Newlands. I often walked by that corner. It bordered Groote Schuur, the former estate of legendary diamond baron Cecil Rhodes. The President and ministers lived within that complex now. The first meeting between National Party and ANC leaders took place there, May 2-4, 1990. I would have given a lot for a glimpse inside, but all I could see from the sidewalk, or the highway, was tree tops above solid ten-foot walls. Rhodes, a young Englishman who came to South Africa in 1871, developed De Beers and died very rich. Before his death, in 1902, he presented his mansion and land to the country as an official residence for the leaders of his country.

Further along, past the University of Cape Town's traditional red brick buildings along a landscaped hillside, we passed the other Groote Schuur: a huge block-like, modern hospital and the site of Chris Barnard's historic heart transplants. On the right, the docks and cranes of the waterfront came into view and beyond, the tall buildings of central Cape Town.

Aldino took the Woodstock off ramp into the District Six emptiness and turned on Zonnebloem and into a long driveway through a primary and senior schools complex. I got out at the building farthest back and climbed steps to a broad verandah. Next to the door, above a large terra cotta pot of geraniums was a plaque: "The Trauma Centre for Victims of Violence and Torture, Bernard Mizeki Centre,

Zonnebloem College, Cambridge Street."

Reading it, I collided with someone coming out, a white man with a gray beard and a jaunty French fisherman's cap covering gray hair. He wore a dark jacket with hooks on metal rods extending from the sleeves.

The office was just inside, off a main hall. The woman behind the desk called Trudy de Ridder's office. I sat in a chair against the wall. The image of the armless man did not go away. What had happened to him? Why? When? Where? In the next chair a little girl of five or six, in a green school jumper and white blouse, sucked her thumb.

"She's waiting for transport," the woman at the desk explained.

"Does her mother work here?"

"No," she replied. "She's a client."

Trudy de Ridder strode in. She wore a long black vest and a sheer, white, sleeveless, calf-length tunic over wide-legged, black silk pants, all of which floated to a stop a second or two after she did. Her hair was straight, jet black and shoulder-length; her skin smooth and luminously pale, like a pearl. She was a vision in black and white, strikingly beautiful, actually stunning. Her handshake was firm and her smile welcoming.

I followed her into the hall, up the painted concrete stairs, and into a staff lounge with aging, frayed-at-the-seams easy chairs and sofas. While she shut the door and pulled a couple of chairs together, I took a quick look at the art on the walls, impressionistic with anti-apartheid titles.

No, I didn't mind if she smoked. Which she did with good-old-days style. Her eyes were an amazing blue with irises that appeared to be outlined in white.

The Trauma Center was started in 1993 specifically for individuals who had suffered human rights violations, De Ridder said. "We worked with refugees, returned exiles, ex-political prisoners, ex-detainees, torture survivors, with any person who had suffered any kind of violence, particularly criminal. Basically, we look at that entire area of trauma. We provide mainly a counseling service and psychological support services."

"Now my role for the last two years, and I think probably the reason the director referred you to me, is providing full-time and ongoing psychological support to those testifying before the Truth Commission here in Cape Town, support to those who testified at Human Rights Foundation hearings and to individuals who suffered at the hands of amnesty seekers as well as Truth Commission members."

"The rest of my work entails working with ex-activists, working with anybody, basically, suffering human rights violations during the apartheid years—to deal with the trauma of the past."

De Ridder's voice was deep, cool and quiet. She listened intently to questions and considered her answers carefully before responding.

A psychologist, De Ridder received training and degrees at the University of Stellenbosch; by correspondence with the University of South Africa; at the University of Cape Town; and University of the Western Cape.

Born in Pretoria in 1959, she lived there until she was 17.

"I am from a mixed family," De Ridder said. "My mother has an English background, my father a Dutch-Afrikans background. But we spoke Afrikaans at home and I would say that was my mother language. My grandmother came from Holland to South Africa when she was 19. She started modern dancing in South Africa and was notorious for dancing barefoot—the first woman to do so here on stage. She became quite involved in Afrikans folk dancing. That side of my family was politically and culturally very involved in establishing an Afrikaner culture."

She paused and frowned. "It was a strange culture. I don't know if one could say there was an Afrikaner culture—or if there is an Afrikaner culture. I think it went along with the need for identity and, alongside that, was the kind of social engineering and nationalism that was taking place at the time in this country. My grandfather, whom I didn't know very well, was the secretary-general to the prime minister."

"The other side of my family were mainly farmers. They owned very big farms and were quite wealthy. During the first and second Boer Wars, or English wars or whatever you want to say, they suffered quite a few losses in terms of the land and the family. But that family decided they wanted to reconcile with the British. I think four of my great uncles married English women. They said, 'If we live in this land, we have to reconcile and this will be the history of this family.'"

"That's how the English part comes into my family, from my mother's side. A mixture of English- and Afrikaans-speaking with a very, very different background. They went to French schools, finishing schools. Both my grandfather and grandmother were university graduates. My grandfather—he did his doctorate in Hebrew and Latin—became the principal of a Jewish school."

"I wanted to be an artist, not a psychologist, but I think on both sides of the family, my mother's as well as my father's, there was an incredible focus on caring for people within the community. My maternal grandmother was a qualified social worker; my paternal grandmother started the School for the Blind in South Africa, in Worcester. My mother was an English teacher. On some level, I grew up with this."

After the assassination of Prime Minister H.F. Verwoerd, De Ridder concluded that there was something inherently wrong with Afrikaners as a race.

"But I didn't really have an understanding of what this involved, only an awareness that people looked at us in a kind of disrespectful way," she said. "All I knew was we were doing something wrong. Perhaps I'd picked this up by sharing a bus to school with English children."

Following a long silence, De Ridder said, "It's not possible to articulate this very well. My father was quite obsessional about the Afrikaner culture, whatever existed at the time. He researched the past in detail and intensely and was quite idealistic about it, not about the present, but about the history of the Voortrekkers and wanting to break away and establish an independent community. I think those were the two factors very important to him."

She stopped again. Her expression clearly said that these areas of her past still disturbed and confused her. "My father wanted to strengthen his belief in the Afrikaner culture by following its rituals and being extremely rigid in these. It was essential to only read Afrikaans, essential to research the history from a certain perspective. We had to do the folk dancing. We had to listen to the music. Very religious: Dutch Reformed. He would not swim on Sunday, not as a Christian or a person, but as an Afrikaner. He was, I would say, desperately trying to establish an identity."

"When I was about ten years old, it became a common practice in Afrikaans primary schools to start gifted programs for children. I was one of those selected. We formed a class of thirty two, boys and girls, and were referred to as the X-class. What they did was to separate us completely from the rest of the school. We would, they said, remain in this class until we completed our primary school education: 'You will not be taken out; nobody will be added.' The most humiliating thing any of us could do was to associate with other children in that school. So a complete elitist group of pupils. It was bizarre, but that was what was created."

"And the competition within this class was fierce and cruel. You must perform in the nineties. If you don't, you will be looked upon as unintelligent and not be socially accepted in the class. If not accepted because you are not performing properly, you will not participate in social activities outside the classroom. It was incredible isolation. There was enormous stimulation as well. They fed us information constantly. We were the guinea pigs."

De Ridder paused: "I was terribly, terribly unhappy, to the point I lost so much weight that, when I made Standard Five, the doctor was quite concerned. He called my parents, said they ought to hospitalize me. Why I mention this is, whatever happened in this class—listening to pop music or whatever, my parents resisted it. So there was no way out for me. I had a very good experience of elitism, of being separated from others, and how to look down on others. So much of the society I lived in was acted out there. That was my first experience, emotionally, of what it's like to be in an elite group, but to be completely unacceptable there, for whatever reason. That kind of discrimination and prejudice. From about Standard Ten, I started shifting away from my parents and it has been a long and very difficult road for me."

De Ridder had two brothers but she was the only one who, at that time, moved in a completely opposite direction from that of her family. "I just became quite rebellious as a child, against everything that resembled that rigid Afrikaner identity. The pressure from all sides caused the shift. It wasn't political, it was more social."

I asked how she dealt emotionally and outwardly with the pressure to conform to Afrikaner standards.

De Ridder considered this, her gaze moving past me. Beauty it seemed, contrary to what I had always and totally irrationally imagined, had not cancelled the usual teen-age girl problems. "I think initially the only way you feel you can cope when you are an adolescent is to break away from things completely. I wanted to come and study at the University of Cape Town, but I was forbidden. I had to go to an Afrikans university. I did, but I decided to do this my way. Try to fit in where I can and if I can't, I will go away. I had a variety of friends. I become quite involved in the art world which already, in a way, was moving away from this very conservative situation, these Afrikaner ideals and this indoctrination."

"It was very difficult to deal with initially. The break, the familial conflict, was quite severe. My mother once told me that when I was born, my father said his dream for me was that I would become the perfect Afrikaner woman. To find an identity for myself and to feel all right about myself was very difficult. Looking back, I don't think there was any other decision I could have taken but to leave home at seventeen and to do it on my own completely, financially and in every way."

De Ridder recalled being more troubled those years by her Afrikans identity than by her country's policy of apartheid. "I was aware of apartheid, but I think that this incredible need for identity with which I grew up, not my need for personal identity but for an

Afrikaner identity, was incredibly destructive. For me as a person. Being critical of my Afrikaner identity started in my high school years. I went to a conservative school for girls from wealthy Afrikaner families, where it was, again, very important to be the perfect Afrikaner girl. The way I coped with that was not to associate with my peer group, but rather with university students. It was a convenient survival strategy. And at the same time, I became very critical of the kind of religionism, the religious codes, forced on us. And becoming very confused about what the Afrikaner is, and who I am, and what is my history, and where am I going?"

She also paid to learn to speak English. "Two o'clock, after school, I would meet up with two Jewish girls from the Jewish high school in Pretoria and they taught me." She explained that she looked to them because she had become aware of prejudice on the part of English-speaking students: "If you're Afrikaner, you're dumb. You don't know what you are talking about; you're lower class. That was the other side. So one is in-between. Where do you go? Who are you?"

De Ridder's years at university were better. "I began to focus on other things more important to me. I also had the freedom to select my friends, to be wherever I wanted to be. I became independent financially—I worked full time and received bursaries—and to some extent, independent emotionally."

After receiving a bachelor's degree, she earned a diploma in teaching, then went on to an honors class in counseling psychology. "With this particular course, at your second year level in psychology," she explained, "you have to do an extra course and pass with 80 percent. Then you go through a selection process to go into your third year, then do your honors."

"Now, I think, because of my experience at primary school, I learned how to study and I learned how to perform academically. 'I'll do the courses. I'll pass my first, second, whatever year.' But I wasn't very happy with the content of the work in my department at Stellenbosch nor of the perceptions of the lecturers. I thought this particularly conservative and very controlled. They would ask, 'How do you define an adult?' And then say, 'There are ten categories, characteristics, of what an adult person is. One: They will be deeply religious.' And I would question that. 'What religion?' 'What about those who are not religious?'"

"And I would be asked to leave the classroom. I was unhappy. I was the outsider. My whole life I felt like the outsider and, eventually, you adopt the outsider identity. You become more comfortable, but this also has disadvantages."

"I think of the political consciousness of the early to mid-'80s. I was then involved with somebody who had a very similar experience to me. He was much older and, on one level, I think a role model for me. He also had these doubts, this confusion about identity and living in this prejudiced and racist society. It was the first time I had ever felt comfortable with an Afrikaans-speaking person."

"He was a very well-known artist in the country and very bright. And also very connected with all the outsiders of the Afrikaner community. We then were invited to meet the ANC leadership who were in exile at that time. That was the Dakar trip, in '87." (A former leader of the parliamentary opposition took fifty Afrikaner dissidents to Dakar, Senegal, for a week-long meeting with ANC leaders.)

De Ridder called that trip an incredible experience on many levels. "Just to see conditions, the bellies of countries, the make-up of Africa. Africa was extraordinary. And the debate between the ANC and the Afrikaner delegation was fascinating, highly skilled on both sides, with a kind of intellect, social and emotional, that was really incredible."

"The discovery of similarity—that was interesting. To see how the ANC leadership was influenced in its youth, how we were influenced in our youth. And in many ways so similar. Just to sing the same songs together in the bars at night. We would sit in a restaurant and one of the ANC guys wants to say something. We can't use English because we don't want to be understood, so we speak Afrikaans. This was using the language in a positive way."

"Came back and lost two jobs, labeled a political terrorist for having gone. This was devastating for my parents. Difficult for me as well. You have a loyalty toward your parents, yet, at the same time, you know they are not going to change and you are not going to change. I came from obsessional and had to be obsessional to fight it. How to find a relatively comfortable compromise."

"Interestingly enough, because I had had the experience of a family who were particularly politically involved, I hated politics. My parents lived for it. Not necessarily my mother, but my father. It was an integral part of his character, his identity. So I have always been very cynical and very critical of politics. I don't believe in political parties, don't believe in political leaders. Joining a political party, looking to the leaders as the fathers. I don't have that. And I've never been a group person. I actually distrust the group. I did not fit in. I did not feel comfortable."

"I think there's politics and racism. They are not completely on the same level, though sometimes these are confused. Historically, of course, the only way racism works is through social and political engineering. I think that was my perception. Not becoming politically active, but knowing that what was happening at the time was unacceptable to me. That we were not treated equally, that was bizarre."

In 1985, De Ridder had been involved in the creation of OAPSS-SA, Organization for Alternative Psychological and Social Services in South Africa. Its members, psychologists and mental health professionals, volunteered to provide psychological support to people in prison.

"I became involved in that. There was a place in Athlone where people were taken and where most group counseling of detainees was done. Psychologists offering these services became very involved with advocacy for what was happening in the country and against racism and so forth."

Another factor that affected her perceptions of race in her country had been overseas travel during her years as a university student. "In 1981, in Brazil, what really struck me was everyone spoke the same language. Yet I could not speak that language nor the language of the majority of people I lived with."

"I think what is interesting, too, is that my parents taught me to respect people. In our home, black people were treated with the utmost courtesy. And that was bizarre. The focus was more on developing this Afrikaner identity and the only way you can develop this identity is to exclude people? Then, when it came to day-to-day treatment of people it was completely the opposite. And the interaction with people on the farm ... There was this other side."

In 1987, after the Dakar trip, she and her partner established a non-racial artists' organization on farms they acquired outside of Paarl.

"There were fourteen houses, beautifully restored Cape Dutch houses, and artists were subsidized to come there and live and create their art. I was the director. We had artists of all races, from everywhere in the country. And that was the idea. They would stay a certain length of time. They had to exhibit."

"Funding? We did get some from overseas, but we struggled like you wouldn't believe. I didn't earn a salary in five years. But we did it. And we worked. We did everything. We built the beds, worked the land. We had mistakes but I think we had many successes. I believe many artists benefited. Writers came too. Several did books."

De Ridder left the arts colony in 1993 to study for a master's degree. "I went to UWC (University of the Western Cape) rather than UCT because, at that time, it was a more representative community of students. More what South Africa was like, with all its advantages and disadvantages. I knew eventually I would begin my career as a clinical psychologist and I wanted that kind of experience, just to add. If I'm going to be a clinical psychologist, I'm going to work with everybody."

"At that time there came an outcry about the children in prison and in '93, at UWC, I did intensive research on children in prison, the first done in South Africa. They had begun picking children up in the '80s, but psychologists or researchers didn't have access then. I did a clinical and looked at the psychological experience and consequences of imprisonment and, more particularly, actual experiences in prison. The whole prison system. And who are these children? Where do they come from? That project kept me busy for three years."

"That study then assisted policy in the new government. That was also the ideal, that it in some way must have some meaning. It must not just go to the archives."

I asked about her findings. "In lay terms, very difficult," De Ridder replied. "These were psychological studies. I looked at personality development. I looked at socio-economic factors. I looked at as many facts as possible, from the outside and the inside. These children, aged ten to eighteen, had been imprisoned for both criminal and political offenses. This becomes difficult to summarize. I think it is more relevant to the criminal violence that exists at the moment, that is so prevalent. What *is* clear from the study is that prison is probably the worst place you can put children. I'm talking about the prisons in South Africa."

"A fascinating part of this study was just the history of the prison culture. I had to learn the prison language, the gang language, the dynamics that took place there. You could not enter if you were not becoming part of it."

"I think the essence of the study was that we all develop strategies to survive. If I look at where the majority of the children came from, the strategies they developed were extraordinarily and highly creative. Although against the normal society, these allowed them to survive. And it will be particularly difficult to break down those defenses and those survival strategies."

"I think what really informed government as a result of this study was that you had a high risk group and you had a low risk group. And what is a high risk group? Most of the youth I interviewed in prison were there for petty theft. But if you actually did a clinical interview, they had already killed at least four people in their lives. It was, what kind of environment can you establish for a high risk group and what kind of environment for low risk youth? And how to separate these. And how to actually start dealing with the individual rather than the category."

"And I would say one of the most important things is—how can I put it—if I read in the newspaper this killing took place, or that killing took place, it is very easy for me to know, that is a prison killing; that is a civil killing. Don't ask me exactly how, I will just know it."

"In my report to Parliament, I mainly focused on identification of the risk groups, what structures have to be put up. And the education that would have to go into the justice system: magistrates must be educated, social workers must be educated."

During that time, while De Ridder worked on her children-in-prison study, the Trauma Center asked her to join its staff. This now numbers thirty, half clinical and half support staff.

I asked how the Trauma Center started. Those involved initially, mental health professionals and members of the Anglican Church, had worked with ex-political prisoners and detainees, she said. They were also connected through Cowley House, formerly an Anglican monastery. When families came to visit prisoners on Robben Island, they stayed in Cowley House. When prisoners were released, they were taken immediately to Cowley House for counseling and support that would help them integrate back into society. Those who had been involved then, she said, recognized the need to work with victims of violence and torture on a long term basis.

"When they became established in '93, I did voluntary work for them, particularly with children. In '94, I did intensive research for them with ex-political prisoners and ex-detainees and torture survivors in the Cape. Basically, we looked at how many people still suffered post-traumatic stress: from government figures down to the unemployed who hadn't gained anything from the transition."

"In '95, certain NGOs, academic institutions and private individuals came together nationally to discuss the process of the Truth Commission. Proposals were made then, before the commission was established, for psychological support and counseling. That group of people in Cape Town was called the Mental Health Response to the Truth Commission. We are the only organization like this in South

Africa. We devote a full time staff to the process as well as the Mental Health Response which is volunteers as well as mental health professionals."

I asked what could help individuals who had experienced solitary confinement, torture and long imprisonment?

De Ridder frowned. "It is difficult to say what helps and what doesn't, " she said finally. "It's definitely talking about the experience. We have to start at that level. But I think it is more complicated than that. You know, the struggle was collective. The trauma that people experienced was a collective trauma. Even in a sense that if your child's been killed, two houses down the road another child was killed. You dealt with your trauma collectively. Your trauma could not be worse than the other."

"Two major things happened, which people did not realize. Of course, they did know, but I am speaking of the psychological perspective. The struggle is collective, but the victory is individualized. We have a government in a democratic, capitalistic society. Suddenly the focus on the collective changes to the individual. What are you going to do with your life? You don't have the community. You don't have that struggle anymore. Now it is about you. How are you going to survive in a democratic, capitalist society?"

"And I think the second thing is that the Truth Commission individualized trauma. People came as individuals to tell their stories. What assists this work is, for the first time you can speak to someone and actually deal with certain aspects of your trauma that you could not deal with because it was collective. And secondly, you have to now deal with your present life and your past life as an individual."

"I do believe that work with individuals, such as we do, does have spin-offs into society. Each individual has a family that reaches into society."

I asked how applicants to the Truth and Reconciliation Commission learned that counseling services were available to them?

De Ridder explained that she got the list of all those who had made statements: "We then designed a pamphlet that described what we did and wrote a letter to each individual. 'Our services are available.' People were cynical, especially about the black community. No way would people come. But the response was overwhelming. Phenomenal. Phenomenal."

"What turned out to be very important, (the hearings) reawakened things. Your son was killed in 1985. The meaning you construct from that killing can differ profoundly in 1997. A new government took over, but you don't see anything that is concrete that is changing. So you construct meaning from that particular loss and trauma. That doesn't only apply to those who suffered under apartheid, it applies to those who engineered apartheid and to a society where new meaning has to be constructed."

"That is why this work is ongoing. And I think it forms part of reconciliation. For me there is quite a difference between reconciliation from an individual perspective and reconciliation in society."

"If you ask what is the most dominant feeling most people experience, I would say anger. And how do you reconcile with that anger? I always ask, 'OK, this person who tortured you, what would you like to happen to this person? Would you like this person to be killed? Would you like him—or her, or them—to spent their entire life in prison? What would you like?'"

" 'I'd like them to be killed. I'd like them to spend their lives in prison.'

'I understand what you would like. Would that change you?'

'No.'

'Would your life change the moment this person disappears from society?'

'No.'

'Why not?'"

"I'm doing this very superficially," De Ridder continued, "but anger is a very common human feeling. And anger can be channeled productively or destructively. Many productive people, what is really motivating them is some form of anger. Anger is not necessarily negative and we don't need to get rid of it. It is how you channel that anger."

"That's the first thing. Yes, you are angry with your perpetrator, but if you remain a victim, you still are completely in the power of that perpetrator. This is what you want to get rid of. And this is what keeps you intensely angry. So this is where it will stop."

"I will never tell a person, 'When you walk out of here, you are not going to feel angry.' This is normal in terms of what has happened to him, or to her. All I'm saying is, 'I don't want you to feel stalled, disempowered, by your anger for the perpetrator, whoever the perpetrator was. 'What are you going to do with your life now? How can you empower your life?' "

"And how to deal with grief: What meaning are you constructing, now, of what happened? Because that is essential in how you are going to channel your anger."

The interview ended abruptly. The secretary from the desk on the main floor called. De Ridder was expected at a conference in another area. As I gathered up pens, papers, tapes and recorder, I asked if she had married, did she have children?

"Yes," she said, she had married and had one child. "My husband is a writer and," she added with a wry smile, "a political analyst."

XVII
🌿 *EKM Dido*

*Some in my family are fair, some like me, in between,
some are dark*

" I t is white to the bridge," Aldino said, weaving in and
out of the heavy traffic, trying to make up time; talking, I suspected, to distract me since he had been
late. "From that bridge to the next bridge is colored. After that
black."

A string of strip malls with run-down stores followed a stretch of
dusty, open land.

Athlone, he said, and one of the first colored business districts.
We passed a bank and assorted shops. A pony cart rattled by. Kids in
school uniforms clustered at corners and spilled over onto the street.
Aldino said on Fridays, the Muslim sabbath, schools let out at 1 PM.

Into the predominantly Indian area, past the soccer stadium and
the Muslim cemetery. Further along, trash by the road multiplied.
Street stalls appeared. Faces on the street had changed to black.
Urban planning under the National Party government called for a
white core extended by spiraling settlements specified for those with
skins of increasing darkness.

Inside the car, American voices sang hymns. Bit by bit, Aldino
had shared his deep religious feelings though he never proselytized.
He no longer attended church services—reasons unknown—but con-
ducted regular religious studies for his family and others in his home.
JC, his son, took his initials from Jesus Christ. His twin was CJ,
Christ Jesus.

After I had known Aldino for awhile, I asked about his listing in the Cape Town phone book, Western Cape Taxi Information. What was that about? At one time, Aldino said, he had organized a Western Cape Taxi Association to establish common standards in his business. That had, over time, fizzled out.

Impressive iron gates marked the entrance to Nico Malan Nursing College and Aldino turned in there. Like many institutions, roads and airports, this one still bore the name of a former National Party bigwig.

I would be ten minutes late for the interview and was a little cross about it. Aldino often referred to African time—meaning someone not showing up when scheduled—but he sometimes operated by it.

EKM Dido came down a hall toward the large, stark lobby as she was being paged. Tardy was not a problem, she said, with a smile. She had just finished the ethos and professional practices lecture to nursing students.

On the way to her office, she explained that nurses' training at Nico Malan was a four-year program. One and two year courses were also offered for less skilled levels.

Dido's job title was chief professional nurse and head of the college's department of general nursing. She was also the author of two novels and that was the reason I had come to talk with her. That evening, she said, she would be speaking about her books at the University of Cape Town. She had returned recently from her first trip outside the country, to Holland, where she had by invitation attended a special event honoring authors of books written in Afrikaans. Cecily, who worked for a publisher, had told me about her. She said Dido had been the only person of color in a group of high-browed Afrikaners. Her books had been the first written in Afrikaans by someone not Afrikans.

While many books by whites had told about the lives of South African coloreds, Dido said with pride, she was the first colored author to publish, and profit, from a novel about coloreds written in Afrikaans.

Dido was a short woman, fortyish, round and with perfectly even, white teeth. Under her white medical coat, she wore a soccer World Cup T-shirt with an American flag on it. Her skirt was black.

I wasn't sure how to address her.

"Dido," she said. The initials that preceded it were those of her own first names—"my granny's and my mother's names, and I don't like them."

She had begun work on another book, also a novel. In it she would explore what she sees as a trend among coloreds and blacks: tracking down and taking back their traditional names. During the apartheid era, Dido explained, many South Africans of color had tried to upgrade their lives by adopting new last names common among the next higher racial grouping. Blacks attempted to change their classification to colored while coloreds sought white status. With upgraded racial classifications reflected in newly adopted surnames, they hoped to improve their job opportunities and their neighborhoods.

"You still get some people who say they are 'white' and then you see they are not," Dido said. "I didn't see any of us choosing 'black boy.' Whether my people like it or not, the fact is that we are coloreds. Although we also struggled in the apartheid era, we have always been the jam between two slices of bread. Most people hate that, but it is a reality. If a pension for whites, for example, would increase twenty percent, the coloreds would get ten percent. But the blacks would get two percent."

"I'm interested in seeing how this change in surnames, going back to the roots, would affect the coloreds who adopted white identities along with white surnames. Quite a lot of coloreds took white ID's and lived as white people. That was a thing in those days. Quite a few of my friends crossed over and are still white."

Dido explained how that worked: "You had to apply to Internal Affairs and you were asked a lot of questions. They looked at your skin texture, your hair texture, everything. And then they paid you home visits as well, talked to some of your people. And if they found you OK, you got that white passbook. You could then change your name."

"My family, some of them are fair, some like me, in between, some are dark." Dido laughed. "I had one aunt who definitely had *not* been among those seeking a white identity. Her one daughter is very fair and my aunt had to struggle to get her a colored ID document. They would always seem to class her as white and then the struggle would go on and on: 'No,' her mother would say, 'She's colored.' "

"Those with blacker skins didn't have such a nice deal because initially what they did was push a pencil through your hair. And if the pencil stuck, they would say"—she spoke in Afrikaans and repeated "You're black" in English. "You can't then change back to colored."

Would she now change her last name to that of one of her white ancestors?

"No. I wouldn't," Dido replied. "I am happy with my own name. I think those of my people with a sense of insecurity or who have a complex about being colored, and there are quite a few of us, they might take a white name."

"One can't help but always remember what Mrs. (F.W.) de Klerk (wife of the last National Party president) said during one of her speeches, and I think her last speech as well, where she defined the colored as an entity. Perhaps some people got stuck with that, perhaps that is why they feel insecure, I don't know."

"I'm proud of who I am and I've also become proud of my Afrikaans language. Especially now that it has become such an issue."

"In the apartheid time, we used to go out of our way not to speak Afrikaans. Not because we didn't want to, but because we wanted to show other people. 'See? We are not the inferior people you think we are.' Out of the house, when we saw a white person, we would immediately switch to English."

"But I've been a rebel since childhood," she continued, smiling. "I lived near East London and when I would go into some of the shops along Oxford Street, and if I saw you and you looked as if you understood English, I would speak Afrikaans to you. It was a game all the time to me."

The use of Afrikaans remained a topic of great debate in the country, she said, even though Afrikaners no longer made the rules. She believed Afrikaans continued to carry a political association, was a symbol of the time of apartheid, and still looked down upon.

"That's why I tend to use it more," Dido explained. "I told myself already, 'I'm only going to write Afrikaans books.' Now I find myself, for the first time in my life, buying Afrikaans magazines, Afrikaans books. I never used to do that."

Why did she do it now? She had just said she believed Afrikaans had political implications.

Dido nodded: "In a way it does. We can't get away from that. But if I admit to myself, 'Yes, Afrikaans is something we should do away with,' then I must do away with a part of my past, a part of who I am. That is the language I grew up with."

"I am also very obstinate. We have eleven languages. Afrikaans is one. So why should it be threatened? We don't threaten the others. If I have morbid feelings about Afrikaans being an apartheid language, it means that I haven't come to terms yet with the past. Therefore, I need to revisit my feelings. Otherwise I'll remain where I am. I will never go forward. I will never see the beauty of life. That is my opposition."

"You can't see otherwise if you want to survive."

XVIII
🌿 *Karen Katts*
What I never did expect, was to be able to vote

"The coloreds of South Africa are the product of the mixing of racial types from many parts of the world over many hundreds of years," said Karen Katts, lecturer to the Elderhostelers when we had been in Cape Town. "The indigenous people were the Khoi-Khoi and the San. The other half of the mix came from Europe and included the Dutch, Portuguese, Spaniards, English and Germans. Others were slaves from the East, mainly India, Bali and Ceylon, as well as West and East Africa."

Katts herself was, in apartheid terminology, colored. She had stood behind the podium in a conference room in an up-scale hotel in Sea Point, a spectacularly beautiful ocean-front section of Cape Town. She was very attractive and petite with a nice figure and a small waist. Her skin was olive. Her black hair curled softly around a face men would look at twice. Mid to late thirties I guessed, but in fact, as I later learned, forty two. She dressed very smartly, in form-fitting denim jeans and matching blue denim shirt accented by heavy silver jewelry. Her voice was high-pitched and she spoke in a sing-song rhythm.

"Between 1834 and 1838," Katts continued, "the slaves were freed and all people of mixed descent were called 'coloreds.' In 1910, when the Union of South Africa was formed, the British Act declared that members of the new Union Parliament had to be of European descent. In 1948, the Afrikaner National Party defeated the United Party which was mainly English-speakers and took over the government. Its policy of apartheid was put into practice. This meant seg-regation or 'separate development.' In short, it entrenched second-class citizenship."

In 1969, she said, the first elections were held for the Coloured Repesentational Council. Since this was in effect a legislative body with no power at all, the elections were largely boycotted by the col-oreds. A 1984 attempt to herd the coloreds into the National Party fold brought the formation of the Tricameral Parliament which allot-ted eighty-five seats to coloreds. Again, few of the latter voted and, she concluded, that was where matters stood until the first democrat-ic election for all South Africans was held in 1994.

After the talk I cornered Katts and explained what I was working on. I asked if I could call her after the tour when I returned to Cape Town. She wrote down her phone number and a week or two later, we sat around the table in Cecily's dining room. She lived nearby, as it turned out, and stopped on her way home from classes. Katts headed the Pre-Primary Department at Cape Town College of Education, a formerly "white" institution in an area called Mowbray. She coordi-nated curriculum for a student body of 450 and worked mainly with those students preparing to teach children three to six years of age.

My intent had been to ask for suggestions on women I might con-tact, but we ended up talking about her. Though Katts did not really fit into any of the categories of women I sought out, she proved of interest because her experience of South Africa so differed from the others.

She had been born in Durban and attended school there except for her final years. Following her father's promotion, the family—she was one of three children—moved to Cape Town where she finished school. Both parents taught. Her mother, a native of Mauritius, advanced to the level of lecturer. Her South African-born father retired as Deputy Director of Education, House of Representatives, Coloured Affairs. This was the token body Katts had spoken of in the lecture.

"They retained a good sense of humor," Katts said of her parents, "and they spoke always of the importance of education despite the

226

color of one's skin. When I was in matric (high school) I wanted to become a dress designer. It was my father who said, 'I don't know where this child comes from. She must first get a certificate of some kind so she can hold down a steady job.' There was a small institution in Athlone that offered a pattern-making course. Though it was called a school of design, it wasn't the design I wanted. It was more so you could work in a factory. There was a school of dress design in Wineberg, but one would have to have a permit to go to such a school because I wasn't white. My father said, 'Oh no. Over my dead body. After you go to training school and get your diploma then you can start with your fancy ideas.' In those days, we received state bursaries and if you took a bursary for three years, you had to work for the department of education for four years."

"After I had worked a while," Katts continued, "my father asked me: 'Do you still want to become a dress designer?' But I'd changed my mind and no longer thought about entering that field. Still, I often wonder what my life would have been like if I'd become a designer."

Obviously, she still thought clothes important. She put the pieces together creatively and wore them with style. I had remembered exactly what she wore at the lecture. And on that day she had on a smart black skirt, narrow and well-cut, with a silky white blouse and black pumps with heels.

I asked if she ever wondered what her life might have been like if she had not been born in South Africa where skin color determined an individual's options? Katts nodded. She did think about that. "But because my parents were well-educated, we didn't suffer materially. I think, to a certain extent, coloreds were privileged. If your skin was dark, life was much more difficult because they knew straightaway you weren't white. I often had people asking if I was South African. If I said yes, they knew I wasn't a white South African. If I said no, they could think otherwise, because there is a bit of Mediterranean coloring."

She paused, giving me a second to consider the strange codes of apartheid. Katts meant "passing," which in the U.S. was a way to say a light-skinned individual of mixed race had been taken as "white."

She leaned forward and spoke with quiet intensity: "Look, I believe whites suffered just as much as we did, but it was a different kind of suffering. They were disadvantaged because they didn't get to know people of color. You lose out when you don't mix with other people. I'm sure now, too, that more and more whites realize their fears were unfounded. If you're not white, it doesn't mean you're a Communist, a dangerous person, a threat to the state. Literature is responsible for reinforcing this because of our associations with color: white is always good, white is right. Black is the opposite end of the spectrum: black is evil, darkness."

"Whites don't seem to realize that some things are rights, other things privileges," Katts continued. "For instance, the right of admission into a public place. If you do not abide by the rules, the owner should be allowed to show you the door. Some believe if they have the money to gain entrance, they can do what they like. They see that as a right. But it is also a privilege to be there. If you don't behave accordingly, OK, you leave. Admittance should have nothing to do with skin color."

During apartheid, skin color had everything to do with admittance to anything, from schools to neighborhoods to restaurants. Even to cities.

I asked her about the changes of the '90s. Katts said she had never dreamed she would live to see a majority government. "We knew it was coming, but not when. What I never did expect was to be able to vote. Before the elections, people were afraid. They stockpiled food. They said war would break out. I remember when the elections came. It was a rainy day in Cape Town. Queues were kilometers long. People could vote anywhere, not just in our areas. And you saw people of all shades standing alongside each other. There were no arguments. No one tried to jump the queue. It was too wonderful." She shook her head. "And it was a shock to see so many people. They came out of the hillsides, so many people, sort of unaccounted for."

Other changes had come about earlier, after Mandela's release and before the election; schools and universities opened to all and race laws scrapped. "For a long time people were very kind to each other, considerate," Katts recalled. "But people at grassroots level expected change rather quickly and when change didn't come about, the mood changed. Many became despondent because they did not have electricity, they did not have water. Their children still struggled in inferior schools. People who lived in abject poverty will tell you their lives haven't changed. Some say, because of the crime, it is worse."

"You saw the townships. In summer it is hot and dry there. In the winter it is cold and wet and muddy. Cape Flats has the highest incidence of tuberculosis worldwide. It is mostly blacks and coloreds suffering from TB because of overcrowding and poor housing conditions. Before 1994 and the elections, people thought they would get free houses. I remember talk about a five-year plan. I don't think the government has been able to deliver. People have turned to crime. They steal bags and attack tourists because they realize tourists carry money."

Katts believed Cape Town remained relatively safe, but she said she warned a visiting English cousin: "Your camera mustn't be visible. Be careful of your bag. Don't walk on your own. They will know from your accent you are not South African so be as unobtrusive as possible."

I was curious about her cousin. "A lot of people left the country during the '60s, '70s and '80s," Katts explained. "That's why we have families across the world. My aunt and uncle left their homes during the Group Areas Act relocations (the razing of selected neighborhoods because of mixed race, illegal, or increased value of the land). My aunt refused to move to a colored area and emigrated to England. She died two years later. Her husband remarried and their two daughters grew up there. My father won a British scholarship in the mid-sixties and when my parents went to England, they met them. But those were still sad times, not long after the death of their mother, and there wasn't much talking."

The two girls married English men, Katts said, and did not return to South Africa, probably because of concerns about their status in the country. Late in the '80s, Katts traveled to England and met them. "We kept up that contact when I came back and my cousins' desire to meet their family became stronger and stronger."

I wondered if her cousins thought of themselves as colored. Katts shook her head: "I don't think they care. They are just English." Family members who remained in South Africa were, under apartheid, both officially colored and officially white. "I was also classified as white," Katts said, "but we had to return that ID. I was then writing my teacher's certificate examination and had to have proof of identification: The ID number and code were checked to make sure you were registered at the right institution. In those days, a white would not have been allowed to enter a colored institution, nor one for blacks or Asians."

She described her father's skin as "very fair. If you had seen him on the streets, you wouldn't have said he was colored. That's why he was quite defiant. He walked into shops when he shouldn't have been there. He was very bold that way. I think he was quite active in the political movements in the '40s and '50s. But I don't know too much about that part of his life."

Her cousin who had visited South Africa found it a culture shock, Katts said. "Meeting all these people of different shades who are her cousins. She's about 48 now and she's been thinking about this a long time. I dare say it's because of English society which is very class divided, according to birth and wealth. In America I believe it is as well. Not everyone is accepted for who they are. I'm basing that on the news bulletins from America and England which we watch on CNN, ABC, BBC, and the films, the stereotypes on television. And the trial of O.J. Simpson, the trial of Rodney King. We listen to Oprah Winfrey's chat shows, to Barbara Walters and Larry King Live."

"Did you know there are still close ties between the Martin Luther King family and South Africa? Coretta King comes here, the son as well. Andrew Young is here often. There are films of the North-South war and then there was *Philadelphia*, with the AIDS case and the only lawyer, a black man, who would take that on."

"I think the difference for me was that in South Africa apartheid was on the statute books, rather than with the Ku Klux Klan. It was difficult, for example, when we had to go to a particular beach for coloreds. Or when you were playing in the park and were tired and couldn't sit on the benches because these were for whites only. And parents had to explain why."

Cape Town, which traditionally had been the most racially-liberal of any of the country's cities, permitted restaurants to admit persons of color before apartheid ended. There was a catch to this, however. Such individuals would have to leave if any patrons objected.

"I remember going into one restaurant," Katts said. "We waited and waited to be served. My husband (Vincent, also a teacher) eventually asked the waitress: 'What is the problem?' She was embarrassed and the manager came. He said he couldn't serve us because they had a liquor license and that could be revoked if someone complained. So we left and my daughter Eloise was crying for a Coke. My husband had to say, 'No, these people will not serve us because we are not white.' Yet we were as well-behaved and well-dressed, maybe better, than people sitting near us."

"My elder daughter can recall these things because she was born in 1977. She remembers my holding her alongside the gutters rather than letting her go into the non-white, or non-European, toilets which were never clean. The younger one, born in 1982, doesn't really know differences of apartheid, though she's become aware hearing people talk. But she doesn't like being labeled and doesn't like others being labeled. People are people, she says."

"Yes," Katts continued, "it's a sad past. But those experiences have also made us stronger. That is why some of us have risen in our jobs. I know my boss, the director of the college, has faith in me. If mine had been an affirmative action appointment and hadn't worked out, he would have told me. I made that quite clear when one or two of my colleagues implied mine was an affirmative action appointment. There'd been five vacancies for heads of departments and seventeen applicants. I was one of the five named and the only non-white. When I heard the remarks, I went to the director and said, 'Look, if this is an affirmative action post, I don't need it.' He assured me that it was not that at all."

We chatted a bit longer and as she gathered up her things to leave, she said, "Now we can look back and laugh at apartheid and see how stupid it really was. Members of the same family, same mother and father, classified differently. There was a time when we accepted what came our way. Now we realize how farcical it was."

When I thought later about Karen Katts, she seemed on the one hand to have survived apartheid better than many South Africans of color. She was college-educated, held a good job, obviously had prospered and lived a solid middle-class life. Yet in another way, she seemed sad to me. Who knows what she could have become? South Africa's Coco Chanel? Another Laura Ashley? Liz Claiborne perhaps? Her style looked made for that. Yet that had not been a career option. Later, she had not even wanted to try. What other women I had listened to in these interviews refused to accept, Katts apparently had accepted.

Also I remembered what Sue van der Merwe had said about '70 percent of Western Cape voters supporting National Party candidates. The supposition being that coloreds voted for the enemy they knew rather than the one they didn't. Apartheid had been so cleverly engineered that it divided not just whites and blacks but colored and white, colored and black. Or maybe the architects of apartheid were not that devilishly clever but just lucky in that all of this worked to keep them in control of the country for as long as it did.

On late Sunday afternoons in summer, free outdoor concerts were held at Kirstenbosch Botanical Gardens, not far from Cecily's house. These gardens were laid out on hillsides below flat-topped granite mountains that in their upper reaches looked like walls of a giant's fortress. Between the mountains and the gardens stretched forests and brush-covered slopes in various gradations of green. The lawns connecting the beds of flowers were packed with picnickers. We walked around until Cecily found a grassy patch for our blanket. We had shade though the stage was down the hill and almost out of sight.

Cecily hadn't known what the program was. The Sunday music ranged from classical to popular, she said. Anything at all was fine with both of us. Just getting out and being at a lovely place was quite enough. And it was fun being a part of a happy crowd in holiday spirits. When the music started, it turned out to be the kind of swing I remembered from the '40s and '50s, the era of music Aldino liked.

Ballroom dancing had become exceedingly popular in Cape Town, Cecily said. We listened to *In the Mood* by a big band led by Iggy-somebody and a medley of Elvis numbers. This propelled two people near us up and on their feet: he, a dapper, colored man about sixty in a straw hat and bright sport shirt; she a well-dressed, heavy black woman from the adjoining blanket. Before long, dancing couples dotted the lawns as far as we could see. Cecily filled the wine glasses again and I spread olive tapenade over a piece of baguette.

On the drive home, Cecily said, "The music wasn't all that wonderful. But you wouldn't have had this anywhere but Cape Town."

XIX
❧ *Sue Power*

It's complicated, working out who should be beneficiaries of land being returned

Cape Town's Campground Road, Cecily said, had the right name since the British actually stationed its troops there during one of the Boer Wars. I looked out the car window at an empty, weed-filled stretch of land bordering the street. It must have looked much the same a hundred years earlier. Further along, the road entered a section of fine homes. Cecily left me at the corner house on Campground and Norfolk roads, the home of Sue Power. Power, daughter of Black Sash stalwart Noel Robb, worked for an organization with the strange name of Surplus People Project.

I rang the buzzer by the gate and Power, large yellow dog by her side, arrived to open it. Her husband read in a gazebo next to a small pool in the walled garden. I followed her along the walk to the house and through a massive wooden door into a high-ceilinged entry with a loft above the living room just beyond. The floors were tile; the walls masonry, their sternness softened by the warmth of wood. We sat across from each other at a large dining table. A striking and brightly colored fabric hanging covered the wall opposite me.

Power was slightly built, not tall and slightly round shouldered. Her hair was graying, cut in a chin-length bob. She wore a loose cardigan over a blue cotton dress. She had a pleasant face and a quietness, perhaps a diffidence, about her, quite unlike the commanding presence of her mother.

235

The Surplus People Project, Power explained, is a non-governmental organization, NGO, involved with land reform and development issues. She worked primarily in Namaqualand, which is in the Northern Cape province. There she dealt with redistribution of land, ownership of these acquisitions and development of institutions for land management.

The organization, explained Power, got its "awful name" from something said years earlier by M.C. Botha, former Minister of Bantu Administration: " 'Surplus people must be got rid of.' In other words, women, old people, children. He wanted work units, that was all."

The present day Surplus People Project had its origins in the early 1980s when it supported South Africa's black communities resisting forced removals, evictions and privatization of communal land. SPP, then a national research project, undertook the first comprehensive study of the impact of forced removals between the 1960s and early 1980s. The project documented some 3.5 million cases in a five-volume *SPP Reports*, published in 1983.

"Obviously, now removals have stopped," Power said, "and it's a question of trying to get back what people lost or getting access to land for those who never had it. So the organization has changed from a resistance group to a land and development NGO."

I asked how she went about trying to get land back to its original owners.

There was, she said, a new land reform national policy with a Restitution Act and other acts assisting redistribution. Land was being bought back from white farmers, or whoever the current owner was, and returned to communities.

"There are two programs," Power explained. "One is restitution, where people taken off land after 1913 now claim the land back. In some cases, it's communities returning to their land. In other cases, in the Northern Cape where I am, for instance, there were colored communities around mission stations. These were nomadic people and they used a whole area. Over the years, starting in the days of British colonialism, their lands became smaller and smaller. They got crimped down. Now they are trying to get back land traditionally theirs. But since they lost their land before 1913, we're having to use the other program, which is the redistribution program, to get back that land."

The Department of Land Affairs allocates money to both programs, restitution and redistribution. Power worries about a trimmed-back budget the next fiscal year.

"It's just proved much more difficult than people thought it would be," she said. "A lot of the money that was in the budget this year hasn't been spent because the process is so complicated. And when there's unspent money, your budget gets reduced and, of course, there are many other pressing needs in the country."

"The main thing is, it is just so difficult." Her shoulders slumped and her measured and even tone changed to one of frustration and disappointment.

"When you have people who, for instance, were on a piece of land and they are not a specific body to whom you can now transfer the land, you have to set up legal entities, work out the rules of how the land will be managed and so on. So that whole process, before you can give the land back, is very long and complicated."

Where she starts varies from case to case, Power said. "What we found is, the restitution cases where you bring people back who were taken off the land, are very, very difficult."

"I worked on one which became quite famous: the Riemvasmaak case, on the Orange River, one of the early ones. Those people were removed twenty-odd years ago. They have Nama, Herero origins; come from Namibia, sent back to Namibia. Others, they said, had Xhosa origins; sent them back to the Eastern Cape. These, they said, look like coloreds, they can move into towns on the Northern Cape. So they split families, quite literally—mother this way, father that way. It was an appalling mess."

Once it became known that land reform was happening, a couple of activists began reassembling their old Orange River community. They were successful and about 1,500 people are now back on the land.

Power recalled, "That was a really long process of tracking people down, traveling around in Namibia, collecting names, getting everyone together, talking about how the restoration process worked and whether they wanted to return."

"But extraordinarily difficult problems have come up. People have now had twenty years away from each other, and you're going to try to put something back together again, and it is just very, very complicated. The power has changed. This group was in power. Now this other group has, over the past twenty years, had certain better advantages, were more politically active or whatever. So it has reshuffled the order."

"And this is a semi-desert area, extremely hot. In the old days, people lived a very simple life in reed houses. Now you've got kids who have grown up in Windhoek (capital of neighboring Namibia), or Cape Town, are used to electricity, water, TV, et cetera. They don't necessarily want to go and live that primitive kind of life. But their grandparents and some of their parents dreamt of those days."

Power's face again mirrored the frustration of dealing with layers of complications. "So there are these intra-family conflicts, huge, huge problems."

I asked how the Orange River land was acquired?

"The government was using it as an army base," Power said. "It wasn't actually easy, because the army didn't want to go. But they didn't have a lot of choice, and it was awarded back to the community. There are still problems going on, now with the parks board, because the parks board used part of it as a rhino breeding camp. There are negotiations around how this could be managed as a joint project so the community gets something out of it."

How did people relocated there make their living?

"They can farm because it is on the banks of the Orange River. But it is very tough country and not everybody's cup of tea. It's beautiful, but not for city slickers. When you've been living in Cape Town for twenty years, married a townie, it's hard to go back."

Leaning back in her chair, Power resettled herself: "On that case,

I worked on preparing the claim, because it is basically outside our area of operations. I keep in touch because I'm interested. I think it's been a case that illustrates the massive problems of trying to unscramble the egg and get back to where we started."

"You've got those kinds of cases, which are very difficult, the restitution cases. And you have other cases—which I'm on a lot of— these colored, rural areas which were almost like black homelands for colored people. They live in a way where they have communal use of the land, so it's a matter of just adding to the commonage, buying farms back from white farmers. It's not disrupting the whole social order of life, which makes it a lot easier than the restitution case like the previous one."

"But it also has things like, how will the new land be managed? How will it fit in with the present systems? How will it be allocated? And those are all issues which potentially are problematic in the community. You're adding resources to people who are very under-resourced."

I asked if this redistribution of land was country-wide?

Power nodded. "There is a land claims court and a land claims commission and they're busy. The commission in the Cape Town branch has over 7,000 cases they're working on. And it's not all rural stuff, it's in the towns. People got put out of the central suburbs and stuck out there on the Cape Flats and you can now claim your place back. And there's a whole process of how that goes about."

Another situation involved Cavendish Square, a huge new shopping center just down the street from Cecily's house. People had been removed from there.

"Clearly, they're not going to knock it down and put houses on it, so that's a case of working on compensation."

What about areas like District Six?

"Well, that is a huge problem."

She sighed, "You know, it's just so complicated; working out who should be the beneficiaries of that land being returned. You had land-lords who had tenants in their houses. Now whom do you compensate? The landlord or the people who lived there and got chucked out to the back of beyond?"

"Those kinds of issues are hugely difficult. Millions of rands are involved annually."

"In a citrus area where we have been working, a farmer's land was brought back into the community and that one farm cost 4 million rands ($444,444 US). It was a very valuable farm and a very valuable area. It is becoming quite a problem as to how this will be funded if you really try to buy back all the land."

"The other problem is that we have, in the Bill of Rights, a private property clause. People have to be paid the market value for their land and, in the redistribution program, it has to be willing buyer, willing seller. You can't just take peoples' lands away. They have to be paid out for it."

"In another area where we are working, a place has been developed in vineyards worth millions and millions of rands, more than the annual budget of the whole land reform program. It's just not a possibility to buy all that up, so there they're negotiating about how people could benefit out of what's going on on the land. Is there any other land that could be given in compensation?"

Power's job with the Surplus People Project—she took it in 1993—is full time and she is one of twenty-six paid employees: five black, five white, the others colored. She works out of Springbok, the major town in Namaqualand, 341 miles (550 km) from Cape Town, driving back and forth every week.

She explained how she became involved in SPP.

"When we were in East London—my husband's a pediatrician and he practiced there—I got involved through Black Sash, the Advice Office: the issues of squatters needing land and so on. Then we moved to Johannesburg for a year. I'm actually an occupational therapist and, at that stage, I couldn't get a job in occupational therapy and there was a job in a similar land agency. I started working there. Then we moved back to Cape Town and this was a sister organization of the one in Johannesburg."

Power grew up in Cape Town, the middle one of Noel and Frank Robb's five children. She attended university in Johannesburg and was not an activist. After graduation, she returned to Cape Town to work as an occupational therapist.

From a young age, she said, the Robb children were probably more aware of South Africa's injustices than their friends.

"I was always a member of Black Sash," Power said, "but in Cape Town it was quite a big organization and fairly academic backstage unless you worked in the Advice Office, which I couldn't do if I were working in another job. I managed to get to monthly meetings, but I didn't do much."

"Then when we moved to East London in the eighties, Black Sash was about five people. People like Val (Viljoen) were keeping it going with a handful of members. If you joined there, you were very busy. It's just a whole different world, East London to Cape Town. There's no university there, no students doing all these things. Black Sash and the End Conscription Campaign were, I suppose, the only 'whitey' political organizations that were involved."

"At that stage there were just so many problems in the Eastern Cape, we started an Advice Office. There had been one previously which had collapsed a few years earlier through lack of volunteers and other problems."

"I used to work there afternoons because I worked mornings at occupational therapy. In the '80s, in the Eastern Cape, they were locking up everything that moved. Basically, black organizations couldn't function. They were harrassed by the police eternally. So our Advice Office became extremely busy, a center of a lot of activity, and got us involved in lots of things. It was the only surviving structure of that sort. We were open five days a week and had queues from five in the morning. We'd give out tickets for as many as we could handle in a day."

"There were," she continued, "many incidences of awful police abuse and all the problems of detainees, and so on. Parents came trying to track down missing family members, after their having been beaten by police and put in detention. For a long time many people were in jail and thanks to our white skins we could get information. Plus all the usual kinds of Advice Office stuff with pensions, jobs and the complications of the Ciskei and Transkei. It was a hectically busy office. Through that, we just got more and more involved with all sorts of other activities surrounding it."

"The Security Police would harass us. They would come when we had meetings and slash our tires. Their favorite thing was these silly little tricks, like they distributed thousands of pamphlets in Mdantsane and all the black townships saying, if you want food, drink, jobs, blankets, whatever you need, go to my house—they had a map—on Monday night, six o'clock. You'll get everything you want."

"Fortunately, some people in the townships knew us, and knew the Security Police, and they warned us. We tried to tell people this wasn't true, because people were desperate. But at about six o'clock, down the road came hundreds of people—to my house. We had a handful of Black Sash members and they were all there."

"We wondered what would happen. And more and more people turned up. Fortunately, we had quite a big house. And there were literally over a hundred people in it—upstairs, downstairs, in every room—and outside. We gave them food and explained what happened, why they had been used."

"Then the police came and said we were holding an illegal gathering." Power paused. She looked as if she enjoyed this particular memory. "Actually this backfired beautifully on them. We phoned the *Dispatch* and they came and took a photo of all these people packed in the house. Next morning, it was in the newspaper. That day I just got thousands of phone calls from people who thought it was terrible, and we got blankets and materials. We took the stuff to Mdtansane and people there ended up doing quite nicely."

"Other times, the Security Police would phone up and say, your auntie was dead, or order flowers in your name, or food or drink. Or they'd phone up and threaten to kill you. That type of rubbish, but they didn't lock us up."

"We had that protection of being white. The other people who weren't white, running offices like ours, had been locked up. It was during that violent period of the '80s and we just got very, very involved in all sorts of community problems through the Advice Office."

"We followed endless cases in East London. There were all sorts of battles around squatter removal. We tried all the time to publicize, to make people aware of what was going on. The *Daily Dispatch* would come—usually they were fairly cooperative—and take photos of people being chucked out or whatever. So this kept a record of what these guys were up to."

"We were not great revolutionaries. It was, I suppose, pretty minor stuff. We tried to educate ourselves as well to what was going on. And try to get people to come to public meetings so they could hear what was going on."

The Powers and their three children lived in East London for twelve years. She joined the ANC there after it was unbanned in 1990.

"Black Sash," she recalled, "would not affiliate to any other organization, so were not part of the UDF (United Democratic Front). Though because East London was so small, we worked with them, probably through the ANC as well, again carrying on similar activities, like squatters rights. In East London, there were a lot of people with land issues and that is probably how I got involved in SPP."

I wondered if she had suprised at De Klerk's announcement of Mandela's freedom?

"You knew it was coming, but it was amazing to hear it. 'Am I hearing right?' I worked in a center for mentally handicapped people then, a workshop. We had a radio and we listened to it. You couldn't believe it. Well, you could believe it, but it was amazing."

Like Power, Noel Robb's other children eventually became deeply involved in anti-apartheid work, professionally and in their personal lives, as well. That was not always the case with the children of activists.

"I suppose that's because we didn't suffer. Their involvement did not cause us any hardships," she said. "We didn't feel deprived or neglected. They made us interested in the issues. If you had a mother who was locked up for years because of these activities and you were neglected, you can understand why people would not want to be involved. But we did not have any of those problems. It wasn't an issue to be kicked against."

About the country's future, Power said, "I know there are problems, lots and lots of problems, but I think eventually we'll sort it out. We were so in boxes that people didn't understand other people's cultures. And there are genuine obstacles with language, religion, which are now mixed and weren't before. People were not prepared. There are difficulties and they don't know how to handle them. I think people get very frustrated because everything isn't cured overnight. I know, in just the little area I'm working in, with the best will in the world, the problems are huge."

"All of this is not something you can cure in five minutes. Money is part of it, obviously, but it's not the only thing. I don't feel desperate, because I can see why it is taking a long time."

A few days later, I found the Surplus People Project offices on a back alley in a Cape Town district called Observatory. The entrance, locked, was hidden in a narrow space between concrete windowless buildings in an industrial complex, empty of people.

Aldino waited until I got buzzed in.

Upstairs, a receptionist said to help myself to informational material and pointed out a vacant office with a table across the hall.

The following, excerpted from *Overview, 1960–1982*, was published in 1983 by the Durban office of the South African Institute of Race Relations.

The people who have been moved have, with the exception of a tiny number of whites affected by the Group Areas Act, been black: disenfranchised, debarred from participating in the government that has passed the laws and enforced the regulations that govern these removals. Sometimes they were ousted violently, their houses bulldozed; sometimes less overtly, through intimidation, closure of shops, schools, new restrictions on existing buildings.

Between a quarter and a fifth of the removals had affected Indians and coloreds. They were moved mainly in terms of the Group Areas Act of 1950 which enforced rigid segregation in residential and trading areas between Indians, coloreds and whites.

Further information came from a Surplus People Project publication: Categories of relocation included farm removals, mission or black-owned properties, "badly situated" tribal reserve areas, urban relocation, group areas removal, "directly political." The largest single category was farm evictions with group area removals, such as District Six, second.

The 1960 to mid-1982 removals SPP had been able to verify could be rounded off to 3,500,000, almost 10 percent of the present population of the country.

Influx control was also a huge factor and the numbers of individuals physically removed from metropolitan areas, as well as those arrested, charged, or fined in terms of influx control, were staggering. From the beginning of 1979 to the middle of 1981, total arrests in eleven major urban centers totalled 289,237.

Between 1960 and 1984, Africans living in homelands rose by 54 percent, according to another source. There will be no more black South Africans, declared Connie Mulder, Minister of Plural Relations, in 1978. In other words, blacks would be Transkeians, or Ciskeians, citizens of some arbitrary homeland, taken to a place they may have never seen.

Mdantsane in the Ciskei, 12.4 miles (20 km) from East

London, was the oldest relocation area surveyed by SPP and had been established in the early 1960s. There was, the publication noted, an almost total dearth of employment opportunities in relocation areas.

XX
❦ *Linda Fortune*
District Six meant everything to me. It was my home

Posters from Norway, Manchester, England, and the township of Khayelitsha hung above a visitors-sign-in-here stop at the District Six Museum. Past that table by the door, a map covered most of the floor—and it was a big, open room—drawn on oilcoth with either poster paints or crayons. Smart Lane, Primrose Street, all the streets in District Six, Arundel, Cowley ... and in each block, squares for the houses on those streets. Many of the squares had been lettered in with family names.

More of the district showed up in mounted black and white photographs on walls around the perimeter. Men stood around a billiard-like table, shooting pucks with cues in a game called kerrem; costumed figures cavorted at a street carnival; shopkeepers behind counters; three men looked at the camera from a doorway; rooftops above Lee Street; a bus conductor; a horse and cart on Upper Darling Street; a white-gowned bride bidding an emotional goodbye to her mother; a wedding in the Aspeling Street mosque; a domino game; street sweeper with push broom; a uniformed Muslim brigade. Individual stories of a place and time gone forever.

Elsewhere were displayed newspaper records, poetry, banners and metal street signs.

Where the map was, pews once lined up. The museum in central Cape Town had been the Central Methodist Mission and for a century had ministered to the people of the district which bordered it.

Cecily whispered that the young man talking with someone across the room was David Kramer, who had co-written *District Six: The Musical.* Kramer wore an orange polo shirt, slightly pegged pants, and a black, flat fedora, a pork-pie hat in the zoot-suit era.

Against one wall stood a stolid relic of apartheid, a bench: "Europeans Only, Slegs Blankes," in black letters on the slats of the back. A stack of books for sale included EKM Dido's.

Another memento of the recent past was a sign in Afrikaans and English:

> For Use by White Persons; These public premises and the amenities thereof have been reserved for the exclusive use of white persons.
> —By order Provincial Secretary

Linda Fortune, author of *The House in Tyne Street: Childhood Memories of District Six*, worked at the District Six Museum. She waved a group of touring grammar school students out the door and we went upstairs and past the choir loft to sit on a bench at the far end of the open balcony.

She carried herself in a manner that suggested she desired a place in the background, to be inconspicuous, and her quiet, even voice reinforced that first impression. She was medium-height and wore dark clothes. Her hair was dark and wavy. With light skin and regular features, her nice face would be hard to remember in any detail.

Fortune was born in District Six in 1950 and lived there until 1971. She began by recalling her memories.

"The rumor was going around since the '60s that the District would be declared a white area," she said. "When it was official and all in the newspapers, things started to change in District Six. People were very worried: 'What is going to happen to us?' 'Where will we be rehoused?' 'Where will we work?' 'Where will our children go to school?' And it was a very depressing time for the grown-ups. I was a teenager at the time and being a teenager you feel it's not your responsibility, it's your parents' problem. They must sort it out."

"But life went on. And then when I got to 22, the final blow came. My dad had died in March and my mother had been left with seven children. Three of us were working at the time. The other ones were at school so my mother was at home by herself when the officials came and forced her to sign the papers to get out of District Six."

That had always been puzzling to me. Often victims must sign something that made what was happening to them "official." Why had government bothered? There was never any recourse to what it said to do.

Fortune said: "This big, powerful person from the Department of Community Development told her that if she didn't sign these papers, he couldn't guarantee she would get another house and, if she kept them waiting too long, they would come and bulldoze our house while we were in it. She was very frightened of this."

"And in a way she bribed him, too. I had a very beautiful pen and I'd left it home that one day. She said to him, if she does sign, will she get a nice house?"

"He said, 'Yes, but only if you give me that pen.' And there were stories going around that officials from the Group Areas Act also, when they discovered there were beautiful girls in the house—and District Six had beautiful women—the young daughters of the people had to go on dates with these men. In that way, they would either move them up higher in the area, before the bulldozers came, or they didn't have to move to the townships almost immediately."

"My mother signed the papers in March and they wanted us to leave right then. But when she discussed it with us, we said we are working, the younger children are at school in District Six, and we'd have to organize them to other schools in the Cape Flats."

"When the man from the Group Areas came again, she told him, as scared as she was, he would have to wait for us to leave in December when the children finished their school year. After they have written their exams, we will go."

Her mother's dream was to buy a house for her family. Linda and her sister promised they would pay the required deposit and bond.

"But," Fortune continued, "when we made application we could not, because my mother was a single parent, my father passed away. They said they had no guarantee that these two young people will keep on paying the bond."

Fortune switched position on the wooden bench, smoothed her skirt and recrossed her ankles.

"My mother was then forced to take a council house in Hanover Park. But because of the pen this man had taken, he gave us a nice house. It only had two bedrooms, but you could make a small garden in front and there was a bit of a backyard where we could put up washing lines."

I asked if neighbors in District Six had moved nearby.

"We discovered only one neighbor from District Six," Fortune replied. "She lived around the corner from us, an elderly lady. We later discovered that others we knew were living in different areas in Hanover. We would meet at the terminus, but that didn't come until later. When we moved in there wasn't anyone. And there wasn't a school, there wasn't a shop, there wasn't a telephone box, a doctor—no infrastructure. There was absolutely nothing in these townships. Only the houses."

Hanover Park was approximately twelve miles from Cape Town.

"When I lived in District Six," she recalled, "it would take me ten minutes to get to my place of work. I was a secretary in an insurance company. Out in the township it would take me an hour and a half in the morning, an hour and a half in the evening. When we took the train to the nearest station, Landsdowne, we then had to walk from Landsdowne through the bush to get to our house."

"Those with cars, they would give people lifts. Then people started using their own cars like taxis and eventually all these minibus taxis evolved. That whole new culture developed because of the removals."

"I was going with someone and a year later, in 1971, I got

engaged; in 1973 I married. I only lived in Hanover Park for two years, then I went to stay in the northern suburbs."

Her husband, a brick layer when they married, had advanced to building contractor. They had three children: a son then 23, a daughter of 19 and a son, 13.

"Whenever I used to read something about District Six—this was now when we moved out—or listened to something on the radio, or even if I met someone in the street, we stopped and talked about the area and reminisced," Fortune said. "When I walked away from that person, I felt a yearning. I am longing for this place. I want to go back."

"District Six meant everything to me. It was my home. The worst thing that happened there was when we were forced to leave. I was going to be married. I was going to find a place of my own. But the mere fact that we were forced out, so—one could almost say—brutally. Because it happened to so many people, it was an exodus, like an exile out of a place. This is the thing I could never lay to rest."

"Like you never said goodbye to someone. People were leaving in all directions. Trucks were coming into the area, moving people all the time. We never even had a chance to exchange addresses, or explain to this person how to get to where we are going, because we ourselves had to go and find out where we are going now. So it was always a longing to see other people from the area."

"You asked how I got connected to this museum. It was because of that interest in District Six. Over the years, though I never forgot about District Six, I also didn't live in the past. I went on with my life, I improved in where I worked, changed jobs a couple of times, had my children."

"Then one day when I got retrenched, I had some time on my hands and started writing all my feelings. And as I started to write, more and more memories came flowing, and then I would meet someone again from the area. They would say something and that would awake more memories. And I'll just go on and jot it down."

"Then I had this manuscript and I was looking for a publisher and it happened there was a talk show on TV with Vincent Kolbe, who was a librarian in District Six. I phoned him up and reminded him of who I was, was one of his library members. He said, 'Yes. Of course I know you. Haven't seen you for so long.' And he put me in touch with the director of this museum."

"She said, 'Come in, let me see what you've written.' In the meantime, I'd taken my manuscript to a few publishers and they'd sent it back to me. It was just before the elections in 1994 and they were all into doing cookery books and books on the environment. So I thought, but I've got to get this published. It's important to tell this story, particularly to young people. It's a part of history."

"I came to the museum and left it with her. This was in about August, and in September I received a letter from the museum: They are going to start with an exhibition celebrating the district and can I attend these meetings? They feel I have some valuable input and some interest."

"In that way, I came to more and more meetings and when they got involved with the setting up of the streets exhibition—as a celebration of receiving the actual signs back—I came as a volunteer."

Fortune stood up and looked over the rail. A group of school children swarmed around the entrance and spilled over into the open area between the wall exhibits and the map. She watched until a man came through from the back to talk to them.

I asked when the museum opened?

Fortune smiled: "In December of 1994. Right here in this old Methodist Church. And it was supposed to be a two-week District Six Streets celebration, but it is still going on because, when we wanted to close the streets exhibition down, we couldn't close it down. We extended the exhibition. And in 1994, more and more schools phoned us up. Can they come and visit this museum?"

"And we have progressed so far. At the end of 1997, we had 10,000 students who visited this museum. In 1997 alone. And now we have a school come almost every day up until April."

I was curious as to what students wanted to know about.

"Their past," she said. "The young children in Cape Town don't know anything about their own history. They've been taught colonial history, about Jan van Riebeeck, but nothing about Cape Town. They've been denied their own history."

"You know, these young children, they are growing up so beautifully, free and easy. They can make their own choices of who their friends will be, even where they go to school if their parents can afford it. They can mix freely. Now that for me is absolutely wonderful. And they can learn from one another's cultures, from one another. And that is how I grew up in District Six."

"Now my 13-year-old son asked me last year, 'What is a racist and what is apartheid?'"

"I said, 'But Kevin, didn't your teachers ever talk to you about apartheid, racism?'"

"He said, 'No, Mommy, I read it in your book.' So I had to go and explain to him how people then were meant to be separate, even in the schools."

"He said, 'But that can't be. People can't be kept apart.'"

"I started explaining. But he said, 'I don't understand how you put up with it. What did you do?' Today's children don't have to go through apartheid like we did. If you liked a particular beach, you couldn't go there if you weren't the right color. You weren't allowed."

Visitors started drifting upstairs where there were more photographs on standing panels. We gathered our things and started down.

Though Fortune came to the museum as a volunteer, she was then an employee. A colleague was also an ex-resident of District Six.

"He used to come here for months, with no payment," she explained, "but he enjoyed being here, because this was the place where he met all of his friends, some of which he hasn't seen for forty years."

I asked where the money came from to keep the museum going.

Mainly donations, Fortune said. "We also have a book store and a table which we call the coffee shop and a donation box there. We are self-supporting, but we did receive some support from the Netherlands, also from the Germans, they sponsored our sculpture exhibition. And if it wasn't for the Ford Foundation, we wouldn't be here. They started us off and it is through their wonderful support—and their blessing I think—that we have come so far."

The King and Queen of Norway were expected soon, Fortune said. On the walls were photos of museum staff with other famous people: the monarchs of Sweden, queen of the Netherlands, Mary Robinson, president of Ireland, then U.S. Vice-President Al Gore.

"Since we started," Fortune said, "we have had the streets exhibition. We've had a sports exhibition which was sports of the Western Cape; we've had a sculpture exhibition; a Steve Biko exhibition. We are now busy with a George Hallett collection. He took photographs in Cape Town as a young man. He put all his work away for about twenty-five years. He was in exile in France and he's come back."

Fortune smiled at a couple slowly strolling past, reading the memorabilia on the wall. "Just last week," she continued, "a lady came into the museum. I at first didn't recognize her. As she walked, I could see she was very interested in what was going on. Then I looked in her face and called out her name and she called out my name and we hugged."

"I said, 'I'm so happy to see you. But where is your sister, Gigi?' Gigi was my friend."

"She said Gigi is living in Durban. She gave me Gigi's phone number and I phoned up that night."

"I said, 'Gigi, this is Linda.'"

" 'Linda?'"

"I said, 'Yes!'" Fortune beamed. "It was so wonderful speaking to her. I hadn't seen Gigi for thirty years."

Many who visit the museum are, like her friend's sister, former District Six residents.

"They come here because they can show their families where they lived. The first time it is very emotional. It is not easy for ex-residents. The first thing they are faced with are the street names. And their street name portrays all their memories and sometimes that is very hard."

"But they do come again, normally on Saturday, so they can bring their husbands and children or granny or whatever. Then they fill in their name on the house in the street where they used to live. On the map on the floor. And they will write their names on the cloth of memories." This was a white sheet, hanging in the back of the room, next to a cup of felt pens.

Visitors include not only ex-residents in South Africa, but district people who have emigrated to Britain, Australia, New Zealand and Canada.

"They bring their families here," Fortune said. "Sometimes it gets very sad—a woman who might have been very young when she left to get married, or to continue her career overseas. They will spend hours in this place. We believe they are remembering and reconciling with the past."

Fortune said her reconciliation with that past began in 1988 when she started her book.

"I had been to see *District Six: The Musical* by David Kramer. I was sitting in that audience and I was laughing and I was weeping and then I thought, if they can write a musical about District Six, I can write my book. District Six was not just a song and dance. There was so much more."

"And that night I don't think I slept. I just wrote and wrote and wrote. I added to it all the time. I had a vision, I had a dream, and I have got to keep at it. Sometimes I would leave it for a little while, but I finished it and the problem then was finding a publisher. This was in the days of apartheid and even though this story is simple, hasn't got anything that qualifies it to be banned, I had the feeling it would be banned. I may even have gone to prison.

"So I had to wait until after the elections. But the editor from Kwela Books—she'd lost my phone number—she sent me a telegram, asking me to call her immediately. This was in 1994. She said the book was well worth publishing, but she had to work on it. It came out 23rd May 1996. My granddaughter was born on the same day."

The House in Tyne Street is now required reading for primary school children, she said with pride.

"I'm also busy on my next book," Fortune said. "It is about a beach where colored fishermen lived in the caves and how they were also forced out of their homes. The beach is 14 km (9 miles) out of Cape Town. About ten families lived in this place, on the beach, in the caves. Children will find this very exciting, because they can actually go and explore the places where I'm writing about."

I asked when she wrote.

"I'm here at the museum, from 9 to 3. Then I have to do the normal things a woman does—cook, see to the children, do all the little chores—and I have to squeeze my writing in between. When my thoughts wake me in the middle of the night, I have my pen and pad by the bed, and I put my light on and I just write, write, write. Even on the train, whenever I have the opportunity, I write down the thoughts which come to me."

We had stopped to talk at the bottom of the old church steps into the main hall. As we prepared to part, Fortune said, her voice quieter but emotional: "If I can just mention, having grown up in the apartheid years was, for me, something very terrible. You weren't paid equally for the work that you did, you couldn't even go to certain places. We were oppressed by apartheid, especially women."

We said goodbye near the entrance. I turned around as I went out and saw Fortune, bent over, engaged in talk with a visiting toddler.

After leaving the museum, Cecily drove into the hillsides below Table Mountain. Adjacent to the blank weediness of District Six lay the Malay Quarter which had been prettily restored: lines of common wall houses, some of them two-story, painted in pastel shades. Architecturally, these looked to be near relatives to Cape Dutch: without ornamentation, cleanly geometric, painted masonry walls with wooden sash windows and tile roofs. They ranged across the hills, up and down the slopes with fine views across District Six to the sea.

Cecily said the Cape Coloreds were descendants of Malaysians and whites, often Muslims, whereas in other areas of South Africa, the majority of coloreds were a mix of white and black.

At the museum, I had picked up a short history of District Six, gathered from newspaper articles written by Don Pinnock and Lucien Le Grange. What follows is taken from that document.

In 1838, the Cape slaves were freed. Many were Muslims of Malay origin. They gathered on the perimeter of Cape Town in temporary housing. Many of those former slaves were skilled and in time came to monopolize many of the skilled trades in the city. Because of the increasing pressure of black labor in the Eastern Province, an unskilled colored proletariat began drifting into the city. This movement was later joined by blacks and whites. By the time District Six was named in 1867, it was already overcrowded.

After 1885, development speeded up. The mining boom brought skilled British artisans and the Boer War swelled the town's population with refugees from the Transvaal. Much building took place in District Six during the war, giving rise to a variety of architectural styles. During the early 1900s "poor whites" fled to the towns which increased the pressure on District Six.

After 1945, little was done to improve conditions in District Six and much of it began to deteriorate until it was generally regarded as a slum. In 1966, the Group Areas Act which designated residential areas on a racial basis, was applied to District Six and it was declared a white group area. All residents were forced to move out, sometimes physically carried from their houses and loaded onto trucks. As houses were vacated, they were bulldozed.

In 1966 more than 60,000 people lived in the District. By the early '80s it was only a barren, windswept piece of land in the middle of a large city.

XXI
⚜ *Melanie Verwoerd*
If there is ever a time to be in Parliament, it is now

In the small foyer off the lobby of the Parliament building, two blonde women at the desk announced themselves as tourists. A heavy-set black man on a couch listened to Afrikaans on a two-way radio. The TV in the corner showed a still photo of the building and a South African flag. When it was my turn, the desk attendant dialed MP Melanie Verwoerd's extension. Busy. He left with the tourists and gestured at the phone on the counter: I should keep trying. When he returned a few minutes later, I still had not been able to get through, but he shrugged and took me to Verwoerd's office on an upper floor.

She was at her desk, still on the phone. I sat in the chair across from her and set out what I needed. Melanie Verwoerd was small, short and petite, young and pretty. She had red hair which was long and wavy. Her dress came in two parts: a long-sleeved top layer, dark blue and sheer with embossing, worn like a tunic over a slip-like dress also dark blue. The frames of her glasses were round. My immediate impression was pert, saucy, straight-forward, indeed as she turned out to be.

She hung up, apologizing. She had been talking to her family. She is the mother of two, one seven-and-a-half and the other just turned five. They live in Cape Town now. Commuting from Stellenbosch just became too much, she said.

"Basically, we're here because of them, the children," Verwoerd said. "Going for a whole week without seeing them awake was getting to me. We decided at that stage to move. My husband is commuting at the moment to Stellenbosch, but that is against the traffic so it's easier. He is back at the university. The last eighteen months he was on unpaid leave, doing research for the Truth Commission."

At the outset, she wanted to say that, despite being a very strong feminist, her story "will sort of flow over my husband's. They are just too interlinked."

"I was born in Pretoria," she began, "and moved to the Cape, to a town called the Strand, when I was five years old, lived in Stellenbosch since I was about thirteen. My parents were very much Afrikans—my grandmother was a Van der Merwe. Both maternal and paternal ancestors are of Dutch descent."

"My father is an academic, at the University of Stellenbosch. My mother is a computer scientist, also at the University of Stellenbosch. Usual Afrikaner story, grew up in a very traditional Afrikans household, white schools, white church—Dutch Reformed—white neighborhood."

"From my secondary years I was at school in Stellenbosch then went on to university. Did a degree in theology at Stellenbosch. I was the only woman in a class of fifty men. Theology was a very strange thing for a woman to do, particularly an Afrikans woman. I was going to do teaching. I did. For a week. Then decided I was going to die if I kept doing it. I wanted to become a minister. I felt quite a deeply religious passion at that stage."

"—Changed a lot in the three years I did the degree. Became very disillusioned with the church, with their sexism and racism. The philosophy too. That came together."

"The sexism part: I was always told that I'm part of the course, but nothing official. Women could not be ordained at that stage. So I did it very much on the trust that things would change. By the end of my third year, in fact, it did change. But my view of that synod when it changed is that they didn't want to address the racial issues, not that there was a fundamental change of opinion. It was either they were going to accept blacks into the church or they would accept women to be ordained."

"Politically, I got sick of the racial comments in class." Verwoerd's grin managed to be mischievous as well as triumphant. "Actually, I got into quite a bit of trouble commenting on the racism of the lecturers."

"At the end of the third year, you get a BA degree in theology and then decide if you're going to continue for three more years. I decided then not to continue in theology. I went on in philosophy and did honors. Also at the end of that year, I married Wilhelm. I'd met him at the end of my first year. Wilhelm did the same as I did: BA in theology—he's a little older than I am, three years—and then he was busy with his MA in philosophy."

Verwoerd is a Member of Parliament and ANC. Growing up in the Afrikaner community, where did she first get the idea that apartheid was wrong?

"My parents, I think," replied Verwoerd. "I always got the impression, from my mother especially, that something was not right. In the sense that she would often throw a side comment about how dreadful things were. My mother, and my father for that matter, had a very strong social conscience—taking clothes to people, that sort of thing—but in a very paternalistic kind of way."

"Still, today, they wouldn't even consider voting for the ANC. My mother would vote for the Democratic Party, which is regarded as slightly more liberal. My father was National Party until recently. But he is part of the RDP Forum—the Reconstruction Development Forum—in his area, which is not hardline."

"In that respect I'm certainly different from my husband who grew up in a very hardline Afrikaner home. His father is the eldest son of the late prime minister."

Hendrick Verwoerd was prime minister from 1958 until his assassination in 1966. Verwoerd, wrote Allister Sparks in *Tomorrow Is Another Country* (University of Chicago Press, 1995), is the name identified more than any other with apartheid. Sparks called him the chief architect and the most ruthless implementer of the doctrine that turned South Africa into the world symbol of racial oppression, "apartheid's Karl Marx and Stalin rolled into one."

Wilhelm, his wife said, was two when his grandfather was killed. "He can't recall him, but obviously the family is very ideological."

At the time we talked, her husband's family was deeply involved in efforts to establish an Afrikaner homeland in the center of the country. His grandmother, widow of the prime minister, lived there in the small town of Orania.

"If I say my view changed in university," Verwoerd continued, "it had, but not yet so dramatically. I've always had a fairly hard head, and I certainly had a very strong idea that people should be equal. But I didn't understand anything about the structure of politics in the country. We never got taught that. Growing up in the kind of Christian national education that we did, you were not only not encouraged, you weren't allowed to question adults on anything. At school questions were not the in thing."

She paused a moment before continuing. "I believe the main part of my change came during my second year. That's why I say Wilhelm's and my stories flow into one another. Wilhelm then got a Rhodes scholarship and on his way there, he studied in Holland for three months."

"This was his first time out of the country and in Holland he landed in a house with mainly South African exiles, mostly ANC. Very hard for him, very big shock—everything. They confronted him with all the South African books and stuff banned here. He started sending some of this back to me, like Donald Woods' book (*Biko*: Henry Holt & Co. 1978, 1987), Mandela's transcript of his trial et cetera, et cetera. Since this was all completely banned in South Africa, we were very lucky not to get caught out at that stage."

Wilhelm's introduction to South Africans with totally different political philosophies coincided with hers. She had begun attending meetings of new, alternative, opposition organizations such as IDASA (Institute for Democratic Alternatives in South Africa).

"People would pitch up at IDASA conferences," Verwoerd recalled, "—banned people—then evaporate again within a few minutes after speaking. Things like that, inside the country, were really influential for me."

"Wilhelm went to Oxford from Holland and we got married a year and a half later in South Africa. We stayed a year in the country. I finished honors and he finished his MA in philosophy here. During which time he also took a study trip into Africa and met some ANC leaders there. Came back and was very much influenced by the whole trip."

"But at that stage, end of '88, we were on our way back to Oxford to complete the Rhodes scholarship. And this was just about when PW (Botha) went down and FW (De Klerk) took over."

She stopped. "I think I must interrupt myself. At the end of my second year, which was '86 and Wilhelm was in Oxford for the first time, I went to visit him the end of that year. During that period I met quite a few South African exiles, Africans, who had fled the country. They just hammered me for nights. And I tried every rational argument in the books about Buthelezi (Zulu chief, considered a sell-out to the government by its opponents), about everybody. After a few nights, the arguments didn't work out very well."

"I came back and I was quite shattered. It was very hard. I felt that every authority figure I had ever known had been lying to me. I was angry, disillusioned. I must have been an extremely difficult student after that."

I was curious as to what her parents thought of her new views.

"They didn't respond very much," Verwoerd replied. "At that stage I was living in the house again, having come back to save money."

"I have a very close relationship with my parents, especially with my mother, to this day, in spite of our difference in politics. I think they just tried to prevent problems. The ANC then was still banned and if you opened your mouth too much, the Security Police, who had people in every single class, in every single hostel—fellow students—would start sort of taking notes. But they were so stupid, it was always very easy to know which ones they were."

She grinned impishly, "Actually, I enjoyed taking them for a ride."

"My parents were a bit worried. It wasn't a nice time. We were in a state of emergency."

"I don't want to make it sound glamorous because it wasn't," Verwoerd continued. "I was dead scared and I didn't do much at that stage except, gradually, to speak out."

"So back at Oxford in '89, middle of '90. We just sort of settled in and became comfortable with the idea that we felt completely different than most other white South Africans. Wilhelm also did a lot of research on his grandfather, to look the ghost in the eye, as it were. It was very painful for him."

They had been at Oxford when F.W. de Klerk announced Mandela's release from prison. Had they anticipated that?

"I think most people felt things were slipping away, but were surprised at the speed, and wondered, why now?," Verwoerd replied. She shook her head. "It was funny. We sat with some Russian friends and some English friends and American friends, watching this little screen for hours. Then out to this bottle store: Did they still have a bit of champagne left? It was frustrating being at Oxford, because things would then begin to happen."

"At that stage, Rhodes scholars get offers overseas. We also had that decision. If we were coming back. At that time, most South Africans didn't. For us that wasn't ever really an issue. We felt very committed, very obliged under the privileges we received from the country. And I think, fundamentally, as much as we loved England and being away from the pressures of South Africa for a little while, we were African. That was one thing overseas made clear to us. We couldn't live anywhere else."

Their first child was born just before they left Oxford in mid-1990. Back in South Africa, Wilhelm began teaching philosophy at Stellenbosch University and they both tried to settle in.

"We wanted to do something, but were very careful," Verwoerd recalled. "By that time we knew the whole ANC issue was going to be a big thing with the family. Also a lot of people, especially whites, came back from studying overseas and did a lot of things which we called 'on the rebound.' They then really hated the whites, hated everybody, hated the country, and did all kinds of dramatic stuff. But after a few months, they just blow off and become good, middle-of-the-road, establishment people again. So we were careful that, A, that didn't happen, and B, people didn't perceive whatever we did as that."

"We waited and we struggled and tried to speak to Wilhelm's parents: to try to bring them along from where we'd been; to show them the pieces Wilhelm wrote in Oxford on his grandfather's role. Wilhelm tried to look at what happened. He had to do that in Oxford. He couldn't do it here."

"In the beginning of 1991, we met President Mandela, then only president of the ANC, at a cocktail function at Stellenbosch. By which stage I had done lots of things. I was working at the university part time, very unhappy, but in need of money, trying to finish up an MA in Feminist Theology—which I only finished up last year. *Finally.* I'd also formed a sort of association to help house workers, domestic workers, because they weren't covered by any labor laws."

"Meeting the president was quite something. Knowing our family background, people felt he would be interested in meeting us. Someone introduced Wilhelm and Mandela to each other. Wilhelm tried to say how sorry he was about what happened in the past and especially his family's role in the whole thing."

"Mr. Mandela looked at him and said, 'No. The past is the past.'"

"Then he said, 'As a Verwoerd, you must think very carefully about where you are going in the future. Because people will stop and look at what you are doing.'"

"He also inquired about Wilhelm's grandmother. 'How is she doing? Is she still well? If she won't resent you for saying this, will you please tell her that I send her my regards and I'm happy she lived to be such a ripe old age.' It was incredibly touching."

Verwoerd's mischevious expression came again: "He'd invited all the old presidents' wives to have tea with him. She wouldn't come. She said she wasn't comfortable traveling anymore. She's 96 now. But healthy still."

"But in a very gracious way—she's a very gracious lady—she said to Mandela, 'If you are ever in my neighborhood, please feel free to call.' And, of course, he called her bluff and went with the helicopters and the whole international press to Orania and had tea with her. Afterward, people in Orania said he'd been treated like a foreign head of state."

"Shortly after our meeting with President Mandela, I remember driving home from work one day, it was 5 o'clock, and watching all these African women leaving this all-white area after having done their work. And I felt a bit of despair. I thought apartheid had been so successful in what it set out to do—which was keeping us apart—that unless one actually did something very dramatic, took a very concrete step, you would not be able to get over those barriers. It will stay with them and us for many generations. All of this came together at the same time."

"I'd been going, off and on, to ANC meetings in friends' houses in Stellenbosch," Verwoerd continued. "That night I went, came home, and said to Wilhelm, 'I'm going to sign up.' He was quite happy with that, but he didn't want to sign up at that stage. I didn't think it would be much of a fuss in the media, but he obviously sensed that it would be."

"He said, 'Look, why don't you try it out? If you decide it's not the right place to be, at least we'll know.' I joined. We asked the ANC, which was very gracious about this, not to make a fuss, and they didn't."

"Wilhlem joined about eight months later. He came to the point where he felt compelled to. He could not find an excuse convincing enough not to."

"Things then went a bit fast for me. Shortly after I joined, I got elected onto the executive of the local ANC branch, at Stellenbosch. Wonderful. I served from '92 until I got into Parliament. Enjoyed it very much. A major learning school. It was free. Nobody knew about it. Learned everything I know about politics."

"I worked in the townships, political mobilization work, organizing mass rallies, picking up issues for people. The nice thing was, being white, I could fool officials easily. They didn't know I was in the

ANC. So I could solve housing problems by getting the officials to talk themselves into a fix and then saying, 'I am actually the ANC.'"

"Then I suppose the next part of the story was that the press did find out about it. Just a line in a column on the back of an Afrikaans magazine: 'We believe there is a Verwoerd in the ANC.' I didn't think much of it. Next day, one of the weekend newspapers also ran a one-liner on it. Then all the newspapers picked it up."

"Someone called and wanted to interview me. I said I didn't want to be interviewed. He said, 'Look, we're going to make a story about this whether you like it or not. Either you cooperate and you can have some editing in this article or else we're going to call anyone who knows you very well, including your parents-in-law.' In trying to prevent that, I consulted with Wilhelm."

"He said, 'My parents aren't going to worry about you too much. Try not to say that I'm involved.' And he wasn't too involved. He wasn't active."

"So we went through the whole interview. The reporter sent me the fax copy. In it he said—maybe it was a trick on his side—Wilhelm wasn't a member. I had to phone him and say, 'You can't actually say that. Why is Wilhelm featuring in this article?' And that was all he wanted from me. He said, 'I have to call your in-laws for comments.'"

"Even though I'd been in the ANC for more than a year, Wilhelm for eight months, having little children who knew everything about the ANC, we had now to inform the in-laws so they don't read it in the newspaper as a shock."

Verwoerd's face reflected a difficult situation that still troubled her. "Wilhelm tried to. It didn't go very well. His father hasn't spoken to us since. That's now been five years. I try not to talk about it too much to the press. I obviously do think about it a lot."

"He does see our children. We make a very special effort, because we believe it's important for our kids to know their grandparents. It's extremely difficult for Wilhelm's mother because she's a very traditional woman who must obey her husband but whose life has gone into her children. For her sake, what we've done is to take the

267

kids there. We leave them and pick them up, because my father-in-law won't interact with the kids when we're there. He will leave the room when we arrive.

"Wilhelm actually wrote a book (*My Winds of Change:* Raven 1997). Basically, it's a letter to his father to try to form some healing there. This has been very hard for Wilhelm, very painful. And his father also chose to go to the press about it. His father very publicly said he wishes to disengage himself from his son."

"It's difficult for me and the children as well. We haven't told them, but I think the older girl senses something. Sometime soon we'll have to sit down and do some hard talking."

"After it went into the media, Wilhelm was asked to speak at ANC rallies. He did. he felt that if he could contribute in any way, he should."

"I was happily carrying on in Stellenbosch, working within the ANC, raising two toddlers, working at the university writing computer programs, and trying to finish the MA," Verwoerd laughed, "—which is a little refrain through my life."

"Then I got asked, out of the blue, middle of '93: 'Will you please come and speak at a rally with Mandela?' I said, 'No. I think you're actually looking for my husband.'"

"I remember very vividly: I was trying to help a mother and I was sitting with this screaming child on my lap."

" 'No,' they said, 'We want you. Definitely you. We need a woman.'"

"And I did it and it was astonishing: 4,000 people, the first time in my life I'd spoken on a stage—the Civic in Cape Town. I was really scared. They'd said I could speak on anything, and I basically spoke on why whites should reconsider their role in South Africa. Thereafter it seemed that Wilhelm and I both constantly spoke."

"By the end of that year I got elected onto the Provincial Executive of the ANC in the Western Cape. Three months later I was in Parliament, so it happened fast. Thrilling and amazing. If there is ever a time to be in Parliament it is now, though it's probably the hardest time in any country's history."

Verwoerd paused a moment: "We had a lecturer at Stellenbosch: in philosophy, an amazing man, who started one of his lectures by walking into the class, looking at the hundreds of students, saying, 'I'm leaving you with one question: What does it mean to be in this class, in this town, in this country, on the continent, at this time of the world's history?' And then he leaves again. I think it is a bit of that. It's amazing to be here at this time. It's very humbling, but it's wonderful."

The legislative committee with which Verwoerd spends most of her time is constitutional development. The section of that that interests her most is local government, involved with a redesign of the entire local government system. Verwoerd was also on the committee dealing with communications and broadcasting and postal services. This she described as big business and added, "I don't like the money side of things."

She remains on many ad hoc committees—dealing with legislation on surrogate motherhood; setting up of a youth commission; salaries of Members of Parliament; whether members should be allowed to "cross the floor," join another party.

That week her husband had returned from the Truth and Reconciliation Commission to the University of Stellensbosh. He had been with the TRC research unit involved in content: determining definitions of gross human rights abuse and whether those in the active military, both sides, could be considered victims of human rights abuses, and under what conditions.

I asked Verwoerd if she planned to run for Parliament in the 1999 elections?

"For the last few years I've been ducking that question very determinedly," she replied. "I'm worried about people who say they want to remain in politics forever. It seems to me they start doing things to get re-elected rather than things they believe in."

"Obviously, with 1999 being an election year, that question is becoming very imminent. One can't keep ducking it. Where I am now, I feel the work is not finished. And I can't think of anything else at the moment I really want to do. It's great to be in a position where if people phone you and need your help, from time to time, you can help them."

Verwoerd stopped for a few moments, then said, "The difficult part is personal. I'm very conscious of the price the family pays and especially with small children. That will always be my painful paying off. One of my biggest fears is that my kids, though they most probably will do this no matter what I do, will say when they're 15: 'You had time for all the other people, but not for me.'"

"For the moment I think, yes. If I get on to the ANC list again which is not a given for any of us."

"Future of South Africa? I'm very—how do you say it in English?—optimistic. But it's not as if I think everything's going to be a rose garden. Actually it's a very realistic optimism I hold, in the sense that I believe that we are going to face enormous challenges, economically, socially, on all levels."

"This country was left, and remains in, quite a bad state. The demands are enormous. People will have to give up things. As long as we don't give up our dreams. The dreaming part needs to stay."

"It's going to be hard, especially economically. I sometimes speak to white audiences on whether they have a future. It actually irritates me to do that because I think we should, in this country, stop asking if we have a future. We should start co-creating that future."

"But it will most probably be hard. Everything is not going to stay as comfortable for the privileged as it was. The euphoria is gone for most people in South Africa I think."

"I believe we must remind ourselves that this truly is a miracle. I don't know that miracle is the right word since it means people didn't actually work for it, don't work at it. But it could have gone so differently and it was very close."

I had scheduled another interview at Parliament after Verwoerd. When I left her office, I checked in again at the front desk. Would they please call Patricia de Lille? The attendant dialed her extension and said I was downstairs. "Not possible," he told me, hanging up the receiver: "Another meeting."

I felt like arguing, or asking him to call again but did neither. I walked out, stood beside the main gate. Pigeons came and went on Louis Botha's stone head—"hero, farmer ..."—and that of his horse. Both looked as if they were guarding the compound from some hordes just over the horizon. After an hour, I asked a guard about the closest phone. Two blocks away, an open booth surrounded by loitering men. I decided not to stop and came back to wait again by the statue.

Aldino didn't arrive for another half hour. He felt badly and explained that he had become involved and lost track of time. At home he said, "This ride's on me."

XXII
〰 *Ela Gandhi*

My children grew up with us being banned

A South African flag whipped in the wind outside Ela Gandhi's dormer window: another tiny Parliament office, a single desk tucked under a sloping ceiling.

Gandhi was on the phone when I appeared at her open door. She wore a long traditional Indian gown with a length of material across one shoulder, both patterned with shades of amber and gold. I imagined India to be made of those colors.

Her phone conversation concerned a convention in Israel in July. While she talked, I looked around. Posters about women's issues—family planning, spouse abuse, equal pay—hung on the walls. One poster was from the Fourth UN Conference on Women in Beijing in 1995. Gandhi hung up. The phone rang again. She sounded annoyed about a missing cassette in a packet on learning Zulu. The book that came with it lay on her desk, on an open daily planner with many, many entries.

Gandhi's voice was soft, childlike, and its sing-song rhythm reflected the Indian heritage evident in her apparel and features. Her gray-streaked hair reached her shoulders and was beautifully thick and wavy. Her skin, the color of cumin, was satiny and unlined.

Her call finished, she explained she would be presenting a paper, "Alternate Methods of Social Work," at a workers conference in Israel.

"As an activist, this is what I did," she explained.

273

Her famous name came from her father, son of Mohandas K. Gandhi. The late Mahatma Gandhi had arrived in South Africa in 1893. He met racism from the start, his granddaughter said.

"Soon after his arrival, he was taken to the court and there he was thrown out because he would not remove his turban. He tried to explain to the presiding judge that this turban does not have the same significance as the hat. You remove the hat as a mark of respect; the turban you wear as a mark of respect. But the judge wasn't prepared to listen."

"Then he got thrown out of the train. He'd sat in a first-class compartment. He had a first-class ticket, but was not allowed in his compartment because the others were white people and a white person objected. On the same day, he'd had to go by carriage from one town to another town. The whites sat inside. He was asked to sit outside with the driver of the carriage. Because he had to get to this place, he agreed. But then, halfway through the journey, a person sitting inside decided to smoke. He wants to sit outside where my grandfather is sitting, so he told him to go sit on the step of the carriage."

"My grandfather said, 'No. I'm not going to sit on the step. Either I sit inside or I sit here.' This man started beating him. Other people stopped this person from seriously injuring him. Eventually that matter was sorted out by this person taking the reins and making the driver sit on the step. All the way he kept swearing and threatening my grandfather. Those were some of the experiences he had that first week after his arrival."

As Gandhi told her story she switched tenses, sometimes talking of what had happened long before as if it were going on at this moment. Several women, I recalled, had done the same thing. There was an immediacy to how they spoke of certain past events. Perhaps every day they relived the instances of injustices and pain they, or members of their family, had suffered and it would be that way for them forever.

Gandhi continued, "He'd led a sheltered life in India as the son of a very well-to-do family. His father was respected, in the position of the governor where he lived. He hadn't encountered this kind of race prejudice until South Africa."

Mohandas Gandhi, trained in law, had come to South Africa on behalf of a family friend who had written asking his help in a court case. The friend had problems trying to communicate with his white South African lawyer. Gandhi spoke his language. The plan was, Gandhi would act as interpreter between the friend and his lawyer.

"It just so happened that after my grandfather studied this case, he decided this is a dispute beween two cousins. Why should they go to the expense of a long, drawn-out court process, where only the court and the attorneys would benefit? So he asked to mediate and resolved the case out of court."

"That's when my grandfather began to think about law serious-ly," she said. "Prior to that he wasn't able to represent people in court in India. He didn't make a success of his legal training, largely because he didn't feel confident enough to go and argue a case in court. When he came here he began to develop that self-confidence."

The phone rang. I listened to Gandhi's concern about conflict-ing appointments and her enthusiastic acceptance of a trip to Robben Island the following day. As she hung up, she explained this would be her first visit to the prison where Mandela and others spent years.

Though Mohandas Gandhi never practiced law again in India, he argued many cases in South Africa.

"He represented all the political cases," his granddaughter said. "In most instances, he did this free of charge. In fact, some of his arguments recorded in court make really good reading."

After that first visit to South Africa, her grandfather returned briefly to India to collect his family. They lived in South Africa for the next twenty-one years. Their son, Ela's father, had been born in India; her youngest uncle in South Africa.

When her grandfather returned permanently to India in 1914, among the projects he left in South Africa was the Phoenix Settle-ment, where she was born in 1940. This was a community on a hundred acres he owned north of Durban. The settlement was dedicated to Tolstoy's and Ruskin's ideas of self-sufficiency. Before leaving, Gandhi transferred ownership of the land to a community trust.

"With that spirit," his granddaughter said, "he asked my father to go back immediately and manage the whole—the farm as well as *The Indian*, which was a newspaper he had started many years back."

"My father didn't have any formal education. That was another issue my grandfather didn't believe in, the kind of education being offered. He felt that to be education for subjugation. He started an experiment on basic education, very similiar to our Curriculum 2005: interrelated, so that you build up the person's character as well as the intellect and you teach them skills."

Mohandas Gandhi, she said, believed no matter what the job, dressmaker or cobbler, these were as important to the good of the community as the practice of law. After equating different types of endeavors, he had concluded the most vital occupation to be that of laborer.

"My grandfather talked a great deal about manual labor and, similarly, my father was taught to live a life like that and do those kinds of things."

"After my grandfather left, many of the Phoenix settlers also left, so as we grew up we don't recall settlers living on the Phoenix settlement, just my family. We adhered to some of the disciplines. Simplicity was one. Gandhi believed in the politics of simple living. He said if each person only consumed what was necessary for that person, there would be no poverty in the world. And when I talk about consuming, I mean everything—water, air, and clothes and whatever, food, the lot."

"Today we suffer because consumerism, greed, has overtaken the world. That's why we have so much poverty, so much suffering. Our family had strict quotas on everything. I remember my sister had to wear old shirts, my father's, converted to a frock. I also had the simple clothes. This was very painful for us because we weren't a group, we were alone. Three children. Five years difference between each of us. I am the youngest."

Until she was ten, Ela Gandhi was schooled at home. She learned a philosophy of life, based on simplicity, from her mother. A British woman who lived with them taught the children English along with educational basics.

"But in time that wasn't sufficient," she continued. "I saw all these people around me going to school and I was sitting at home. I rebelled. I said to my parents, 'Send me to school; otherwise I will go away.' Eventually they did, but they said it wasn't going to be easy for me. If I wanted to go to school I'd have to walk. The nearest school was about two kilometers (a mile) from home so I walked that distance daily. They thought after a few days I would give it up. But I said, 'No. I do want to go to school.'"

But she frowned at the memory: "It was actually quite terrible, a state-aided Indian school. Because of the Bantu Education Act, there was no way anyone could run a mixed school. So although mainly our neighbors were Africans, I went to a school which was Indian. Many students walked twice as far as I did."

"But I liked school. I think it taught me a good attitude. I got my book knowledge—history, geography, that kind of information— basically from school, but I got my grounding from home. I was lucky."

"High school was in Durban and that was even more difficult. I had to walk to get a bus; the bus took me to the station; a train took me from there; then I walked two or three kilometers to the school."

Following another brief phone call, Gandhi continued. "It used to take me two hours in the morning, two hours in the evening. By the time I got home, it was usually 5 o'clock. After that I went to university. The University of Natal at that time was only for whites. For us, so-called non-whites, we had classes in the evenings. Go by bus to university, start at about 4:30, go on to 7:30 or 8. Fortunately, at that time bus service was good and it was quite safe for us to walk in the night. Most of the time my parents would fetch me from the bus stop, or send my brother, so I didn't have to walk home alone."

"I was very interested in political philosophy and thought political science a good course. It was part of the law curriculum. You did a three-year, BA course, then you did two more years and you got a law degree, in those days it was Roman Dutch law."

"So I did the three years, but before I could get to the two-year course, I was banned."

Yes, she had asked for reasons why she had been banned, she told me, but the government doesn't explain. Bannings were for various reasons; for instance, activists such as she, in a particular political movement, were believed banned to kill that movement.

"I suppose," Gandhi said, "they felt it was my political activities even though I was involved only marginally. I'd been elected vice chairperson of the Natal Indian Congress. What usually happens is, if you get banned, other people are afraid of the same thing because they don't know why that person was banned. And that's perhaps why they don't give reasons for banning."

"Banned and house arrested in the '70s. That lasted five years, then they renewed that for another three and a half years. So eight and a half years. Lifted in '85 or so."

During that time, Gandhi continued her studies by correspondence with the University of South Africa.

Another phone call. Also short.

"Banning was difficult," she continued. "My children (she had five; the youngest twins, now 27) grew up with us being banned. They didn't know what it was to go to a beach, to have a picnic."

"From Saturday five o'clock until Monday morning we were not allowed to leave the house, both my husband and myself. He was also banned and house arrested."

"They had three kinds of banning. One just precluded you from participating in political organizations, in social gatherings, being in an educational institution, a factory, anything like that. But you could move, go anywhere in the country."

"The second order limited your movement to a political geographical area, so you couldn't leave that area."

"The third banning was the house arrest which restricted you to your home for a certain number of hours. I had all three orders served on me, also my husband. Like me, he could work from seven in the morning to seven in the evening. But he was an insurance agent and usually insurance work is after hours. He couldn't go out in the evening and he couldn't have visitors. This affected his business. Thank god for what our parents taught us. Because of that, we were able to survive."

Gandhi was a member of the United Democratic Front (UDF) political party, and before her banning, a founding member of the Natal Organization of Women.

"Even during the time I was banned," she said, "because I was a social worker, I did a lot of community organizing. In places without water, for instance, or with housing problems, we would talk to the people, get them to be organized. We would help them with marches, or petitions, or any kind of action they would decide to take. We would be the back-up for those actions. But always, in the end, it was the community that did the work."

"That banning order," she continued, "made me all the more determined to see things changed in this country. The community needed my help and as long as the community needs me, they are the only ones who can throw me out, not the government. I was active all the way through the banning order. I think my life continued to be the same. It hasn't changed even now. If you want things, you still have to work."

Once again, as often happened when I heard these personal tales of oppression, I wondered: Would I have continued to defy authority under such threatening circumstances?

De Klerk's 1990 speech came as no surprise to Gandhi. As a member of the UDF, she had visited Mandela just days before his release from prison. She called him inspirational.

"Since the first congress of the ANC," she said, "I've been active in the ANC Women's League—I'm on the Provincial Executive of the league. Prior to that I was the treasurer of the Southern Natal Women's League. Wherever we went, we encouraged people to form

Women's Leagues as well as ANC branches. I felt I must only take on what I can fulfill, so I didn't stand for any position in the ANC."

"I think one of the Women's League's greatest achievements was during the negotiations with the National Party. The entire negotiations could have happened with only men at the table. It was only because the Women's League fought for representation that we were there. Then, slowly, we got on the Gender Commission and received more recognition."

"There were a lot of little battles we won. On the Transitional Executive Council, we had a sub-council on the status of women and I was on that."

I asked about the Transitional Executive Council. "It was a sort of shadow government to ensure the elections went smoothly and everybody participated and so on," Gandhi explained.

"In that council we made a lot of submissions. We made an input into defense. You just have to read the old defense law to know how male chauvinist the law was. Women were not even allowed to wear the uniforms men wore. They had to wear certain types of clothes, and no matter what rank a woman reached, she always was subordinate to the male."

"There were a whole lot of harsh, anti-women provisions. With the help of lawyers, we looked at the act and then pointed out these things to the defense sub-committee. We had to work very hard to raise their consciousness, because these were men who had always thought women had to be in the kitchen."

The Women's League had nominated Gandhi for Parliament. She will not run for another term. To her, community work is more important and that's what she plans to return to.

Social workers today, she believes, incorrectly perceive their role, the world, people with whom they work and how change occurs.

"To me, bringing about change is the most important role. That is what social work is based on. A professional must be a catalyst for change, whether it is personal change or environmental change. When you interact with people, you bring about change so they can function in a different way."

"The point of it is, how much of a real change are we making and how much change do we have to make? Do we have to make people accept their situation? Is the situation one we must accept? That is the crux of it."

Like her grandfather, Gandhi believes the world's population must become more self-sufficient, learning to live more simply and to consume less.

"We are saying that people have to change so they can accept this is how society must work. You find your role in that society. You can't change the society. You can change yourself. And that is what social work is all about."

"Now we are doing more harm than good in the community because we are only getting people to accept their position. We are not getting them to change their position. That is what I want to do."

"I feel people need, firstly, to have confidence in themselves," Gandhi continued. "But I don't want acceptance. Yes, by all means, become self-confident and fight for your rights, but change the society as well, become a catalyst. In that way get people to take their rightful place in society, begin to make a difference."

"I really want to see that we don't marginalize the poor, women and children, and the disabled. And society is marginalizing them. I want to organize groups at community level, I want to see that they begin to talk—start off small and let this spread."

Cecily and I had dinner that night with longtime friends of hers. They lived quite close, maybe two or three miles away, in a charming small Victorian house with a verandah, on a lot only slightly larger. A small garden in front; in back a narrow bricked patio followed the house around a corner; pots of flowers and a table under a canopy of mulberry leaves; the other side a high wall covered with vines. We drank wine, munched home-grown, home-cured olives and then ate a long meal outside under a full moon. Around that table interesting individuals talked with knowledge and passion about events and issues and people.

At some point, the host, a TV reporter, mentioned he would be making a trip to Robben Island the following day with Ela Gandhi. Gandhi had taken his call while I was in her office. So much seemed connected here. Trudy de Ridder had talked about a grandmother who had started the South African School for the Blind in Worcester. That had been one of the stops on the Elderhostel tour. EKM Dido had lived near East London and had shopped on Oxford Street. So had I. Noel Robb was on the board of the District Six school attended by Aldino's children.

In the U.S., I felt totally unable to affect change. I voted, wrote the occasional letter to my congressman but never, ever, did I even fantasize that my voice would be heard, much less that anything, ever, would come from what I wrote or said. In South Africa, a connectedness existed that gave me hope. It made me believe that this country could build a good future for those who worked together.

I returned euphoric to Cecily's little room. If only I could stay in this country forever.

XXIII
Lizzie Abrahams
I've got knowledge to share with other people

By now, the tiny, single-windowed cubicle was familiar, though it still didn't look as if it belonged in such a grand building. This particular office was Lizzie Abrahams', ANC Member of Parliament.

She came out from behind her desk and shook my hand, smiling broadly as she did so. Abrahams was medium-height, her body enveloped by an ankle-length dress in a bright, multi-colored African pattern. It hung loosely from her shoulders. Her gray, curly hair was cropped close to her head.

After a brief exchange of pleasantries, Abrahams sat down heavily in her desk chair and moved papers around on her desk until she found a spot to rest her forearms.

"I was born in Paarl in 1925 and I went to the Bethany Congregational School," Abrahams said. "It's still there today, but they're not teaching any more."

When her father, a brick maker, became ill, Lizzie, third oldest of eight children and in standard seven, left school. She had to earn money for the family. She found a job at the canning factory where her mother worked.

"While I was working in this factory, I joined the union, the Food and Canning Workers Union," Abrahams said. "It started in 1941 and was then multi-racial. In the factory there were coloreds and Africans who worked there, but there were very good relationships between those two races."

"And then a law was published to say that the coloreds must have the Food and Canning Workers Union and the Africans must have African Food and Canning Workers. They must be separate. Then we had to decide what to do. We decided, in our committee, we are not going to split, we are only going to go into separate groups."

"I started from the bottom. I was a member of the union, a committee member, then the branch treasurer and then I became the general secretary. I was very busy when I was working for the union: I had to negotiate, had to run up and down, up and down, then I lost two babies. I was married three years, then I lost the first one. Another two years, I lost the second one. I have now one child, adopted."

"While I was working," Abrahams continued in her husky voice, "I had to go away a lot, but I was lucky. My mother was near and she took care of my child and if my husband needs something, she gets it. I worked in the factory for fourteen years, then I was banned."

"Why? If you tell the worker his rights, that was the biggest crime in South Africa. They've got rights. They've got the right to stand up for these rights. They've got the right to speak for themselves, to say 'we are not satisfied.' And that's what I was doing. I was working for a legal union. It was not illegal. We were registered."

In 1958, Abrahams was restricted to Paarl. "I couldn't keep working," she recalled, "couldn't go to the locations; couldn't go to buildings where printing was being done. I couldn't go to church. For five years, I just stayed home. If they come to check you and you are not there, there are problems."

"One of my sister's children was confirmed," she said. Abrahams laughed. She sounded good-humored, not bitter. "They asked me to be the godmother and I even had to go to the magistrate to get permission to do that. And I had to report to the police in Paarl every Monday morning."

"In your banning order," she explained, "it says you are banned from this date until that date. Then they come to you and say your banning order is expired. That was in 1963. When they come they say, 'You mustn't do this,' and 'You mustn't do that, or you will be banned again.'"

"After the five years, I was asked to come and assist the union again. Our union was big, well established, but it had so many problems. It was the hardest hit. All our people in the union were banned—general secretary, president, everyone—on both sides, Food and Canning and African Food and Canning. I was general secretary, Food and Canning, just for the sake of the inspectors who come to check. Oscar Mapetla was general secretary of the African Food and Canning. But we work together, like we did before. In one office, with one meeting."

She said that employers didn't like the two secretaries working together, coming together to talk about employee issues. The working committees in the factories, which had been organized by representatives of the two unions, could not understand why they had to talk to the bosses separately. "They protested," she recalled. " 'If the others can't come, we won't do this.' So at the end, they allowed us to go in together."

After her banning, Abrahams became very nervous about resuming her union activities. Upon being asked to do that, she explained her fears to union members and management.

"They called a meeting and discussed my position," she said. "They asked a person called Jan Theron to come and be the general secretary. He agreed. But he always came to me and discussed things so we worked together."

"Then they said I must come nearer to them because they must be able to talk to me any time they want. They were in Cape Town. Our office was on Plein Street. Then they hired a little office in Market Street and I used to work with them from that office. It was nearer for them than to come to Paarl. I came by train. I still lived in Paarl."

"But before I got this office there was a big strike at Mones and Fatties, the factory where they make macaroni. That was also organized by Food and Canning. I was always in the union office then, in the hideout at the back. The strike was big, about seven hundred people.

Oscar Mapetla was the general secretary. He was in East London organizing. He was not here. Jan Theron was not here either. He was organizing in George. So when the strike came, there was no one experienced and I had to come back in the open. I must assist the workers. I think this was about two years after my banning order expired."

"The negotiator was a comrade of ours. Jan, the general secretary, was responsible for the negotiations. From George, he contacted the employers to try to settle the strike."

I asked what the strike was all about.

Abrahams replied, "The strike was partly about wages, but mostly the problem was discrimination. They'd dismissed five colored workers. The whole factory felt it was unfair. The other employees, coloreds and Africans, consolidated behind these five workers."

"We had a meeting the night before the strike and I attended this meeting. The workers said, 'Look, we are going to strike tomorrow. We are not going to allow them to shut out those workers.'"

"The next morning," she continued, her voice becoming more intense, "after they'd had a meeting, they will send a message to me. If they say the baby is not sick, the strike is off. If the baby is sick, the strike is on. They phoned me: 'The baby is sick.'"

"There was a law that said if workers strike, they may not be outside the gate. If they're locked out, they must go home. I had one of our local chairmen come to assist and we went to the factory. All the workers were still standing there. We knew if they were going to stand there longer, the vans would come and take them to jail."

Abrahams laughed. She had a head-back, full-body laugh. "We asked all the workers to go to the station because they can't arrest them while they are waiting for the train ...."

"Now, Oscar's not here; Jan is not here to start negotiations. So our local chairmen came into the office on Plein Street and we discussed what to do now. We decided we must have meetings with the workers, try to negotiate with the employers, bring reports back to the workers, and so on. Both sides. So we went on and on."

"The negotiations were very hard. And there were the contract workers, also on strike, who go on holiday to their homes. They now couldn't go because they need them and if they don't get paid, they might not come back."

The strike continued for seven months. I asked Abrahams how strikers and their families survived without paychecks?

The union, she explained, appealed for donations to other unions both in the country and overseas. Members also staged fund raisers.

"Every week we paid the workers strike pay," Abrahams said. "And though it was not the money they earned at the factory, at least they could carry on."

I was curious as to why the five workers had been fired.

"This was a racist thing," she explained, "because the Africans supported the coloreds. To them, the employers, it must have been the African union should not have supported the colored union. They should have allowed the coloreds to go on their own with the protest and lose the strike."

"This was a South African-owned factory, but they sent products overseas. We contacted their customers, told them the history of what was happening here and they boycotted. The company owners try to drag, drag, until they can't take any more. It was difficult for the company when workers united. So this was a very successful strike."

After seven months of negotiations, a settlement was reached. Dismissed workers were reinstated. Those who had annual holidays coming were given bags of food, blankets for their families and transportation back to Transkei or to another homeland.

"After that strike," said Abrahams, "I worked for awhile for the union in Cape Town. Then trouble started again in Paarl, with the branch secretary who had worked for the union for many years. She made a statement in the paper to say—I forgot the legal name of the law—that you must only hire coloreds in a certain area, that work must not be given to Africans because they are taking the bread out of the colored people's mouths." Abrahams shook her head in dismay at the memory.

Even though the African Food and Canning and the Food and Canning unions were officially separate, their history of cooperation had been long and solid. Therefore, the statement by the colored union's branch secretary was, Abrahams said, "very, very against our policy. We were a partnership. So she was dismissed from the union. But before she left, she made such a lot of trouble. She organized little cliques and so on."

"When this problem broke out, the management, the executive from the Paarl branch, wrote to the head office and said, 'Please try to get Lizzie to come and work for us, help us to solve this problem'"

"So I went to start work again in Paarl. We had three factories, but we'd had one chairman, one secretary for the branch, but she had split the branch. We then had two secretaries, two chairmen, one for each union, black and colored. When I went to Paarl, I explained to the workers that the meaning of this was to weaken the workers. And the workers understood. And we had one branch again. They elected again one chairman, one secretary and treasurer."

"Luckily, I'm from Paarl and the people knew me so it was a little bit easier for me to try to reorganize things. But still, it was a difficult time. Our union had registration and they had provisional registration. It meant they got some rights, all rights we had."

But Abrahams worked it out and went on from there to organize workers at a dried fruit factory in Upington. One night, driving home from a meeting there, she was in an accident—ribs broken, a knee fractured, other injuries. A union car drove her to a hospital in Malmesbury.

"I really couldn't come right there," Abrahams said, "because they didn't do good treatment. They treated me on medicine for three weeks—broken ribs, broken leg, broken hip, injured neck. And the pain, terrible, terrible, terrible."

"I complained to one of the doctors and he couldn't understand why I was being given only aspirin for a broken leg and broken everything. They then referred me to Paarl Hospital and there I stayed. I saw a specialist and I got better treatment. Then I got better."

"I worked for another three years. But because I didn't get proper treatment, I was in pain every day. So I told the union it was no use. I retired."

"After I retired, the ANC Women's League branch in Paarl asked me to assist them. That was in '90 and the ANC was unbanned. When the ANC was banned, I was not a member at that time. Why? The ANC was for Africans only. But, of course, working with Oscar that is a member of the ANC, we always had discussions and I knew what it was about."

"So next, I was elected chairman of the ANC branch in Paarl for two years. Being the chairman of the ANC, I attended meetings, explained to the people how it worked. But mostly my duty was to try and build the ANC branch into a strong branch. We usually had meetings once a month, members meetings, also once-a-month executive meeting. Sometimes we had open air meetings and asked a speaker from Worcester. We'd then go to Worcester to speak. Up to now there is a strong branch at Paarl."

"After the ANC," Abrahams said, settling back in her chair, "I was elected to serve on the Paarl council and while I was on the Paarl council for three months, I was called to come to Parliament."

She laughed, still sounding suprised at where she was.

Abrahams did not join Parliament after the 1994 elections but came a year later. She explained that those further down on the ANC list of four hundred moved up when some accepted other positions in the new government. Abrahams had begun at number thirty-seven on that list.

In Parliament, she serves on communications and public works committees.

She nodded. "It is interesting. But you must always learn, learn, about this committee. You meet two or three times a week. Today is communication, tomorrow is public works. I'm alternative on justice. Sometimes you sit in these from nine o'clock to six o'clock. And sometimes Parliament will meet from two o'clock in the afternoon until one o'clock in the morning." Abrahams shook her head: "A really difficult job."

Since she still lives in Paarl, she drives an hour or longer each way. "And not only that, as an MP, you've got constituency offices. Now I have a constituency office in Wellington and a satellite office in Franzhoek. Both are farm areas. And even if you are an ANC MP, you must work for the other parties in your constituency."

I asked about the problems brought to her: "The most difficult issues we are facing in our constituencies is the farm workers problem, domestic workers."

"Say, for instance, this one asking for assistance is a member of a union. It's difficult to help a member of the union, because you haven't got the agreements, you haven't got their policies. Then you refer them to that particular union. If you're a food worker, we send you to Food and Canning; if you're a leather worker, you go to the leather workers union; a wood worker, you go to the wood workers union. There is now a farm workers union, but it is still very weak."

"If we see it's problems about relationships—'This foreman shouted at me and he swore at me. He kicks me,' and so on, this is ill treatment. Then we'll make an appointment with the employer and say, 'Look, we've got a problem. We've got to complain. We'd like to discuss it with you, otherwise we'll take the matter further.'"

"Some of the employers are ready to speak with us. They'd like to get it settled before it goes to court. Let me give you an example. At one farm, a wine farm, there'd been a strike for three days already and they could not settle. And they called us. They did not want to call the labor department. The workers knew me from the trade union days, so they insisted they should call me."

"We went there. We discussed. The workers had been underpaid, worked for long hours, and so on. We settled the problem and asked the employer to work with the union. And he says he's got no problem. And he recognized the union and he began even deducting subscriptions. You get employers that like to cooperate but not all do."

"So," Abrahams settled back in her chair, "that is what we do in our constituency offices."

I asked about the federation for unions.

"There's a very strong umbrella body, COSATU, Congress of South African Trade Unions. All the local unions affiliate with COSATU. If a union's got problems or needs assistance, it can go to COSATU."

"In my time, South Africa Congress of Trade Unions, SACTU, that was the umbrella body. I think there were problems and they didn't continue and after that, COSATU. There are other umbrella bodies, NACTU, National Congress of Trade Unions, but there are few unions that belong to that. COSATU's got the majority."

I asked if she planned to stand again for Parliament?

"I don't think so," Abrahams said. "Depends on my health."

I asked if her husband objected to her long hours in Parliament.

"I am a widow," she said. "But when I worked for the union, it was very difficult, because he was not interested in anything and it's difficult to be married to that kind of person if you are an activist."

"We were always trying to work it out. At one time it seemed we never would. But then I said to him, 'I'm not prepared to leave my work.' I was forty then and I'd got so fond of the people, solving their problems. It was a real part of my life. I always said to him, 'There are thousands of workers out there who need me and you are only one person. Why must I consider one person and leave?'"

"It was terrible when I was working. I go there seven o'clock, come back tomorrow morning, three o'clock, two in the morning. Then he doesn't open the door. I must stand there 'til daylight. That kind of life I had. I gave him the choice, 'I must go or you must leave me.' Then he started to understand."

What would she be involved with if she did not continue in Parliament?

Abrahams shook her head: "I don't know. That's the problem. It all depends on how I feel. If I feel like I can carry on a little longer, I'll do so. Once you're seventy, you're not so strong in the legs, but I've got knowledge to share with other people."

"The future? I've got hope for South Africa. I think things will

291

change for the better. There still are lots of things that must be ironed out, but you know, being among the people, hearing what they say, some people got hope for the future."

Riding the elevator back to the lobby, I remembered that, part way through, talking about her work during the apartheid years, Abraham had asked some of what she said to be "off the record." Shutting off the recorder then, I felt an old, but familiar fear: She shouldn't be saying these things; I shouldn't be listening; who is watching?

An instant later, a great relief washed over me. South Africa was not like that anymore.

XXIV
〰 *Annette Cockburn*
The Homestead helps street children reconstruct their
shattered lives

The guard at the Chiappini Street entrance to Homestead Projects pointed to the far end of a long and several storied building. Aldino drove into the walled complex and along one side of a tarred play field where boys kicked soccer balls and aimed shots at a basketball hoop on a pole.

A woman in a small main-floor office of Patrick's House led the way up a couple of flights of stairs against walls with bright, primitive murals. Painted by residents, she said. Annette Cockburn's office was off a room filled with ledgers, files, books and computers.

Cockburn remained behind her desk and got right down to business: "I'm director of an organization called the Homestead which helps street children reconstruct their shattered lives. In a glance, this is our mission." She picked up a booklet, flipped to a photograph of a child wrapped in a blanket that covered all of him except his haunted eyes: "From this—" she turned over a half dozen pages to a photo of three young men in school uniforms, slacks, jackets, ties and white shirts—"to that, in a number of extremely difficult steps." She dropped the book with the photos onto her cluttered desk top and kept going. She talked rapidly and in a deep voice.

"We have six programs at this stage, three of which are non-residential, three residential. It's a phase rehabilitation program from the first step, which is outreach to the kids on the street, to the second step, a drop-in-center where kids come—not to sleep, but to access

293

basic resources, like ablutions and food and secondhand clothes. At that point there's an attempt on the part of this program, Masithethe, which means 'let us speak,' to reunite them with their families and communities of origin."

Cockburn said that children who are eligible and willing could refer themselves to the intake center. It is required that they come of their own accord and must be street children sixteen or under. All facilities are open door: no one is kept under lock and key. Once a child settles in at this phase, he is moved to either the Bridge or to Patrick's House. At that stage, the aim of the program is to put a child back into formal school, with the help of a non-formal educational program, also conducted at Patrick's House.

"In this program," Cockburn continued, "they relearn structure, receive a bit of remediation so when they do go back to formal school, we have a sense of what standard they should be in and where the big cognitive gaps are."

"They might stay here for a term or a year or two years, catching up. The other agenda in these two programs is to reestablish links with their families from which, in many cases, they have been alienated for years."

A social worker directs each program and child care workers are on duty 24 hours a day.

"Very few of the children have not been to school at all," continued Cockburn. "Most of them have two or three years of schooling, dropped out. Without being in school, after a year or two they are no longer literate. That is a big problem."

I desperately wanted Cockburn to slow down, to maybe ramble a little so I could jot down words to help recreate her later. I wanted words to get a sense of her and her work space. I wanted to make a note when she said something I wanted her to get back to. But she kept going full speed.

"Usually a street child becomes a street child by degrees," she said. "He doesn't just decide one day, 'I'm leaving home.' He will, in most cases, come from a family of abject poverty, characterized the world over—not just here in South Africa—by overcrowding, unemployment and some form of alcohol abuse, drug usage, in the family."

"Families become dysfunctional in many cases through no fault of their own: families benumbed by the minimum circumstances of their lives; flooding into the urban areas, looking for jobs, houses, money. Finding none of them. The children become the casualties, drifting into the city streets. Part of that drift is dropping out of school. When a child stops going to school, irregularly starts sleeping out from his family, these are indicators of high risk. In most cases— I would say 99.9 percent—the circumstances at home are untenable. In a way, it's an indication of a desire, a need, to survive that drives kids onto the street where they eke out an existence."

Homestead programs, she said, touch a couple of thousand children a year.

"We keep a number of stats," Cockburn said, "but to know how many kids get through in one go is difficult. They might be readmitted a dozen times in the next two or three years."

She said at any one time, about one hundred and twenty children are in residence at Patrick's House, the Bridge and the Homestead intake shelter.

"That first contact? The networks on the street are good. The kids all know about us, word of mouth. But the street workers' job is not to bring them in. We don't recruit because we believe the prognosis for rehabilitation is a lot better when the child is there because he wants to be, rather than because the policeman has brought him in, or even a member of the public."

"So while the street workers do not recruit, they do disseminate information about resources: This is where food is accessible; This is where you can sleep the night; This is where you can get a shower. Where are your parents? Do you want us to do a visit?"

"There are traditional ways of working with street kids. Very especially, rounding them up and locking them up does not work. They simply run away. They have to be somewhere where they want to be. That's what is difficult to communicate to an impatient public who wants them out of the way. They're a nuisance. In some places, they are perceived as a danger. But very few children under sixteen are actually in trouble with the law. And the generic term, street children, is used by the media in the most profligate way," Cockburn rolled her eyes and looked and sounded annoyed, "for anybody with a black face, who's fifteen and on the streets, and especially when he commits a crime. Street child is more emotive, more sensationalist than 'juvenile' or 'Young Man Mugs Tourist.'"

"Many times street workers investigating such incidents find the 'street child' is nineteen, or twenty-three. But the press never prints a retraction."

"The other thing which I try to get across constantly, in newspapers, TV, and on the radio, is that most children begging in the streets, or mugging or shoplifting, or stealing or parking cars, live in the community. Like children throughout the world, they come into town on a daily basis to make a buck. Comparatively few eat, sleep, exist, on the street full time."

Cockburn said street workers had done a 3 AM head count in Cape Town a year earlier and found one hundred and nineteen children under the age of sixteen sleeping on the street.

"Where do they hang out? In groups. Although these children are individualistic and don't move in gangs, they do tend to crowd together at night for protection and warmth. And they'll sleep under any overhang, vacant lot, church stoop, water bank, where there is some protection offered."

A woman from the other room brought in a tray with coffee, distracting Cockburn for a minute or two. Cockburn had a deep, cigarette-husky voice; wavy, shoulder-length hair between blonde and brown. She wore something dark red, shiny and drapey. She was big-boned, five-feet, eight or nine inches, looked healthy and exuded energy. Everything about her, from her posture at her desk, the way she dealt with the coffee cups, to facial features to voice, said focused, strong, determined, committed.

Homestead, she continued, had a paid staff of twenty-five, most of them child care workers. Volunteers helped out too. Cockburn believed public money should be spent on service not personnel. There was no receptionist, no gardener or phone answerer. There was a part-time bookkeeper, part-time typist and a project manager who worked for all programs.

"I think," said Cockburn, "that part of the success of the Homestead is attributable to the fact that it has a track record. We've been around for a long time, since '82. We have a trackable infrastructure, impeccably audited accounts. Every cent that comes in is receipted, et cetera. The service is third world, nothing elaborate, but a range to meet the children's needs where they are"—she banged the desk with her fist—"at this stage"—*bang*—"at this stage"—*bang*—"at this stage"—*bang*—"at that stage." *Bang*.

I asked about funding. She said project funding comes from a variety of sources.

"For those children who are committed, we get a state subsidy which I imagine accounts for perhaps a third of our income. For the rest, we fund raise and we really have had over the years very generous responses from the public, from businesses, from churches, from embassies, schools, private individuals, trusts. But our funding is fairly modest. I don't believe in giving kids the notion that out there, back in the community, they're going to have four pairs of shoes and a domestic worker. I think one has to be, and they need to be, realistic about their expectations of life in the community, because, obviously, that's where we want them."

"I believe that children's homes that ascribe to a first world model, for instance, create in those children expectations that are not going to be met. We try to keep the whole material quality of these places simple, clean, bright. Nobody's got thousands of clothes, but everybody's got enough and everybody's responsible for doing their chores, making their beds, cleaning their rooms, for washing dishes, et cetera."

Primarily, it is Cockburn who raises funds for the project. She believes that people want to help and just need to be told what will help. Many donors give year after year. There is also a very large mailing list from a donor base that receives a multi-page annual report. She described this as a very well-done work with photos of the children, synopses of what is done at each facility, case histories and good quotations.

The woman who worked in the office beyond came in. As they talked, my eye was caught by the name of the writer and the words on the cover of the 1996 annual report on Cockburn's desk:

> Our ability to reach unity in diversity
> will be the beauty and test of our civilization.
> —Mahatma Gandhi

After the worker left, I asked Cockburn if these reports were money raisers. She nodded her head vigorously. These raise about 40,000 rands ($4,444 US) a page, she said.

The project began in 1982. Cockburn joined it in 1986, in answer to an ad for a coordinator for Patrick's House, the first home for children.

"At that stage," she said, "there was just an intake shelter, started by concerned citizens, with a social worker from child welfare seconded to establish this first street children program, the Homestead. Over the years this has evolved into the name of the organization as well as the name of one of the programs. At the time I came it was only this," she swept the space with an arm, "sixteen boys, a couple of parishes involved, St. Paul's, the cathedral, St. Barnaby's, but always non-denominational."

The building where we talked was part of a cluster called the Salesian Institute, and belonged to the Catholic Church. A nearby structure was owned by the Anglicans. Homestead paid rent on both buildings.

I was curious as to what prompted the different Homestead programs.

"All of them," Cockburn replied, "evolved from the bottom up, rather than the top down."

"Children decide, 'we need' and each one starts to become a reality. Most projects, here and in other developing countries, start through some kind of a feeding scheme, soup kitchen. They come for food. There might be a social worker there attached to an agency, or maybe citizens who saw a need. Once the kids start coming regularly to the soup kitchen, they say, 'Where can we stay?' And out of that evolves the need for a shelter. When there's a shelter, there's the question of what do they do with their time? They must have an education program of some sort. Once they've settled into the shelter, they must move on to make room for the new kids."

"Kids said to the street worker, 'You find us on the street. That's great, but where can we find you?' Because the street worker, by definition, is not in an office. Then we started the drop-in center where the street worker could be found some part of the day. This was an expressed need on the part of the children."

"What they want there is, basically, somewhere safe. They've spent all night running away from a policeman, or a security guard, or dogs, or whatever. Almost always they want food. Many of them want to shower, an opportunity to wash clothes. Some of them are looking for something more—educational and recreational opportunities, a chance to play soccer, do some handwork, watch a video."

"Some of these will refer themselves to the intake. The more incorrigible will continue to come to the drop-in center. Don't want anything else; don't want any more structure. Life on the street, for some of them, is more attractive than the rules and structures of the intake center, which are minimal—no drugs, no knives, and you've got to be in at a certain time. But even that, for some, is too much to cope with."

I asked Cockburn about the steps that led her to the Homestead.

"I come from an academic background, teaching in universities and schools," she said, "and they were looking for a principal, someone to run these two programs, the Homestead and Patrick's House. They wanted a registered social worker, which I'm not; a male; someone who was black; and a committed Christian, which they didn't get."

"What I figured they needed was an educationist at this point when the big dilemma was: how do we get these kids back into school? Part of the diploma I did was adult education. I designed this informal education program, and we began that and subsequently handed it over to the Salesians, a Catholic order, whose priests run it here."

Cockburn is a third generation South African. One grandfather came to the country from England, the other from Italy. She was born in 1942 in KwaZulu/Natal, formerly the province of Natal. She went to school in the nearest city, Pietermaritzburg, then on to university in Durban.

Cockburn paused. "I can't remember what I'd planned to do, but I spent most of my life before forty teaching. I married at nineteen or twenty and had three kids. Got divorced when they were small. During that time, I taught in a variety of schools, none of them state schools: black schools, private schools that to some degree determined the education they offered. I didn't send my kids to state schools either. I have a problem with dutiful, mincing conformity. And in any case, in those bad old days, one would rather be in an alternative educational environment."

I was curious as to when she became aware of how things were in her country?

"My family was quite conservative and I think it was only when I went to university that I was exposed to any real questioning of the status quo. Then I did get involved with the struggle, as most people in my generation did—NUSAS, that kind of thing, then Black Sash."

When her children were quite young, she moved to the country and taught them at home for a year. Later they all went off to Italy and lived there a year.

"I believe the sorts of experiences my kids had when they were growing up were, in a way, far more enriching than standing in lines," Cockburn said. "And they all went on to university. Didn't seem to suffer at all. I think we had a rich and varied time."

"And, of course, being a teacher when they were small was an ideal job. In many cases I taught in the schools where they were. We did lots of camping and traveling. Often we lived in communities of the schools where I taught which, in some cases, were residential so the kids grew up in a community with access to swimming pools and horses."

Her final eight years in education, Cockburn lectured in drama at the University of Natal. To me, she had a theatrical air about her and, as it turned out, she had directed plays and, indeed, had done "a bit" of acting. The move from Durban to Cape Town came because her daughter, now a doctor, wanted to go to medical school and there was none in Durban.

In Cape Town, Cockburn taught acting in a ballet school. "Briefly, what happened," she said, "was that suddenly I had the sense that if I had to listen to another Antigone monologue, or Juliet ... 'Uh. Uh. I actually want to be with kids who aren't as privileged or advantaged' and then this came up. And this has been my passion. This job more than any other."

But after twelve years, Cockburn finds that what she signed on for has changed. She is chairman of the Western Cape Street Children's Forum, has been deeply involved with a Committee for Youth and has taken on a number of assignments from its minister in the cabinet to cover the whole area of policy-making for street kids. She has helped establish similar programs elsewhere, has been featured at international conferences on the subject and has published articles. She works with the city council and also at the provincial level to formulate policy on homelessness with regard to street children.

"All of this is extremely time consuming so at this point in my career, I'm kind of ricocheting beween the needs of the organization and the demands on my time and expertise on a wider platform."

I asked how she could move to the next level? "That," she replied, "is what I'm wrestling with now. We may put in an operational manager with more responsibility. We do have a projects manager, but that person doesn't do the fund-raising and the writing, and someone heading operations would leave me freer to deal with the policy stuff."

"The only thing is, that's not what I get up for in the morning—

to sit around a desk at city council. I get up for"—she tapped the book with the photographs—"these children. And when they're not here in front of my eyes, I'm not sure why I do this job. I think I'm very much a cliff-face person who is being dragged unwillingly, though I realize it's necessary, into the political arena."

"This is the mission," she waved toward the page with the three dark-suited alumni, "and a graphic illustration. This kid left last year and now he's a got a job. This one did his matric. This one dropped out."

"Oh, we've got lots of success stories. One of ours, he belongs to a circus, been to Denmark, to Los Angeles, to Amsterdam. Unconventional, but he's made it."

She got up, gathered reports and newsletters and thrust them into my hands: "There's some stats." I followed her into the adjoining office. "Annie will show you a bit downstairs," Cockburn said, extending her hand.

Annie led the way down a floor to the dormitory for residents. Most of the boys are tri-lingual, she said, speaking Xhosa, English and Afrikaans. For seventy percent, Xhosa is the mother tongue.

The dormitory was a very large, open room with double deck bunks placed in such a way as to divide the room into sections. Nearby was a recreation hall with pool tables. Colorful murals done by the children decorated most walls. Other than that, the facility was neat, but stark and institutional.

We walked down a hall and past two or three closed doors. "There's a couple of rooms for the coordinator of the drop-in center and the housefather," Annie said. "There are always two staff on duty."

Children hung out in the halls, played pool in the rec room and, in the large kitchen, sat around tables with the radio playing. The TV stood in one corner.

Annie called the kitchen the heart of it. The reason for children around on a weekday was that their teachers were marching with others in the city to protest cutbacks in school staff. All children, everywhere, she said, would be affected by cuts in the education budget. The newspaper had reported class sizes would go to seventy or eighty.

In the new South Africa, unlike the old, all children were guaranteed an education. But budgets for that and every other kind of social service were not only straitened but meager.

Another office down the hall was occupied by a social worker. At that time, Patrick's House had thirty-four residents but was registered for forty. Going down the stairs, we walked past a colorful mural. I stopped to jot down a part of it:

> Think son of Africa,
> What it is you wanted to be
> Think of your dreams and take power
> And the power will help set you free

The building we were in, Annie said, had been built for orphans almost a hundred years earlier.

On the next floor down was a staff room and the office of coordinator of the educational and skills programs: Daniel Brown, a member of the Catholic order of Salesians and in his fourth year at Patrick's House. A bespectacled man, he was short, perhaps in his early fifties, with a pleasant expression and a round face.

"I was a boy here," he said, "and came back as principal when it became a technical school. Like other mission schools, it closed down as a result of National Party government policies. It then became a hostel, before finally going back to the reason for the founding of the Salesian order in Italy in 1855: the education and training of street youth which its founders had worked with since 1841." In 1990, the order took over the the school programs for Homestead.

"So," he said with a smile, "after an interval of a hundred years, we are back to educating street children."

Part of the building is used for the Learn to Live School and part for the Learn to Live Skills program. In the latter are street youth over the ages of sixteen, or grade ten, the age and standard when education no longer is compulsory.

Those who come off the street are aggressive and definitely not ready for conventional schools, he said. The aim of the school is to get the children calmed down and to put a bit of a structure in their lives.

"We take a lot of nonsense from them," Brown said. "Initially, a good number have tremendous need for physical contact, to hold our hands, to hug us. They go through a naughty stage and we are here to get them through it, to get them ready to work with adults, all that sort of thing."

About forty children have been recommended as ready to return to school. Not all want to go. The drop-out rate is as high as a quarter, Brown said, but they come back and "we try them for another year."

We walked through classrooms on the same floor. "We are a child-friendly school," he said, "and schools out there are definitely not child friendly."

I asked about general characteristics of the children. "Their behavior is to shock people," Brown replied. "It is par for the course that they use solvents. This is almost a given. If they come to us under the influence of solvents, we send them away. They are a temptation to others, and we can't do much with them in that state."

"They also can't bring weapons. Gradually, as they stay, they calm down. We teach respect, which is very important. You will see religious symbols throughout the buildings. We firmly believe religion and God is a solid foundation on which to build self-esteem and a sense of worth."

"The staff have to take each moment as it comes. These children act out of thoughtlessness rather than malice. We try to remember a child has been damaged terribly, but there are limits to misbehavior. We prepare children for school, but have problems preparing the schools for these children."

School opens at 9 AM with a half hour of "rousing" hymn singing. After that comes an hour of solid school work. The work may be easy, but staff are encouraging and try to build self-esteem. The school day ends at 1 PM.

A classroom, bright with murals, had a line of perhaps ten or twelve desks and chairs. The number wouldn't go over fourteen, Brown said, since the children's volatility requires individual attention.

Outside the building, on a wide, covered walkway, children batted at balls and shot pool. We stopped at the doorway of a room where youths worked with wood. They were older than the children who played outside.

Brown explained that the young men spend a full day in the workshop and learn to work a full day with the elementary skills of the trade. They first make something simple to sell, using mostly hand tools except for a wood-turning lathe in the corner. Students also learn to repair furniture.

"If somebody comes and needs a worker, we find one here," Brown said. "The job may not be permanent, but it is a good experience. They learn to work with a boss. They can come back, but never under the influence of anything. They can carry on producing here after they complete the course, but then must pay for materials. When they're learning, all is free."

Further down the walk was the leathercraft room. A radio inside played rap. Those working in it had been making purses and belts and were just learning how to do sandals. Everything was hand stitched. The basic course was seven weeks.

"The idea again is to make something they can sell," Brown said. "In the early years, many of the older youth left Learn to Live but could not go to school and thus ended on the street again, so workshops were added to teach a skill it is hoped will keep them off the streets."

Beween eight and ten youths worked in each crafts room.

Outside, we waited for Aldino. One child, chest-high, puffed on a cigarette. Without comment, Brown walked over and took it out of his mouth.

Some of the children around us looked to be as young as five or six. One or two of them lived with their parents on the streets, he said.

As Aldino drove in, the Signal Hill cannon boomed. This happened every noon. The cannon, left behind from the days of war and the announcements of the arrivals of tall-masted sailing ships, sat on a hill above Cape Town.

The scene opens with a group of Street Children playing dice, sharing a loaf of bread and a litre of Coke, wrote Director Cockburn in a review of the Homestead's 1997 Christmas play. The overhead projector casts a pool of light onto the stage and a street girl comes into the light and hears the age-old message from a voice-over: "Behold, I bring you tidings of great joy." Joseph is not convinced. "This is not my child. Don't give me this rubbish about the son of God." Another pool of light, and Joseph is severely reprimanded by a stern angel in the wings. Briefly he apologises to Mary and they set off to find a place for the baby to be born. Some groups of Street Children on the stage say: "There is no room here, not in our territory."

There is also an encounter with the police—very stereotypical—but it elicits waves of laughter and feelings of identification from the boys in the audience. The policeman tells the strollers and Mary and Joseph to push off (though rather more graphically)... Three representatives from the SA Police Services, who have for the first time ever come to this concert, are laughing their heads off!

Eventually Mary and Joseph end up under the bridge at the bottom of Napier Street and the people there agree to build them a shack. The scene moves to jugglers and acrobats in the street and we see a virtuoso display from the children.

Some chairs are placed in a line and they become a taxi complete with the tout. They are picking up Wise Men from Khayelitsha. The wise men are well-dressed and want to go to see the baby born under the bridge in Cape Town. They are bearing gifts. The Street Worker runs onto the stage.

"Come and see the baby," he shouts, and everyone rushes off.

In the next scene the baby is there, one month old—and real. There is a token sheep in a gray blanket who says baa, baa, on an ad hoc basis. The Wise Men arrive and offer their gifts, elaborately wrapped in see-through cellophane: eight tins of baby food, a packet of nappies and a parcel containing some vests.... I bet, concluded Cockburn, the real Mary would have preferred these gifts to all that frankincense and myrrh!

XV

🌿 *Patricia de Lille*

We've achieved political freedom. There's still a long way to go

Early afternoon on the fifth of February I was at Parliament when a series of alarms, like those for fire drills, signalled the opening of the year's first session. Patricia de Lille's offices were across the street from Parliament's chambers and office annex, in the Marks Building. Once again I was lost in a long hall bordered by empty offices and very relieved to see what turned out to be her aide signal in the distance.

De Lille was one of five Pan Africanist Congress (PAC) Members of Parliament and the party's chief whip. PAC dated back to 1959, founded by ANC members who objected to their party's cooperation with other racial groups. Robert Sobukwe, formerly with the ANC Youth League, became its leader. It had been Sobukwe who had organized the March 1960 campaign of defiance against pass laws that provoked the Sharpeville massacre. A month later PAC and the ANC had been banned. They remained illegal until De Klerk launched the new South Africa.

In January 1991, when Mandela called for an all-party congress to negotiate the route to a new government, PAC initially cooperated. But before the meeting took place, the PAC backed out citing differences of opinion on format, players, etc., and accused the ANC of cooperating with the National Party.

In the run-up to the election, the PAC military wing, the Azanian People's Liberation Army (APLA), had been suspect in the attack on a church in Cape Town and the murder of American Fulbright scholar Amy Biehl, and had claimed responsibility for a number of other attacks on whites in King Williamstown, Queenstown and Cape Town.

De Lille was on the phone when I arrived. That first impression lived up to her reputation for dramatic—a floor-length African robe in a purple and gold print; hair in long, thinner-than-a-pencil braids; painted, perfect nails curved far beyond her fingertips.

Her office was twice the size of others I had been in, with ample space for four bookcase cabinets beyond the standard furniture. Her desk looked busy.

De Lille hung up from what she explained was a call to her son and picked up the ringing cell phone. She would call back.

Her children are 23 and 25, she said. De Lille didn't look more than 35 herself. She lived in Cape Town, born in 1951 in the small Eastern Cape town of Beaufort West. She described her parents as Afrikaans-speaking, very poor, working-class people. Her father taught school, her mother looked after their seven children. The family left Beaufort West when her father was transferred to a school in Stellenbosch.

Though university had been an option, De Lille chose to take a job to help support her family. She worked first in a textile laboratory in Stellenbosch and became active in the union. In 1974, she moved to a job in a paint factory. There she started a chapter of the South African Chemical Workers Union. Since unions were legal during the apartheid era, De Lille said unions assumed the role of the banned liberation movements, addressing not only socio-economic but also political issues.

"I stayed in the factory for fifteen years and remained involved in union activities," she said. "I was elected as vice-president of one of the trade union federations. But when they unbanned the liberation movements, I decided to work for PAC full time."

"Why PAC? I had been in PAC since 1976. PAC was the only organization that had no problem with identity. The ANC and others still spoke of coloreds, Indians, and whites and blacks. But PAC had no description for its members. PAC had a definition of 'What is an African? A person who is born here; whose only loyalty is here; a person willing to be subjected to African majority rule.' If you were prepared to accept the definition in those terms, you were an African."

African was the only identity De Lille sought for herself. Any term other than African was for apartheid purposes. "I never accepted there were colored," she said. "I don't today." From that statement, I made the correct assumption that in the days of racial designation, she had been classified as colored.

I asked how PAC's goals for the country differed from those of the ANC.

De Lille began by describing both as liberation movements. PAC had been the youth wing of the ANC, she said. "They come from the same historical background; they had the same objectives. We may differ in how to achieve these."

Had not PAC historically been considered more militant?

De Lille nodded. "Yes. But also because there was a deliberate campaign to paint the PAC as more radical. We still say, today, that this land belongs to the African people. This is a fact. And because we're stating a fact, people say, 'You're militant.' 'You're radical.'"

"We've always believed the land must be returned to its rightful owners. We were colonized and this country was colonized more than three hundred years ago. When they started to say Namibia was the last colony in Africa, we said 'No, but you're wrong. South Africa's also colonized.'"

"And we said, 'It is not only apartheid that is the problem, it's colonization *and* apartheid. When the ANC focused more on apartheid, a sort of human rights type organization, we focused on decolonization of our country."

I asked how decolonization could be realized?

"You've got independence now," she said, sounding slightly out of patience. "Doesn't that make the country for everyone? Not at all. Not at all. We've achieved what we call political freedom. There's still a long way to go."

All the ills, the legacies of the past, certainly had not been resolved, nor reversed, with an X on the ballots, she said.

"We still have to get equitable land distribution to the people who belong here. And we have to find mechanisms and policies to deal with the redistribution."

"You've got a choice whether you want to belong here. We've got many people who don't want to belong here although they live here. We say those who choose to belong here, they are Africans."

Newspapers had been running stories about a suit De Lille had brought against Parliament. What was that about?

De Lille said she couldn't go into details since it had not come before the courts. What she could talk about were the principles of the case. De Lille had been given a fifteen-day suspension from Parliament by members. She refused to accept that suspension and sued Parliament for her banning.

"What happened to me," she said, "was clearly abuse of a majority vote. Parliament wanted to discipline me for what I said in Parliament. Basically, I'm asking whether some people I've named can confirm or deny that they worked for the previous government. Were they spies?"

That was not a new question, she said, and she had raised it this time as a representative of the public, in a public chamber.

"And members felt because it is ministers I've named and premiers and so on, I should be disciplined. So that's the first wrong principle. The Constitution gives the right to all of us to speak whether we come from a minority or majority. And I'll be the first one to accept that no right is absolute. Then again, it needed to be tested. Just what is freedom of speech? How do you use free speech? In what manner? There is no precedent in this country."

"And another issue is the one of Parliamentary privilege. If you've got this special right assigned to a Member of Parliament, why this extra right? Now they claim I have abused my privilege by naming names."

"I then said, 'Then how do I use my privilege? And who determines that? And where do you draw the line? Who determines when it's use and who determines when it is abuse?'"

"I also felt that a committee established by Parliament was not competent to address those rights because these are constitutional rights. A judge or court of law, but not a committee. The same committee who charged me, adjudicated and found me guilty even before they began any hearings."

"The whole process was really a farce. And I thought, it is much wider than this."

The phone rang. De Lille dealt with the caller briskly and curtly.

Right from the beginning, I realized I had experienced a coolness from, a distance to De Lille. And strangely for whatever reasons, I felt a bit uneasy and thought her a bit scary.

Such a case as hers, taking Parliament to court, was unprecedented in the country's history, she continued. By testing the rights to free speech and Parliamentary privilege, her case could provide legal certainty and interpretation to these rights that would be valuable in the future.

"That is what I'm doing," she said. "Not only for me, but for the rest of the country."

The case would be heard early in April. In the meantime, her fifteen-day suspension to Parliament, imposed by a vote of its members, had been lifted.

I asked how she came to be in Parliament.

She had been a member of PAC's National Executive Council, she said, and her name came up on PAC's list of candidates for office. In Parliament she chaired a standing committee on transport and served on a number of other committees including home affairs, housing, health, rules and welfare.

How did PAC's vision for the future of South Africa differ from that held by the ANC?

De Lille said, "Our vision is, let us see where we are right now. We are in a transitional period from an old order to a new order. At the same time we are transforming our society, our organization of government."

"My vision is that we have to move toward a situation whereby we have our loyalty *only* to this country, when we can proudly say, 'We are all South Africans' and not refer to ourselves as white South Africans, black South Africans and so on. My vision is that we should work very hard to achieve that sensation of being proud to be South African. We don't have this at the moment."

"That and also the elimination of poverty. The political freedom we gained will be very short-lived if we can't change the life of the majority of the people of this country who are poor."

"The thing is, the money is in this country. We just need to reprioritize. We also need to inculcate a mind set amongst our people that they have to do things for themselves. Right now people have the expectation that because they voted in the 1994 elections, government is going to deliver things to their doors. They don't believe it's necessary to work. They believe there is some entitlement."

"If you have the money and don't change the mind set of the people, it's not going to last."

"And," she continued, "we've got the goodwill of the rest of the world, which I feel we are not capitalizing on. We should be saying to the world, 'Yes, now we are free politically, but we still need your help. Not in the form of aid, but in the form of assisting us to rebuild the moral values, to rebuild society, to rebuild the economy, because we inherited a desert.'"

"There are many ways, but I know there are no easy ways. We'll have to take tough decisions, but at the end of the day, you must not say up front, it's not going to work. You can never say for certain that something is not going to work until you've tried it. I think we have not tried yet in South Africa—all of us—to see how to make this work as a collective responsibility."

I asked how the people could be reached with that message?

"We were able to reach them to ask them to vote for us. What's wrong with reaching out to explain what we've inherited? And to explain to them what we are trying to achieve? And to explain we don't have the money? People are very reasonable out there. They will be able to understand. But there's now a vacuum that's developed between ourselves and the people out there."

"What I'm saying is there's the whole issue of reconciliation which must finally bring us to one nation. The second is the issue of rebuilding and reconstructing this country. But before we can do this, those who benefitted in the past must acknowlege that they benefitted out of the system which didn't work for the majority of the people. Those who benefitted now say, 'We worked for it.' Those who didn't benefit say, 'Now we've got our government. We're entitled.'"

"Once having acknowledged, we need to move forward together: To say 'How do we move from point A to point B? Do we have the resources? How are we going to use them?' That basic conversation process, public participation, is not taking place."

De Lille also believed that lack of communication is why "people perceive others as disappointed, disillusioned."

"It's not that bad. The reason why I'm hopeful is that I found the hope out there, too. These are the same people who have been waiting over three hundred years and who suffered under apartheid. They still have hope. And I think while we still have hope, a way can be found. I don't have all the answers. I'm just saying a way can be found."

Instead of taking the elevator down, I walked. On one of the main floor corridors, I came upon an exhibit of paintings. I stopped there for some time. Much of the art was startling and difficult to look at: bold slashes of blacks and grays, dismembered bodies, tortured faces, prison bars; memorial titles—to Steve Biko, to Robert Sobukwe, to other martyrs of the country's racist past.

A plaque titled *Art Against Apartheid* read:

> The majority of the works presented here was assembled at the beginning of the 1980s. The aim of the 'Artists of the World Against Apartheid' was to take part in the interna-

tional campaign which was committed to denouncing, to fighting this crime against man, this crime against culture which is known as apartheid.

These works were presented in several museums and cultural establishments all over the world.

As a tribute to Picasso, to his demands concerning Guernica, we hoped that once apartheid had been abolished, these works could be offered to the first free and democratic Government of South Africa, to be selected through universal suffrage: 'One man, one voice,' said Mandela.

That day has come—and our action has formed part of the efforts of the international community and those of the South African people who worked towards the day when the works would leave for Africa ...

Outside on Plein Street which bordered one side of Parliament, I watched for Aldino. That day must have been the hottest so far. Next day I would leave. The sorry-I'm-late scores should then have been about even.

Some hard to identify distant sounds moved closer. First around the corner appeared three, maybe more, high and wide armored troop carriers. Behind these marched twenty or thirty policemen followed by rows of kids grouped by different school uniforms and periodically yelling "Viva." The parade of students must have been a block long. After them came another contingent of the same vehicles with police officers bringing up the rear. The protests against government cutbacks to education continued.

XXVI
✹ *Patricia Matolengwe*
Construction is hard work which we, as women, don't know

I walked the Liesbeek River trail for the final time that morning and stayed on Main Street to the Cavendish Square mall. I went down a flight to Exclusive Books and found a couple of books for Aldino's twin sons. One day he had picked them up at pre-school on the way home from an interview. They were darling litle boys: appealing, bright-eyed and beautiful three-year-olds. I'd gone in with him to the pre-school child care facility in District Six. Appropriately, it seemed to me, "Granny Black Sash" Noel Robb, one of the first women I had talked to, was still a member of the school's board. I took the underpass to get back across Main Street. "Fuck you kaffer" (*sic*) had been scribbled over "White SA repent" since my last time through. Kaffir was Afrikaans for nigger.

The night before we had gone to the Open-Air Theatre in Wynberg, a few miles from Cecily's neighborhood. The theater's summer season of plays with professional actors was an annual event, she said. Cecily brought a hamper of food and wine, as had six of her friends who met us there. We all sat on blankets spread on the grass under the trees. The park was large, picnics going on all around. Dishes were passed and wine poured.

At dusk, we trooped into rows of seats facing the set: a small, white, plastered Cape Dutch style house with traditional chimneys and classic concave, convex, curved gable. Next to the house was a lanai; in front, a dock, white sand and water. The setting was a Cape colored fishing village. Half an hour or so into the play, a full moon rose behind the exotic foliages of for-real bamboos and palms silhouetted beyond the set.

The dialogue was difficult for me because of the heavy Cape colored accent, but the audience laughed a lot. The music, set and speech were all "very Capey," Cecily whispered. The dialogue was faithful to Shakespeare, she said, and exactly fitted the setting, the situation and flamboyance of the Cape colored characters.

The music was by David Kramer. He had done the District Six musical and had been at the District Six Museum on the day we visited.

On that last morning before twenty-seven hours in limbo, I waited for a group of students before daring a crossing in the heavy traffic. A sign on the side of a delivery van going by read "Poultry in Motion." I followed a couple of maids up Palmboom and met the man in the ragged clothes who came around Thursdays, which was garbage pick-up day. He loaded his rusty supermarket cart with bottles, flattened cardboard and newspapers in plastic bags that sat waiting for him alongside the garbage containers.

Talking above *Second Time Around* sung by Frank Sinatra, I read the directions Patricia Matolengwe had given me to Aldino: "Take Landsdowne Road, before old Crossroads township, turn opposite Ikapi Town Council, houses being built right side; go to foot of bridge, turn right. Ask anyone: 'Where is Mxenge?'"

The road passed a former military base. Middle-class coloreds lived in houses on the right. Past that were low cost developments and farm lands, all of it flat, bleak and treeless.

Hanover Park. Aldino said, "I lived there for twenty-five years after we left District Six." Past Manenberg, described by him as high risk, gang-infested.

Trash increased, blowing across the road and the flat lands before coming to a stop at stands of weeds and barbed wire fences. We crossed a bridge, out of colored into black; Guguletu, then Khayelitsha, then Crossroads. Aldino stopped a couple of times to ask where the Ikapi Town Council was. After the second stop, he turned the car around.

"Crossroads was the main squatter area in the past," he said. "Now the squatters are all over."

We passed the new Crossroads community, Nelson Mandela High School and a new library.

"This was a war field," Aldino said. "A lot of people died in this area." He turned onto a side road. People walking in the street moved out of the way. A calf stood in dirt next to the street. We drove past cement block houses in various stages of construction and stopped in front of one used as an office.

A number of individuals inside waited or talked with the tall woman obviously in charge. Photos and framed newspaper clippings hung on the walls above cheap folding chairs, a couple of desks and some book shelves.

A laborer asked a question in Xhosa. A couple of white men came in, picked up rolled blueprints and left without speaking to anyone. A framed certificate, from the Institute for Housing of South Africa, named Patricia Matolengwe 1996 Western Cape Housing Person of the Year. A steady stream of individuals and phone calls flowed by Matolengwe.

Her talk with me went on between calls and in-person interruptions. Depending on need, Matolengwe responded in English, Xhosa or Afrikaans.

She said she had attended a conference on the eradication of poverty at the United Nations in New York in October 1997. The UN Displaced Persons project funded the South African Homeless People's Federation, which supported her project and had recommended her for the trip.

I couldn't resist asking if she liked the U.S. She laughed, "Oh yes. Oh yes."

Matolengwe was a tall, slender, handsome woman with a great deal of presence. She wore an ankle-length gown in a mostly red,

African-patterned, cotton fabric. Her hair was black, short and curled. She wore fashionable red sandals with bright red polish on her toenails. Her voice was low-pitched. She spoke with confidence and she smiled and laughed often.

Her organization, the Victoria Mxenge Housing Savings Scheme had its start in 1991. A conference of homeless people had been organized by the Roman Catholic Church, Matolengwe said. "People were discussing housing and how are we going to overcome that problem in our country?"

"At that conference, we had also other international visitors, like Indians and Italians and Mexicans. People are sharing their experiences of what happened to them after their freedoms in their countries."

Obtaining housing for the poor proved to be a major problem throughout the world, a longtime process dependent on frequently unfulfilled government promises.

"So was to set up groups: Women come together and set up housing saving schemes. We also liked this idea and we take it from there to share among ourselves, how South Africans are going to do this."

"We are coming from all over South Africa, then also we started in '92, based in Khayelitsha. What we did, we tell women we are starting this. Because most of the people want to start something that is voluntary. They felt to hesitate, unclearness on this is going to happen. But we say, 'Let us try.'"

Those at the international gathering in New York who had described such programs in their countries had warned it would not be easy to sell their communities on the idea. But participation by residents, especially squatters, would strengthen and unite the community.

"So," continued Matolengwe, "we take the idea and we spread it in the communities. Then, after we started, we organized more people to join. It was fortunate for us that most of the people interested were women more than men. We now have 280 women; six are men."

Women worked out better than men, she said, because they understood each other and were better at working together.

The background noise of pounding sounded closer and Matolengwe spoke louder.

"We are also drawing from the poorest of the poor, the unemployed, because they are the ones always disadvantaged to get money or any resources. We target them."

"We agreed that every day people must save. If they survive, even though they are not employed, they have to tell us, 'how do you survive?' We elect treasurers who are responsible for this collecting on a daily basis."

"We said each and every individual must feel free to save as much as they can, from their way of surviving. If you have little amount, just put it. Forget how much do you have. At the end of the day, you find yourself you save *so—o—o*—much."

There are both collectors and treasurers and what comes in is kept in one fund. Amounts given range from betwen ten cents (1 cent US) and a rand (9 cents US) daily and usually are different every day.

"The more they see in the books and the records from the small amount they save, is the more they get motivated. I couldn't believe myself, can't ever think, myself, that small amounts can make me have wealth."

"When we started, we were twelve women. But we organized more and decided to close the number at two hundred. Then we said, not restrict, just keep a smaller number (in a group) in order that they understand each other."

A smaller unit works together better than a larger one, Matolengwe explained. Since they talk more, they motivate each other to save as much as possible. Cooperation, when it comes to the actual process of building, will make it easier for everyone as well. Construction would "need participation and it is hard work which we don't know. Especially as women."

Over a long period, those involved came together at regular meetings. At these sessions, they did more than talk about the houses they would build: "We build you as individuals," Matolengwe said earnestly, "the understanding of the organization first, in order for you to be able to take the responsibility of the structure which you are going to build."

It requires about a month to understand how the money is saved, how to read the records, and to know the activities of the organization, she said.

"From then, the technicalities of what you are going to do; the technicals of what kind of material, the availabilities. And when you talk about the material, how are you going to use this, come up with your dream of the structure? What are the reasons for that, compared to the existing shack where you are coming from? How much are you going to afford? How much did it cost to build the shack compared to the future house which you are going to build? The cost of the material to the big companies—how do we relate ourselves with them, to the factories, and to the suppliers of the materials?"

"That process alone takes very long. It goes along with the land which you are going to use. You have to know to whom does the land belong to? If it is yours, what are the proofs you have that the land belongs to you? Because we will use (building materials) which is not going to be easy to demolish if the land does not belong to you."

"Most of the people do not have land. The process takes years for them to negotiate because the questions of the land is an issue everywhere."

Throughout the conversation, people drifted in, sitting in chairs along the wall to listen. Occasional coughs came as reminders of an audience.

"As we started in '92," Matolengwe said, "people learned from us because we negotiated for the piece of land which we are using. It took us nine months. And it was unserviced land. Then it was another process (to put in water, electricity and sewer) before we put the structure."

Was that here, this site, I asked?

She nodded.

I asked how much land was involved.

"Three hectares (eight-and-a-half acres), to accommodate 148 houses," she said. "Ninety-six houses up already. Ten slabs under construction. So we are close to finish."

"After this they'll move on. There is another group which is going to build across the railway line. So also we negotiate for this land. The owner is selling the land when we bought the land for the group. So another development will take place there very soon. We are also going to assist them."

I asked where funds came from?

"First thing, we depend on our own capacity, like the savings which I'm talking about. And secondly, as we are a national movement now—through the country we have more than one thousand groups—we set up a fund which is called the Utshani Fund." That she explained is a Zulu term meaning grass roots.

"If," Matolengwe continued, "there are resources which are coming from outside, like the UNDP (United Nations Displaced Persons) fund, these must not come to the funds we are generating on our own so we can see our strength."

Outside contributions, she said, go into a revolving national fund. "We do not depend on the outsiders. By so doing, if those funds dry anytime, we can sustain ourselves by depending on our own savings."

In the Western Cape, all such housing groups put their collections into a single account. But each contributor has a personal savings record. If the individual's savings won't cover costs of building, the fund kicks in.

"So there is," Matolengwe said, "a reason for the fund which we set up originally for those who want to borrow for whatever they like, they must come to the original fund for help."

"If you want for income generation or to improve your house, you can come to this fund and get the loans and do whatever you like. Then you pay it back so we do not use the fund which is restricted according to the funders so they can be able to account for that."

"Even though there are men who are part of us now, every individual woman who wants a house has to involve herself to her house. The money we are going to use is only for material costs. For labor each and every individual must involve him or herself in the work which is taking place. We are helping each other build the houses."

"At the beginning there were no men interested in this because of the income. We told everybody that there is nothing going to be benefited by anybody. Almost all are the women because they are the ones who are always out of jobs. So they are more in the work we are doing on a daily basis."

"The houses that are going to be built here are 148, so we divide that number into twenty families. Each and every twenty families they are responsible for their houses. What we are doing, as an entire group, is to monitor the situation. It may happen that another twenty has got people who are scared to understand this, so we swap members to go help where there is a lack and checking the work which is being done that it is in the correct manner and also correcting each other."

One of the newspaper clippings on the wall reported a house built for 8000 rands ($888 US). Could a house actually be built for 8000 rands?

"Oh yes," replied Matolengwe. "But we build that structure in 1995. Each year the cost of the material has gone up, so now this very same size, last year, was 11,000 rands ($1,222 US), this year maybe up another thousand. It is only after we finish to know exactly how much."

I was curious to know how she became involved in the issue of housing.

Matolengwe smiled and paused. "I cannot say how, because I was out of job. At the time I was doing the domestic work, in the '80s as well. Then someone approached me that there was an NGO called Peoples Dialogue. It is about land and shelter. This NGO was also part of the conference which I mention to you. They need us to organize ourselves in the communities."

"Then I organized my area. I learnt a lot from that. But I was always in the community, also involved myself voluntarily in work where we also guided ourselves as women."

This earlier group, she explained, involved mothers' savings clubs to purchase school clothes for their children. But in this plan, the women were required to put a certain amount away each month. She believes that the current idea of participants feeling free to save whatever they can is far better.

"And the loan from our savings is also different from that one in terms of interest. Because to this one, the interest is one percent. But the interest for the other was two percent of the amount, so to those ones, the interest is extremely rip-offing."

Matolengwe also believed that if the amount of savings agreed upon becomes too much of a burden, saving stops. That does not happen when the amount saved is determined daily by what is available.

"So that is the way which I used to be part of. And after I was out of a job, then I decided to sell the meat and reorganize all the people who are selling: 'Let's form a co-op of some sort. We are going to discuss about the prices and all that and the unity among ourselves as people who are selling, and how do we proect ourselves?' I was used to working with people because of that. That also was at Khayelitsha."

Matolengwe had been born in 1955 in the Transkei homeland in the Eastern Cape. She had attended school full time through Standard Ten, then part time to finish. In 1980, she came to Cape Town to work

"I am not married," she said, "but I do have responsibility, one daughter, seventeen now."

She and her daughter "live in a shack at the present moment. The house is not yet started to build."

I was surprised. I imagined her house would have been the first built.

Matolengwe shook her head. "Members decided they did not want to because they said every time when people come up with the initiative, they are always the ones who benefit first. I said on my side, I was not likely. They said, 'No ways. If you are sincere in what you come, you are going to benefit last. So we can see first if it's working or not. Because we used to involve ourselves in something which sounds like nice. At the end of the day, people who come with those initiatives are the ones who benefit first. So we are not going to allow you to benefit first.' That is the reason my house has not risen yet."

"I have no problem with that at all. Because they see now, it's only now they realize that that is true what I said."

I asked where the name of the project, Victoria Mxenge, had come from. She said it is the name of one of the lawyers who fought for Nelson Mandela's release.

Project houses come in different sizes depending on what the owner has saved. A standard 54-square meter (650 sq. ft.) house has two bedrooms; 65-square meters (780 sq. ft.), three bedrooms. There is also a 72-square meter (860 sq. ft.) model. Lot sizes are the same.

"We encourage everyone to build what they can afford," Matolengwe said. "If you can't afford, we advise you as a group because we know each other. We know everything of the family because we share in these every day. It is not easy for you to bluff us and say 'I can afford this.'"

"Even the collectors and the treasurer will advise you: 'You tell us you can afford. We don't see that. So maybe you can start building this size. Maybe in future you can extend it. First build a house which you can afford and finish so you can have a roof. Improve later and get another loan.'"

"What they repay each month is different according to the affordability. You tell us how much you are going to afford a month then, according to that information, we calculate how much you can get. You repay what you said to us."

An emergency vehicle, siren going full blast, screamed down the road.

Matolengwe said that the South African homeless program gets visitors from inside the country and outside and sends its own representatives out "to work and to share whatever experience we have and they have. We're staying a week or ten days together, especially to our sister organizations in other areas where is that common understanding."

"We are set up on an international network. We have countries like India, Sri Lanka, Philippines, Thailand, and Brazil. We have

African countries like Zimbabwe, Namibia, and are slowly starting to go to Zambia as well."

Matolengwe is in charge of the Mxenge project; the overall director is head of the South African Homeless Peoples Federation. Matolengwe receives a stipend rather than a salary.

"We do not encourage anyone to regard this work as a source of income," she said.

When the interview ends, I ask to look at some of the houses. She walks with me around the development where eighty families now live. Prominent among the one-story dwellings is a two-story community center under construction. This will house the project office, a pre-school and creche.

Thanks to efforts by the community, children are bused to their school on the other side of the busy main road which lies just beyond a line of roofs.

We pass a sign: P. Matolengwe Street.

So far, the major disappointment had been the government side of the cooperative effort. "It is taking its own time to get us what they promised," she said.

The group applied for housing subsidies in 1994. An amount of 15,000 rands ($1,666 US) per house was approved in 1996.

"They haven't finished paying," she said. "They still owe us twenty subsidies."

Many of the houses we passed, though occupied, with curtains on the windows, looked unfinished. "You move in when the walls and roof are in place," she explained. "You improve your house as you live in it."

We went into one of the houses. A teen-age girl in a school uniform watched TV from an easy chair. The living room was completely furnished, down to a rug on the concrete slab.

A sheet of paper tacked to the wall between living room and kitchen was labeled, "House Cost for Elsie Qungqisa." The house was 72-square meters in size and cost a total of 20,445.86 rands ($2,271.76 US). Under that was an item-by-item accounting, subdivided under walls, foundation and slab, and roof. The biggest expense had been 3,000 rands ($333 US) for 1042 external blocks; the least, 38.71 ($4.30 US) for hoop iron.

The house took two weeks to go up. "First a roof and gradually they keep improving."

We walked back to the community center and went inside. Children being cared for in a private home would move to the creche in the center the following week. When the office moves there, Matolengwe's house will be built on its site.

Six women painted shelves in a large room at the back of the building. This would become a "tuck shop." Proceeds from sandwiches and snacks sold there would benefit the creche.

The women were having a great time. They talked in animated, clicking Xhosa punctuated by laughter. In the main area, two women opened bags of cement while others smoothed a part of the slab with trowels. The partition between that room and the shop was the side of a ship container. Outside I saw that a section of wall not yet plastered was stacked containers.

A parade of women workers started past, on their way to lunch. As Matolengwe and I shook hands, I asked how much longer she expected it to be until the project was completed?

She said, "As long as homeless cannot end, this cannot end. If you really understand what is homelessness and when homelessness started and how it ends, it is an endless thing. So it is not easy for us to say we can end. As long as there are people who are homeless, we have to give support to them. Even if we can finish our area, we have to give the advice and support to those who are starting. We believe it is not possible to tell ourselves we can stop."

Afterword

When I think about what South Africa was and how it is now I am amazed. Change happened and it didn't take a war to get there. As I wrap up this book, I feel regret as well. How I wish I could have remained in South Africa and been a part of the march toward freedom and equal rights.

I have not been back since I did the interviews in early 1998. Because I do not read about troubles in the country—and I look for those datelines—my assumption is that the system put in place so well is operating with no big bumps.

I knew before I began this project that South African women actively participated in the workings of their country, speaking out on issues of racism and injustice and striving to provide social services to those in desperate need. Until I questioned them about what they had done, I had not realized the extent and the scope of their contributions. During the '70s when I wrote for the *Daily Dispatch*, any involvements that opposed official positions were not only off-limits to newspapers but could draw police attention to individuals linked to such activities.

I am a journalist, not a historian nor an academic. During my adult life, I have concentrated my attention on what is happening in front of me, what people are talking about, what newspapers and magazines are reporting. Given that limited focus, I can recall no revolution in which women played such a major role. Is that why the transforming changes in South Africa unfolded as they did? Is it possible, perhaps likely, that the South African revolution was more evolution, at least in part because of the work of these women and others like them? They clearly established a civilizing influence, an on-the-ground and friendly workforce of creative problem solvers.

Establishing an alternative political system in other former colonial lands of Africa has, so far at least, proved destructive to the land, people and economy, and largely unsuccessful in providing even a

prospect of prosperity and peace. At the beginning of the 21st century, South Africa showed a different face. After years of oppression
based on race, the country operates now under a Constitution, a Bill of
Rights and a Parliament that represents and reflects a diverse racial
and ethnic population. A Truth and Reconciliation Commission
helped to bury the shameful past with decency and compassion.

I had not put a frame around what I had witnessed until my friend
Cecily came to visit in 1997 and we talked about what had happened in
South Africa. But, looking back, the signs were there. For instance, my
first trip to South Africa was in 1972. A newspaper article which ran in
the *Daily Dispatch* a few days after I arrived in East London reported
three women elected to the City Council. No big deal. Other women
served on the Council. The newspaper at Ventura, California, which I
had left, had run a front page story on a woman appointed to the Planning Commission. A first, at least in recent history.

Several times during those years in South Africa I covered evening
meetings of Black Sash, listened to speakers talk about pass laws or
lawyers discuss detentions and bannings. I heard reports by Sash
members who had attended hearings and spoken out on issues affecting the country's disenfranchised majority. Though they inevitably
were silenced immediately, they showed up at the next meeting. I sat
in on an Advice Office session and detailed the stories of a succession
of impoverished blacks seeking help negotiating the spider web of
white bureaucracy. I followed Trudy Thomas on her rounds of the
mission hospital wards. I saw a population of mainly women and children in the rural areas. The men had gone off to the mines or the cities
to work, leaving women to raise the children, find ways to bring in
money, grow crops and tend the livestock. Sometimes the husbands
came back on annual leave. Sometimes they didn't. A matriarchal
society had evolved.

Other factors contributed to the changes in South Africa, of
course. It is impossible to imagine the country developing as it has
without Nelson Mandela. What if 27 years in prison had embittered
him? What if he had given up? What if the leader tapped by De Klerk

for release had been a militant? What if the entire white population, rather than being divided politically, supported the National Party government?

What if television remained banned? How much of a factor was allowing TV into the country in 1976? From the beginning all programs were pre-screened and censored, news came from the official government perspective. A big part of the South African population could not afford a TV, but they found places with sets where they watched. I always mused about what they absorbed subliminally: the backgrounds, the sets of those soap operas and situation comedies from England and the US. In South Africa a miserably poor and discriminated-against part of society could see people leading lives free of pass laws, living in houses with running water and comfortable furniture, cooking foods in gleaming kitchens, talking on telephones.

Ah yes, timing. Timing is everything. All the elements to produce change percolated to the surface more or less at the same time. I guess my point is that without the ground work laid by women who fought on for years with little hope of changing the system, the revolution might have unfolded in a far different way. They laid a groundwork of good will and reason. They arrived with knowledge.

I admired them all greatly. Everyone from testy Elsa Joubert who told her Afrikaner tribe about the *Poppies* in their kitchens, to Noel Robb who stood all night in the rain to protest a racist law, to Patricia Matolengwe who, with the women she had rallied to build their houses, shoveled dirt and put up walls.

How I wish I had been there.

331

Index

X